GOTHIC THINGS

Gothic Things

DARK ENCHANTMENT AND ANTHROPOCENE ANXIETY

Jeffrey Andrew Weinstock

FORDHAM UNIVERSITY PRESS   NEW YORK 2023

Copyright © 2023 Fordham University Press

All rights reserved. No part of this publication may be reproduced, stored in a retrieval system, or transmitted in any form or by any means—electronic, mechanical, photocopy, recording, or any other—except for brief quotations in printed reviews, without the prior permission of the publisher.

Fordham University Press has no responsibility for the persistence or accuracy of URLs for external or third-party Internet websites referred to in this publication and does not guarantee that any content on such websites is, or will remain, accurate or appropriate.

Fordham University Press also publishes its books in a variety of electronic formats. Some content that appears in print may not be available in electronic books.

Visit us online at www.fordhampress.com.

Library of Congress Cataloging-in-Publication Data available online at https://catalog.loc.gov.

Printed in the United States of America
25 24 23   5 4 3 2 1

First edition

Contents

PREFACE: THREE BEGINNINGS   vii

Introduction: Ominous Matter   1

1. Gothic Thing Theory   19
2. Dark Enchantment and Gothic Materialism   41
3. Body-as-Thing   72
4. Thing-as-Body   91
5. Book: How to Do Things with Words   115
6. Building: Bigger on the Inside   137

Epilogue: The Ominous Matter of One's Ordinary Life   171

ACKNOWLEDGMENTS   173

NOTES   175

WORKS CITED   181

INDEX   195

Preface
Three Beginnings

Like most stories, this one has multiple beginnings.

The most obvious starting point for this project, which has been developing over the course of a decade, immediately followed a panel on which I participated in October of 2011 at the George Washington University, where I presented a paper with the title of "What Monsters Mean." Post-talk discussion turned to recent trends in cultural and critical theory and, in particular, the approaches being referred to as Object-Oriented Ontology and New Materialism. Feeling myself sadly behind the curve, I solicited suggestions as to where I should start to get myself up to speed and assembled a list of names, including Jane Bennett, Graham Harman, and Timothy Morton. What followed was then a deep dive into these works and others broadly categorizable under the rubric of the "nonhuman turn"—Richard Grusin's phrase for the constellation of modern theoretical paradigms "engaged in decentering the human in favor of a turn toward and concern for the nonhuman, understood variously in terms of animals, affectivity, bodies, organic and geophysical systems, materiality, or technologies" (Grusin 2015, vii).

This post-talk discussion is the obvious moment at which the trajectory of the project originated because it set wheels in motion; however, it is also a kind of non-beginning because the new works I was reading in Object-Oriented Ontology (OOO), Speculative Realism, Vibrant Materiality, eco-criticism, and so on didn't seem at all new to me. In fact, the concepts and tropes introduced—"thing-power"; enchantment; the intrusion of the "outside"; hidden depths to objects; the "entanglement" or "enmeshing" of the human and nonhuman; the decentering of the human; the rhetoric of apocalypse, spectrality, and monstrosity; weird realism, and so on—were all strangely familiar. This, I realized, is because of a second, more diffuse beginning point: my research into the Gothic, which prompted the realization that these are exactly the concepts and tropes that the Gothic as a genre has been obsessed with since its origins in the eighteenth century. The Gothic, as this study will develop as its central argument, has always been about how human beings relate to the nonhuman world, what happens when objects assume a kind of mysterious animacy or potency, and what happens when human beings are reduced to the status of things among other things. It insistently decenters the human, showing human beings to be enmeshed in networks of human and nonhuman forces mostly outside of our control. The Gothic, in short, turns out to be the uncanny doppelgänger of twenty-first-century critical and cultural theory everywhere lurking beneath the surface (and sometimes explicitly surfacing) as it haunts considerations of how human beings interact with objects and their environment. The Gothic, I will argue, has been making the claims of New Materialists, Speculative Realists, and Object-Oriented Ontologists for them since its inception—and has exerted significant pressure on these frameworks, shaping their discourse in both obvious unacknowledged ways. "New Materialism," it turns out, is just the repackaged "old materialism" of the Gothic with a different affective valence—and what the Gothic shows us is the troubling side of "staying with the trouble," as Donna Haraway puts it in her 2016 book *Staying with the Trouble: Making Kin in the Chthulucene*. Acknowledging our entanglement within webs of actants can be revelatory; it can also be terrifying—and the Gothic not only makes clear that being considered a thing among things can be frightening, but that, as Kyla Wazana Tompkins reminds us, certain groups of people have "never been considered quite human enough" in the first place ("On the Limits" [2016]).

The realization that the Gothic functions in some respects as the uncanny doppelgänger of twenty-first-century critical and cultural theory was then driven home for me by a third beginning point for this study: Drew Goddard's 2012 horror comedy film *The Cabin in the Woods*. Itself a metatextual reflection on and critique of the formulaic nature of cinematic horror, the film early on focuses insistently on objects, making the role of what Jane Bennett, in *Vibrant Matter* (2010, 6), refers to as "thing-power"—"the curious ability of inanimate things to animate, to act, to produce effects dramatic and subtle"—in Gothic narrative a central theme. Having arrived at the isolated titular cabin, five college students descend into a basement packed with mysterious artifacts—among them a music box, a necklace atop a wedding dress, drums, a puzzle sphere, an amulet, a ceremonial dagger, a telescope, a gas mask, a toy chest, doll masks, and a diary. Everything about the staging of this scene invests the setting and these items with an almost palpable aura of dread. What we later learn is that all the objects serve as "summoning artifacts" to be used in "The Ritual": an annual ceremony humanity must perform to placate "The Ancient Ones," monstrous Lovecraftian entities that must be entertained with scenes of blood and sacrifice to ensure humanity's continued existence. Each artifact correlates with a particular monster and, when handled, summons that creature. Then, if things go as scripted by a shadowy organization overseeing events, the summoned creature dispatches or devours the unlucky summoners and humanity gets to survive for another year.

The basement in *The Cabin in the Woods* is the cellar of the Gothic, the place where its various trinkets and curios and souvenirs have all been tucked away, and what it reveals is just how deeply invested the Gothic has always been in a kind of New Materialist theorization of objects. While the film emphasizes objects associated specifically with the horror film tradition, the movie nevertheless more broadly foregrounds the central role uncanny objects have played in Gothic narrative since Manfred was crushed by a gigantic helmet and a figure stepped down from a portrait in Horace Walpole's 1764 *The Castle of Otranto*. Were the hapless students in *The Cabin in the Woods* to rummage even more deeply into the cellar, no doubt they would pull a drop cloth off of a creepy portrait with eyes that move or that has aged poorly in comparison to its subject; they might wipe the dust off a magic mirror with a sticky surface that stretches when touched and that functions as a window or portal into another dimension; perhaps they would come across a battered trunk housing a voodoo doll or mysterious idol, a marionette imbued with the will to do evil or a hateful "talky Tina" doll or a manic wind-up monkey toy with clanging cymbals. Certainly, there would be a whistle that summons a mysterious malevolent entity, a Ouija Board that permits one to contact the great beyond, and a cursed videotape (in an equally cursed antique VCR) or a gold doubloon or a violin with a disconcertingly red finish. They might even come across a volume of accursed lore, a skin-bound grimoire such as the *Necronomicon* or *The King in Yellow* or *The Babadook*. And if cabins in the woods have garages (in addition to basements), no doubt there would be a malevolent 1958 Ford Fury named Christine parked there. Like the warehouse that holds the Ark of the Covenant in Steven Spielberg's 1981 *Raiders of the Lost Ark* (itself an uncanny object that exerts agency as it effaces the Nazi insignia off the crate that contains it at the end), the Gothic's basement extends endlessly off into the distance in order to accommodate all the accursed matter of the Gothic. It is labyrinthine and no doubt, like a House of Leaves, larger on the inside than without.

Like elements in a dream (or nightmare) then, the story *Gothic Things* tells is inevitably overdetermined, traceable back to multiple points of origin: a discussion after a talk and a very metatextual horror film situated in relation to the Gothic genre, cinematic horror, and developments in twenty-first-century critical theory. It has taken me a while to work out the ideas here, which I've been trying out in bits and pieces over the past decade and then some, and I've sometimes worried that I've taken too long; but the essence of the Gothic is disturbing tales, and belatedness is the nature of ascribing meaning to traumatic events—so perhaps, given all the trouble human beings confront in the twenty-first century, a consideration of what the Gothic can tell us about the anxieties of embracing the "thingness of the human" and the "potentially actant qualities of the material and non-human world" (Tompkins 2016) is more pressing than ever.

GOTHIC THINGS

Introduction
Ominous Matter

The Gothic as a genre has generated a substantial body of criticism that has sought to define the category in a variety of ways. Perhaps most influentially, Fred Botting, in his overview of the genre in his book *Gothic*, defines it as the literature of transgression. Tracing the development of the Gothic from the eighteenth century onward, Botting characterizes the genre as "a writing of excess" (Botting 1996, 1) that is preoccupied with locating and overstepping cultural expectations and boundaries. "In Gothic productions," writes Botting, "imagination and emotional effects exceed reason. Passion, excitement and sensation transgress social proprieties and moral laws" (3). "Encouraging superstitious beliefs," continues Botting, "Gothic narratives subverted rational codes of understanding and, in their presentation of diabolical deeds and supernatural incidents, ventured into the unhallowed ground of necromancy and arcane ritual" (6). Through representations of unrestrained desire, the Gothic raises the "awful spectre of complete social disintegration in which virtue cedes to vice, reason to desire, law to tyranny" (5).

In coordination with Botting, other critics have emphasized the mechanics of Gothic plots and recurring generic conceits—what Eve Kosofsky Sedgwick refers to in her study of the genre as the Gothic "formula" (1986, 10)—and their participation in creating an atmosphere of dread. Nick Groom, for example, helpfully proposes "seven types of obscurity" that prevail in Gothic novels:

1. meteorological (mists, clouds, rain, storm, tempest, smoke, darkness, shadows, gloom);

2. topographical (impenetrable forests, inaccessible mountains, chasms, gorges, deserts, blasted heaths, icefields, the boundless ocean);
3. architectural (towers, prisons, castles covered in gargoyles and crenellations, abbeys and priories, tombs, crypts, dungeons, ruins, graveyards, mazes, secret passages, locked doors);
4. material (masks, veils, disguises, billowing curtains, suits of armor, tapestries);
5. textual (riddles, rumors, folklore, unreadable manuscripts and inscriptions, ellipses, broken texts, fragments, clotted language, polysyllabism, obscure dialect, inserted narratives, stories-within-stories);
6. spiritual (religious mystery, allegory and symbolism, Roman Catholic ritual, mysticism, freemasonry, magic and the occult, Satanism, witchcraft, summoning, damnation);
7. psychological (dreams, visions, hallucinations, drugs, sleepwalking, madness, split personalities, mistaken identities, doubles, derangement, ghostly presences, forgetfulness, death, hauntings). (Groom 2012, 77–78)

These forms of obscurity, propose Groom, "aim at sublimity through mystification in order to probe the consequences of history and the telling of secrets" (79).

While intermingling stylistic elements with thematic ones, and far from a complete list, Groom's catalog of recurring Gothic conceits is nevertheless particularly apropos to my purpose here because it highlights so clearly the centrality of human/nonhuman interaction to Gothic narrative—that is, the roles of weather, place, architecture, objects, and so on in creating suspense, dread, and terror for Gothic protagonists, as well as for consumers of Gothic narratives. What Groom's recipe for the Gothic illustrates is in fact the central premise of this study: that the Gothic has been insistently about objects and the material world as possessing what contemporary theorist Jane Bennett refers to as "thing-power" (2010, xvi and *passim*) and people as enmeshed in networks of human and nonhuman forces since its eighteenth-century origins. The Gothic, I will argue, since its beginnings has been consistently preoccupied with the nature of matter itself and the relation of the human to the nonhuman, and this sensibility informing early contributions to the genre continues to structure literary and visual contributions in the present. With this in mind, my purpose here is to reorient Gothic studies onto what one might refer to as "Gothic materialism": the centrality of objects within Gothic narrative, the ways that the Gothic calls into question conventional distinctions between animate and inanimate, and how, in place of autonomous human actors, the Gothic redefines human beings as Latourean actants within constantly shifting networks of relationships.

Beyond a focus on the uncanny animacy of the material world and the ways that human beings are objects participating in networks of objects, however, what also distinguishes the Gothic as a genre is its characteristic affective orientation: dread and horror elicited by a sense of categorical confusion as humans and nonhuman beings and objects swap places. Consumers of Gothic narrative are meant to share the confusion and dread of Gothic protagonists as they are buffeted by challenging environments in their attempts to negotiate dark and confusing spaces and are forced to contend with malevolent and occult forces to avoid being transformed into corpses. Put differently, in Gothic narrative the animate world acts as an antagonistic force—in concert with and often eclipsing the threat posed by any human villain.

Thinking about Gothic materialism as the affect-generating machine of the Gothic genre then collapses the familiar distinction between terror and horror outlined by eighteenth-century Gothic author Ann Radcliffe in her 1826 "On the Supernatural in Poetry." There, Radcliffe distinguishes terror as an anticipatory affect evoked by obscurity from horror, which she associates with revulsion elicited by confrontation with the abject. "Terror and horror," she writes, "are so far opposite, that the first expands the soul, and awakens the faculties to a high degree of life; the other contracts, freezes, and nearly annihilates them" (Radcliffe 1826, 149). Drawing on the philosophy of Edmund Burke, Radcliffe associates terror with the sublime: awe and dread elicited by expansive powers. Horror, in contrast, is considered by Radcliffe as a lesser emotion provoked by crude representations of violence and physical decay. Glossing Radcliffe's distinction, Devendra Varma writes in *The Gothic Flame* (1957) that "the difference between Terror and Horror is the difference between awful apprehension and sickening realization: between the smell of death and stumbling against a corpse" (130). However, whether the source of anxiety and dread within Gothic narrative is the awful obscurity of the mazelike forest or the loathsome spectacle of decay, the smell of death or the corpse itself that one stumbles upon soon after, the affective response is evoked through a confrontation with the physical world in which matter asserts itself and the agency of the protagonist is circumscribed. Whether it is the humbling sublimity of the natural landscape or the spectacle of decay associated with the corpse, the world, we might say, is always too much with us in the Gothic, which is the source of its dread—not in the Wordsworthean sense of being out of tune with nature, but rather in the sense of being overwhelmed by objects and natural forces that, as Timothy Morton develops in his discussion of "hyperobjects" in

Hyperobjects: Philosophy and Ecology After the End of the World (2013a), "humiliate" (in the sense of humble, bring low) the human (17).

The Gothic genre, therefore, is indeed the literature of transgression, as Botting proposes, but its transgressivity goes beyond representations of illicit and unconstrained desire; this study will argue that at the core of the Gothic is its transgressive undercutting of human anthropocentrism through the foregrounding of the agential qualities of "ominous matter." This is the master narrative of the Gothic genre as it repeatedly upends the human/nonhuman hierarchy entirely by endowing things with uncanny life at the expense of human agency—and it is a story that has remained remarkably consistent since the genre's origins. What I am calling Gothic materialism then invests this rethinking of the nature of the human and the relationship of the human to the nonhuman with dread, rendering matter as sinister and menacing, human mastery of the natural world a fiction, and human existence as precarious. The Gothic in this way can be said to offer a kind of philosophical meditation on the entanglement of human beings with the nonhuman world—and, in this, it corresponds in striking ways with the contemporary critical paradigms Richard Grusin assembles under the rubric of the "nonhuman turn" (2015, vii and *passim*), but with a different affective valence: one that substitutes horror for hope. As such, a return to the Gothic can help elaborate the challenges that New Materialism, Speculative Realism, Object-Oriented Ontology, and other twenty-first-century attempts to rethink the relationship between the human and the nonhuman confront as they seek to decenter the human and challenge the primacy of what Sylvia Wynter refers to as "ethnoclass Man" (see Wynter 2003, 262 and *passim*) in ongoing efforts to develop more just, humane, and sustainable ways of living. Indeed, as I will develop in Chapter 1, the Gothic turns out to be the uncanny doppelgänger of the theoretical paradigms associated with the nonhuman turn, informing their approach and suffusing their rhetoric.

How Do You Solve a Problem Like Cthulhu?

Donna Haraway, in her 2016 *Staying with the Trouble: Making Kin in the Chthulucene*, is clear that her notion of the "Chthulucene" as a name for an alternate version of our current epoch is not derived from or related to horror author H. P. Lovecraft's interdimensional tentacle-faced monstrosity, Cthulhu. As opposed to "SF writer H. P. Lovecraft's misogynist racial-nightmare monster Cthulhu" (Haraway 2016, 101), her Chthulucene, which names "a timeplace for learning to stay with the trouble of living and dying in response-ability on a damaged earth" (2), "entangles myriad temporalities and spatialities and myriad intra-active entities-in-assemblages—including the more-than-human, other-than-human, inhuman, and human-as-humus" (101). The web Haraway weaves of "speculative fabulation, speculative feminism, science fiction, and scientific fact" is, she asserts, a vein of SF that "Lovecraft could not have imagined or embraced" (101). Embraced, certainly not. The twentieth-century introvert who longed for the days of the eighteenth-century gentleman would have wanted nothing to do with feminism or other movements seeking to empower the disenfranchised and address historical inequities. But imagined? That's another matter. Not only did Lovecraft clearly imagine what Haraway refers to as the "more-than-human, other-than-human, inhuman, and human-as-humus," but this revaluation of the human as relational and material is in fact the source of the dread that pulsates through its fiction.

Lovecraft's decentering of the human is reflected by his cosmicism—his belief that, as summarized by Trung Nguyen in his *History of Humans*, "there is no recognizable divine presence, such as God, in the universe, and that humans are particularly insignificant in the larger scheme of intergalactic existence" (2016, 160). Lovecraft weaves this perspective throughout his fiction, in which human civilization is presented as both ephemeral and precarious. Human civilization, his fiction proposes, will eventually decline and be replaced by something else later on—in his "The Shadow Out of Time" (1936b), a race of beetles is proposed. And the decline of human civilization is not necessarily an extended process—at the heart of Lovecraft's cosmic horror is the existence of powers and forces in the universe that could blot us out of existence should they actually take note of us.

Lovecraft's cosmicism, on full display at the start of his most famous story, "The Call of Cthulhu" (Lovecraft [1928] 1999), is in fact quite amenable to contemporary theoretical paradigms that seek to decenter the human—and, despite its pessimism, is certainly implicated in Lovecraft's twenty-first-century popularity. Lovecraft starts his tale by foregrounding human limitations and insignificance:

> The most merciful thing in the world, I think, is the inability of the human mind to correlate all its contents. We live on a placid island of ignorance in the midst of black seas of infinity, and it was not meant that we should voyage far. The sciences, each straining in its own direction, have hitherto harmed us little; but some day the piecing together of dissociated knowledge will open up such terrifying vistas of reality, and of our frightful position therein, that we shall either go mad from the revelation or flee from the deadly light into the peace and safety of a new dark age. (139)

We human beings, asserts the opening of the tale, despite all our pretensions to grandeur, just don't know what we're getting into, what we're doing, or what we are up against. We think of ourselves as masters of all we survey, penetrating the secrets of the universe, when, in fact, we've barely scratched the surface of what there is to know and are not prepared for the revelation of our own impotence and insignificance when we put the pieces together. After this opening, the rest of the story then serves to illustrate this premise through the introduction of Cthulhu, one of several interdimensional Lovecraftian monstrosities whose powers so far outstrip those of human beings that all we can really do is keep our heads down and hope not to attract their attention.

Cthulhu—and the pantheon of extraterrestrial deities called The Great Old Ones of which it is a part—are for all intents and purposes what Timothy Morton refers to as "hyperobjects": things like black holes and global warming that are "massively distributed in time and space relative to humans" (2013a, 1). Interdimensional, powerful beyond comprehension, and seemingly immortal, Cthulhu exists outside of human time but nevertheless has a global influence, with a greatly dispersed network of worshippers and an effect on the dreams of those with the requisite sensitivity. Indeed, Cthulhu works surprisingly well as an avatar for climate change—a massively dispersed threat to human survival that can't really be fought directly. In this sense, we really are living in the Cthulhucene, spelled in the Lovecraftian way. To "stay with the trouble," as Haraway directs, would then mean staying with Cthulhu—which would entail rejecting human hubris, acknowledging our insignificance in comparison to hyperobjects and in light of deep time and interstellar distance, accepting our enmeshment within Latourean networks of human and nonhuman actants, and so on—all of which would be in keeping with Haraway's philosophy of *"sympoeisis"*—of "making kin" (2016, 2 and *passim*) with creatures human and nonhuman and creating the world together.

Lovecraft certainly did imagine "myriad temporalities and spatialities and myriad intra-active entities-in-assemblages." The problem, however, is that imagining them filled him with dread. Where Lovecraft runs afoul of Haraway's posthumanism—and that of all those who have followed in her wake—is in his horror at "impurity," which reflects Lovecraft's notorious racism. As author of weird fiction China Miéville explains, Lovecraft's racism wasn't simply a lamentable detail or aspect of his writing that can be bracketed off from his fiction; it is, rather, the motor force that propels it. According to Miéville, the "antihumanism one finds so bracing" in Lovecraft is a product of his racism—his "race hatred" (Miéville 2016, 241)—which cannot be divorced from his writing. Put differently, Lovecraft's horror fiction is not effective *despite* his racism, but *because* of it (Miéville 2016, 242). Abhorrence of miscegenation arguably is the force that propels Lovecraft's fiction and is present both in his dismissive attitude toward non-white races and what he refers to as "mongrels" and "half-castes" in particular and in his human/nonhuman hybrid monstrosities more generally—Cthulhu's humanoid shape with tentacled face, the fish-people of "The Shadow Over Innsmouth" (Lovecraft [1936c] 1999), Wilber Whateley's monstrous brother in "The Dunwich Horror" (Lovecraft [1929] 2001), and so on. That Donna Haraway, the philosopher famous for celebrating the cyborg in "A Cyborg Manifesto" ([1985] 1991) as a concept that undoes rigid human/nonhuman distinctions, would hold Lovecraft, an author who can find only dread in the undoing of those distinctions, at arm's length is not surprising. But isn't the trouble with Cthulhu—that is, with Lovecraft's worldview, including his racism and its intersections with colonialism, misogyny, exploitation of the natural world and environmental despoliation, predatory capitalism, homophobia, ableism, and with everything Sylvia Wynter, Alexander G. Weheliye, Kyla Wazana Tompkins, and other theorists of race associate with "Man" as a "genre of the human" (Wynter 2003, 288)—isn't this trouble with Cthulhu precisely the root cause of much of the trouble with which we have to grapple in the twenty-first century?

Haraway's insistence that when we hear Chthulucene we shouldn't think Lovecraft falls flat because it is almost impossible not to see the connection between the two—not simply because Cthulhu is so immediately connected with Lovecraft (and the fact that Chapter 2 of Haraway's book is titled, "Tentacular Thinking," when Cthulhu is most notable for its tentacled face, doesn't help distance the two), but also because the notion of the Chthulucene is Haraway's inverted response to the Lovecraftian Cthulhucene. We need a politics and practice of *sympoeisis* precisely because of the divisions sown by Man. To stay with the trouble is to stay with Cthulhu.

Haraway's disavowal of Lovecraft is useful in this context because it offers a particularly convenient example of the move a broad swatch of twenty-first-century critical theory makes, disavowing the Gothic even as it employs Gothic rhetoric and conjures up Gothic images. Collected by Richard Grusin under the umbrella rubric of the "nonhuman turn," these approaches to the relationship of the human to the nonhuman, including Latourean actor-network theory, affect theory, animal studies, New Materialism, and varieties of Speculative Realism including Object-Oriented Ontology, are united, writes Grusin, in their "decentering the human in favor of a turn toward and concern for the nonhuman" (2015, vii). Insisting that "the human has always coevolved, coexisted, or collaborated with the nonhuman" (ix), these different approaches join in rejecting human exceptionalism (x) and share a "resistance to the privileged status of the autonomous male subject of the Western liberal tradition, especially in their refusal of such fundamental oppositions as human/nonhuman and subject/object (x–xi).

The framing of such approaches is often—precisely as in Haraway's *Staying with the Trouble* (2016) or Tsing, Swanson, Gan, and Bubandt's ambitious 2017 study *Arts of Living on a Damaged Planet*, which I will discuss in more detail in Chapter 1—toward living more deliberately, sustainably, harmoniously, and justly with and in relation to other humans and nonhumans. Bearing in mind the state of emergency that is the Anthropocene, the nonhuman turn of contemporary cultural and critical theory frequently frames its project as a kind of provocation to live more gently, to cultivate an "ecological sensibility" (Bennett 2010, xi), and to restore a capacity for "wonder" (Bogost 2012, 124). The goal is to "catalyze a change in our circumstances, a turn for the better not for the worse, in that everyone who wants to participate, human and nonhuman, will get their turn" (Grusin 2015, xxi). If we—human beings—are to stay with the trouble and manage the crises presented to us by the Anthropocene, these perspectives assert, we need to stop pretending that we are masters of the universe and the center of all things. We must let go of the "correlationalist" perspective that "if things exist, they do so only *for us*" (Bogost 2012, 4) and instead acknowledge our entanglement with the stuff of the world. Human beings do not stand over and apart from the nonhuman; rather, we must realize that we are all actants in Latourean networks, defined by our relationships to one another and the nonhuman world. Ironically, this perspective is still generally about the human even when the focus is on the necessity of being less anthropocentric, but for a good reason: survival. Taken broadly, the affective orientation of these works is toward *hope*. Eschewing defeatism (or at least trying to steer clear of nihilism for the most part), these studies are bolstered by a kind of cautious optimism: We, humans, have done lots of bad things to the world and to each other, and time is running short, but it's not too late. We can still change (and we must because the alternative is bleak).

But, like Cthulhu lurking in the shadows of Haraway's Chthulucene, the Gothic offers the dark reflection of nonhuman turn affirmation, shifting the valence and substituting horror for hope. The Gothic shows us that we live in scary times, that surrendering power is difficult, and that confronting the unknown is more difficult still. What Gothic tales of ominous matter bring to the fore is the anxiety underpinning the nonhuman turn and, indeed, of the Anthropocene: fear of losing control, of not being in charge, of being reduced to the status of a thing among other things, of the world ceasing to exist only for us, of the world ceasing to exist at all. What the Gothic shows is actually how hard the nonhuman pivot is to make because the Gothic highlights human fragility, blindness, and impotence—all those things that have gotten us into trouble and that we prefer not to acknowledge. The Gothic is the boomerang effect of the nonhuman turn, shifting the focus back onto the human poised on the edge of a precipice—it is the panicked response of the human to its own decentering.

Ominous Matter I: Debris

While I will go deeper into the dark basement to excavate the repressed Gothic substrate of "Thing Theory" and the nonhuman turn much more fully in Chapter 1, some brief attention to a particular moment in Jane Bennett's *Vibrant Matter: A Political Ecology of Things* (2010) may help to make clear just how gentle a nudge considerations of nonhuman agency need to collapse into the affective terror of the Gothic. Early in the first chapter, in a section titled "Thing-Power I: Debris," Bennett describes her experience of viewing a tangle of junk on the grate over a storm drain consisting of "one large men's black plastic work glove, one dense mat of oak pollen, one unblemished dead rat, one white plastic bottle cap, [and] one smooth stick of wood" (4). While she admits to being "repelled" by the rat and "dismayed" by the litter, she nevertheless emphasizes the way in which this particular and peculiar assemblage of objects suddenly became "vibratory—at one moment disclosing themselves as dead matter and at the next as live presence: junk, then claimant; inert matter, then live wire" (5). For a moment, Bennett explains, she was able to appreciate these objects—and their peculiar assemblage—as "*things*, that is, as vivid entities not entirely reducible to the contexts in which (human) subjects set them, never entirely exhausted by their semiotics" (5). She was, in short, "surprised" (5), momentarily experiencing a sense of what Bogost would call "wonder" (see Bogost 2012, 124).

Bennett presents this encounter as a kind of revelatory experience—the momentary undoing of correlationalism in which she "caught a glimpse" (2010, 5) of the things in themselves rather than as, narrowly, objects for us. Briefly, a "window," as she puts it, opened onto "an eccentric out-side" (5). While it is hard to say if Bennett achieved some insight into what Graham Harman would call the "real qualities" of the objects—their qualities apart from how they are perceived (see Chapter 3 of Harman's *The Quadruple Object* [2011])—the things did emerge in their singularity for her: "*that* rat, *that* configuration of pollen, *that* otherwise utterly banal, mass produced plastic water-bottle cap" (Bennett 2010, 4). Bennett's story here is very much in keeping with—and echoes the language of—what Bill Brown says in his essay "Thing Theory" from 2001:

As they circulate through our lives, we look *through* objects (to see what they disclose about history, society, nature, or culture—above all, what they disclose about *us*), but we only catch a glimpse of things.... We begin to confront the thingness of objects when they stop working for us: when the drill breaks, when the car stalls, when the window gets filthy, when their flow within the circuits of production and distribution, consumption and exhibition, has been arrested, however momentarily. The story of objects asserting themselves as things, then, is the story of a changed relationship to the human subject and thus the story of how the thing really names less an object than a particular subject-object relation. (Brown 2001, 4)

Borrowing from Heidegger, objects become things when we glimpse their specificity outside their intended function. What's important about Bennett's telling of the story for my purposes here is her interpretation of this glimpse of the "out-side" as affirmation. She explains that she has worked hard to cultivate a capacity to be surprised, and her "hope" is that "the story will enhance receptivity to the impersonal life that surrounds and infuses us, will generate a more subtle awareness of the complicated web of dissonant connections between bodies, and will enable wiser interventions into the ecology" (2010, 4). Her project aims to "encourage more intelligent and sustainable engagements with vibrant matter and lively things" (viii).

But there are things and then there are things—and not all surprises are pleasant. The Gothic version of the same story is one emphasizing not the exuberant surprise of vibrant matter, but the terror associated with the defamiliarization of the world and the breakdown of conventional explanatory paradigms. Bennett's experience outside a bagel shop in Baltimore on a sunny June morning borders on the sublime: insight into the inexpressible, that which goes beyond human language, the secret life of things. But if Bennett's experience is one that takes her outside of herself, the Gothic is what brings us back. Insistently anthropocentric, the Gothic narrates the human experience of a world that surprises us in chilling ways—it is a world in which meaning falters as a result of misperception, madness, or the suspension of the laws of reality as we know them. The Gothic is a world in which the vibrant materiality of things is received as ominous—if the Gothic teaches us anything, it is that it is never, ever good when objects stop working for us, assert themselves, and transform from "dead stuff" to "live presence"—consider, for example, zombies and all manner of murderous dolls, robots, puppets, and "inspirited" objects. And when one catches a glimpse of the "out-side" in the Gothic, it is menacingly inhuman—a space of Lovecraftian madness and cosmic dread, a *Stranger*

Things "Upside Down," an alternate dimension, or roiling elemental substrate inhospitable to human life.

Bennett's story is essentially about the defamiliarization of the world as she is "surprised" by the unexpected "vibrancy" of objects, which she embraces as hopeful—the seeds of a renewed sense of wonder that can prompt a more thoughtful and deliberative engagement with the world. But with just a very minor twist, Bennett's experience of that sunny June morning could become vertiginous as the ground of meaning gives way and one tumbles into the affective terrain of the Gothic. Indeed, the Gothic has been lurking there from the start; Bennett admits to bracketing off her repulsion over the dead rat and her dismay over the litter in order to experience the bracing surprise of the objects as things. In fact, the Gothic is present in her account from the moment she describes the tangle of junk as "debris"—waste, ruins, remains, detritus, the aftermath of human activity and elemental forces. There is already a story present here implied by the chronology implicit in "debris." The aftermath of a storm, a dangerous access point to a dark underground world, vermin, a corpse, a missing human being, decaying vegetation—the tableau Bennett has chosen to make her point is a ready-made Gothic tale overlaid with powerful affective associations. One need not be conversant with the Gothic to be anxious about storm drains (even before Stephen King's 1986 novel *IT* and its cinematic adaptations parents were cautioning children not to play in or around them), to be repulsed by dead rats, or to wonder what happened to the worker whose hand fit the glove.

I am, of course, doing exactly what Bennett is trying not to: imposing meaning and a narrative on the assemblage of objects on that storm grate. For Thing Theorists of the associated schools of thought such as New Materialism, Vibrant Materialism, Speculative Realism, and Object-Oriented Ontology, the challenge is to avoid correlationalism—to think objects and their qualities in their specificity, outside of their particular meaning and use for human beings. Bennett describes an almost mystical moment of experiencing the objects as things outside of networks of personal and social meaning; but surprise, even carefully (and oxymoronically) cultivated, can only be momentary—as human beings, we cannot stay perpetually suspended in the non-meaning of surprise, cannot do more than briefly glimpse the "eccentric out-side" (2010, 5) before we tumble back into meaning. This surprise, I suggest, depending on circumstances, could just as easily evoke the affective uncanniness of a world upended as it could wonder. The Gothic version would experience this glimpse of the "out-side" as a chilling moment of defamiliarization and cosmic dread—an uncanny upending of the world. The Gothic then amplifies that sense of dread by reassembling the objects present into a mesh of meaning tending toward a tragic outcome—a renarrativization of experience conditioned by the chilling glimpse of the out-side.

I offer this consideration of Bennett's anecdote here for several reasons: first, because Bennett's *Vibrant Matter* was a starting point for this project. When first reading Bennett, I was struck by her notion of "thing-power" and the counterintuitive sense of wonder evoked by the surprising animacy of material objects. In the Gothic, this is the stuff of nightmare; second, her brief account of the vibratory storm drain assemblage and her response to it illustrate the curiously Gothic unconscious to the nonhuman turn: the storm, a drain, a dead rat, a missing human, debris. Bennett's provocation is to see these things in their singularity, bracketing off meanings and associations. But such moments are ephemeral, and then they collapse back into affect and meaning—in Bennett's case, revulsion, dismay, and presumably a wary sidestepping of the cluttered storm grate. As I'll develop in Chapter 1, where the Gothic subtext here is implicit, for other Speculative Realists, New Materialists, Object-Oriented Ontologists, and other practitioners of the nonhuman turn, it is explicit. Indeed, the master tropes of twenty-first-century cultural and critical theory are insistently Gothic, orienting as they do around the themes of spectrality, monstrosity, and apocalypse. Third, I'm particularly interested in Bennett's claim that "if matter itself is lively, then not only is the difference between subjects and objects minimized, but *the status of the shared materiality of all things is elevated*. All bodies become more than mere objects, as the thing-powers of resistance and protean agency are brought into sharper relief" (2010, 13, emphasis mine). The Gothic, as I will address in Chapters 3 and 4, is skeptical of this claim and obsessively depicts what happens either when things are more animate than humans or when the human body is considered as a thing numbered among other things—and it reminds us that some bodies have always been considered more thing-like than others.

When the Gothic as a genre originated in the eighteenth century, it was the dark underside to the Enlightenment, giving vent to everything the Enlightenment tried to challenge and keep in check. As Smith and Hughes explain, "this challenge was developed through an exploration of the feelings, desires and passions which compromised the Enlightenment project of rationally calibrating all forms of knowledge and behaviours. The Gothic gives a particular added emphasis to this through its seeming celebration of the irrational, the outlawed and the socially and culturally dispossessed" (2003, 1). The Gothic universe was one of transgressive desires, ungovernable passions, of superstition, of irrational, malevolent forces in an inscrutable universe. The Gothic, I will argue, functions in a similar way today as the dark underside to the nonhuman turn articulating Anthropocene anxieties over the decentering of the human. At its core, the Gothic is about what happens when things acquire uncanny animacy, what happens when humans are numbered as things among other things, and how the human relates to the nonhuman. This is why going back to the Gothic tradition is useful—its prominence in both critical discourse and popular culture indicates the challenges theoretical paradigms that seek to decenter the human must confront. That theorists and critics use the very same tropes and narratives they hope to disrupt to forward their arguments makes plain the difficulty of creating new narratives that seek to compel both urgency and hope. Put differently, it is difficult to move forward into the Chthulucene with Cthulhu's tentacles still wrapped around your neck.

This study has a kind of looping trajectory. It starts by outlining more fully the close correspondence of twenty-first-century critical paradigms associated with the nonhuman turn with the Gothic. Kyla Wazana Tompkins's description of New Materialism is a perfect case in point. In her consideration of the field and its limitations, she offers this overview:

> At its heart, the New Materialism explores the potentially actant qualities of the material and non-human world—New Materialism then is interested in relations between things, objects, phenomena, materialities, and physical bodies, as well as the relations between those things (things with each other) and humans (humans with things). New Materialism also considers the thingness of the human, the materiality of human bodies, and explores consciousness, feeling, affect, and other circulatory and shared social phenomena as they rise out of the substance of the world. (Tompkins 2016)

My argument is that one could everywhere replace "New Materialism" in this definition with "The Gothic" and have an entirely accurate and insightful overview of how the genre functions. This kinship between the contemporary theory and the Gothic then points to the limitations of the former—indeed, that New Materialism and related paradigms can be recast as a kind of horror story with relative ease seems to align with certain critiques of it—notably, that its "flat ontology" that considers all objects equal in existing "suppresses the question and problem of difference" (Tompkins 2016) and fails to consider that some bodies have historically been considered more human than others. Recognition of the Gothic as the dark reflection of contemporary nonhuman theoretical paradigms should thus raise a note of caution when it comes to strategies of "decentering the human."

After Chapter 1's consideration of the insistently Gothicized rhetoric of what I will address as Thing Theory, Chapters 2 through 6 focus squarely on the Gothic with an emphasis on modern texts, illustrating in detail the various ways in which the Gothic explores the agential properties of matter and the "thingness" of the human with attention to privileged categories of ominous matter within the genre: the body (Chapters 3 and 4), the book (Chapter 5), and the building (Chapter 6). In the epilogue to the project, I then return to the initial observation of the correspondences between the Gothic and nonhuman theoretical paradigms to speculate both on the pleasures derived from narratives of Gothic materiality and the implications of this for human attempts to negotiate the challenges of the Anthropocene.

My purpose here is neither to defend Thing Theory from all attacks nor uncritically to adopt Thing Theory as a framework for interpreting what I refer to as Gothic Things. My argument, rather, is not only that the Gothic has been doing a kind of Thing Theory all along, anticipating twenty-first-century decenterings of the human through the foregrounding of the agency of matter, but also that close attention to the Gothic shows how it anticipates some of the same concerns contemporary critics have voiced against Thing Theory—the difficulties of escaping from the correlationalist mode and, notably, the potentially pernicious consequences of thinking of human beings as objects. It may be true that objects have a life outside of the ways they are perceived and made meaningful by human beings; nevertheless, objects in Gothic narrative, however mysterious they may be within the context of the tale, are very much repositories for human anxieties and desires—even their unknowability reflects human anxieties about limitations placed on knowledge. The story here is thus about the intellectual and affective relationships established between the human and nonhuman within Gothic narrative.

This study, I should also add, is not intended to be Historical Materialist in nature. It is not my purpose here to defetishize the magical objects addressed, reinserting them back into networks of social relations, nor will I be tracing in detail the real-world histories of Ouija Boards, magical books, haunted houses, and the like (however interesting and useful such projects would be). Instead, I will be exploring how the Gothic, through its ominous matter, narrates anxieties about the place and role of the human amid a universe of uncanny things. The Gothic in this sense is thus a kind of philosophy that speculates on the nature of the human and its relation to the nonhuman. In this, it shares kinship with Eugene Thacker's approach to horror in *In the Dust of This Planet* (2011).

As Clive Bloom notes, "Gothic" and "horror" are often used interchangeably (2012, 211). Bloom goes on to assert that there may be Gothic tales that lack horror elements and vice versa, but maddeningly doesn't elaborate on precisely what that means (see Bloom 2012, 211). Xavier Aldana Reyes offers a bit more precision in his consideration specifically of Gothic cinema when he writes that the Gothic is a kind of aesthetic mode marked by recurring sets of characters, settings, motifs, and themes (along the lines of Groom's "Seven Kinds of Obscurity" from his *The Gothic: A Very Short Introduction* referenced at the start of this chapter) that generally work in concert to elicit "negative" affect such as fear and suspense but are recognizable as Gothic even separated from affective response (Reyes 2016, 17). Horror, in contrast, is "premised on emotion and not bound by time for setting" (Reyes 2016, 25). Gothic works, in short, share a recognizable aesthetic and catalogue of tropes and devices; they generally seek to elicit dread and horror as affective responses but can still be categorized as Gothic even if eliciting horror isn't their primary goal (cf. Catherine Spooner's seemingly oxymoronic concept of "happy Gothic" in *Post-Millennial Gothic* [2017]). Works of horror, in contrast, can be defined primarily by the affect they seek to elicit from consumers.

In keeping with Reyes, my consideration of Gothic materiality will attend to Gothic works that use familiar Gothic conceits concerning objects to evoke negative affect. This will encompass some works generally classified for marketing purposes as horror but that, by virtue of using familiar Gothic elements, can be accommodated by the Gothic rubric. In Thacker's *In the Dust of This Planet*, he describes horror as a kind of thought experiment that seeks to explore the world outside of our attempts to know and domesticate it—horror addresses "the enigmatic thought of the unknown" (Thacker 2011, 8–9) and is, in Thacker's opinion, thus "a non-philosophical attempt to think about the world-without-us philosophically" (9). My approach to the Gothic, which draws inspiration from Thacker's, adopts a similar tack in its consideration of how the Gothic, including its intersections with what Thacker refers to as horror, insistently thematizes the connections of the human to the nonhuman, investing these relationships with dread. That dread then is an important obstacle to be confronted when attempting to think how best to negotiate the challenges of the Anthropocene. Whereas Thacker is concerned with how horror lets us address limitations on human thought—it is about the "paradoxical thought of the unthinkable" (9)—my argument is that the Gothic genre lets us contemplate a world in which the human holds no privileged place.

I should add that the constellation of theoretical approaches I'm calling Thing Theory that serves as the starting point for this project has received its fair share of criticism—notably from those who argue that thinking of objects divorced from the historical conditions of their production results in a pernicious depoliticization obscuring their implication in broader forms of exploitation and inequality. Kimberly DeFazio, for example, offers a stinging rebuke of New Materialism in which its exclusion of historical processes in the consideration of objects renders it unable to assist us in "class understanding of issues in their material totality" (DeFazio 2014). Ironically, New Materialism, from DeFazio's perspective, ends up shockingly immaterial—that is, as a form of idealism. Wesley Phillips accuses OOO of a form of "commodity fetishism" in which the value of an object seems divorced from the social relations that produced it (Phillips 2012, 298; see also Simon 2013)—New Materialism is taken to task for not being Historical Materialism. Katherine Behar, in the introduction to her 2016 edited collection *Object-Oriented Feminism*, voices a related concern about the idea of a "flat ontology" in which all objects are equal in existing when "all too many humans are well aware of being objects, without finding cause to celebrate that reality" (5). Her proposition of an Object-Oriented Feminism seeks to address the "ontological stakes" (21) of what it means to be considered an object. Then there are those who critique OOO in particular and New Materialism in general as bad philosophy. Andrew Cole, for his part, suggests that Object-Oriented Ontology cannot escape the trap of correlationalism because, even while attempting "*not* to project the human into the heart of things," we inevitably continue to speak for the things (2013, 106). Peter Wolfendale has in fact authored an entire book relentlessly taking issue with OOO's claims to have escaped correlationalism (see Wolfendale 2019).

Again, it is not my purpose here to defend the truth claims of New Materialism, OOO, and other variants of Thing Theory. Rather, my point is that these contemporary philosophical approaches tell a particular story of the human relationship to the nonhuman that mirrors in compelling ways the story the Gothic genre has been telling since its eighteenth-century origins; indeed, as I will outline in Chapter 1, Thing Theory often seems deeply invested in Gothic conceits and rhetoric, which it then represses, focusing on hope instead of horror. Reading the Gothic together with Thing Theory in some respects performs the same kind of critique as that voiced by the critics mentioned previously. Behar's concern, in particular, concerning the reduction of human beings to things is one shared by the Gothic, as developed in Chapter 3 here.

I would add finally that my attention to the Gothic genre as essentially the repressed substrate of contemporary Thing Theory is not intended to negate the proposition that there are literary works that regard the prospect of animated objects in ways other than horror. Certainly, another approach to Thing Theory could explore its inheritance from nineteenth-century Romanticism and its varying attitudes in relation to nonhuman life. My concern here, however, is specifically with the Gothic's correspondences with contemporary theory as the former takes up the problem of the animated thing in ways that both resonate with and diverge from theoretical explorations of the same problem. This study thus seeks to weigh in on a set of present-day concerns through a reading of how contemporary criticism and the Gothic respond to and play off each other. As the rest of this book will argue, the Gothic and contemporary Thing Theory are two sides to the same coin, telling the same tale but with very different affective valences. What Thing Theory often presents with hope, the Gothic regards with horror—and a lot hinges on how we respond to challenges to human exceptionalism.

1
Gothic Thing Theory

The approach to Gothic materiality developed in this study was initiated by my consideration of contemporary "Thing Theory"—the constellation of twenty-first-century theoretical approaches including Speculative Realism, New Materialism, Object-Oriented Ontology, and Vibrant Materialism that share a critique of anthropocentrism and a focus on the primacy and agency of matter. Jane Bennett's idea of "thing-power" in particular, "the curious ability of inanimate things to animate, to act, to produce effects dramatic and subtle" (2010, 6), as she puts it, resonated with my understanding of the Gothic, prompting me to reflect on the fact that the uncanny animacy of matter is exactly what the Gothic as a genre has emphasized since its origins in the eighteenth century. Amplifying this association still more was then the curious tendency of twenty-first-century philosophers and cultural theorists to illustrate their ideas using language and examples that either implicitly or explicitly evoke the Gothic. Accordingly, this first chapter will explore the Gothic as contemporary Thing Theory's shadowy doppelgänger—that is, as a generic framework that shares many of Thing Theory's central preoccupations but with an inverted affective valence: horror rather than hope.

Before focusing on particular examples from Thing Theory, however, it's worth highlighting the overwhelming insistence of Gothic tropes across twenty-first-century critical and cultural theory in general. The prevailing structure of feeling of the twenty-first century may well be what we might refer to as Anthropocenic anxiety, as both critical discourse and popular culture draw repeatedly upon the Gothic as a means through which to express concerns about human impotence, hubris, and our future disappearance. In the critical literature, particularly that group of approaches categorized by Richard Grusin as the "nonhuman turn" including Latourean actor-network theory, affect theory, animal studies, New Materialism, and Speculative Realism, Gothic figures and tropes abound as humans become things, things acquire uncanny animacy, and we brush shoulders with Lovecraftian monsters, serial killers, zombies, and other weird creatures (see Grusin 2015). In popular culture, Anthropocenic anxiety is expressed more directly through Gothic narratives of human decentering and apocalypse. This is particularly evident when considering the mainstreaming of speculative literature and media featuring narratives in which human autonomy and presumptions of mastery are challenged or the human race is threatened with extinction. Such narratives take many forms and range from Lovecraftian tales of cosmic dread to eco-catastrophe stories to wish-fulfillment superhero narratives in which only the intervention of secularized deities saves the world from some otherwise unstoppable force.

Three master tropes of Gothicized discourse have proliferated across contemporary theoretical paradigms that together express a twenty-first-century structure of feeling undergirded by anxiety over the fate of the human: spectrality, monstrosity, and apocalypse. Spectrality encompasses the weird, eerie, and outside of things; monstrosity addresses the in-/post-human; and apocalypse concerns anxieties over the fate of the human when confronted by potentially cataclysmic events and effects: climate change, global pandemics, nuclear annihilation, and so on. Despite the frequent attempt to spin or repurpose these tropes as ethical provocations to live more justly, gently, and deliberately, their proliferation and overlap in critical discourse and popular culture express the irony of the Anthropocene: the anxiety that the pinnacle of human achievement has been the creation of the conditions of our destruction.

Spectrality (Geist as Zeitgeist)

The first of the three master tropes of contemporary Gothic discourse is the one that has been most fully addressed from a metacritical perspective: spectrality, together with the associated concept of haunting. Taken broadly, spectrality can be considered as that which does not materialize fully; haunting is what the spectral does. Writ large, both have to do with incompleteness. As María del Pilar Blanco and Esther Peeren address in the introduction to their *The Spectralities Reader: Ghosts and Hauntings in Contemporary Cultural Theory* (2013), the publication in 1993 of Jacques Derrida's *Specters of Marx* is typically considered the catalyst for the so-called "spectral turn" of critical and cultural theory. However, long before the concept of spectrality ironically crystalized with *Specters*, spectrality had emerged as the organizing premise of both psychoanalysis and deconstruction. Fundamental to psychoanalysis is, of course, the idea of the return of the repressed, while Derridean deconstruction focused on the idea that concepts must be understood in relation to their opposites and that meaning is nowhere present but rather consistently deferred. As I wrote regarding the "spectral turn,"

> Because ghosts are unstable interstitial figures that problematize dichotomous thinking, it perhaps should come as no surprise that phantoms have become a privileged poststructuralist academic trope. Neither living nor dead, present nor absent, the ghost functions as the paradigmatic deconstructive gesture, the "shadowy third" or trace of an absence that undermines the fixedness of such binary oppositions. As an entity out of place in time, as something from the past that emerges into the present, the phantom calls into question the linearity of history. And as, in philosopher Jacques Derrida's words in his *Specters of Marx*, the *"plus d'un,"* simultaneously the "no more one" and the "more than one," the ghost suggests the complex relationship between the constitution of individual subjectivity and the larger social collective. (Weinstock 2004, 4)

In divisions ranging from "spectral media" to "spectral places" to "haunted historiographies," Blanco and Peeren's 2013 anthology collects selections testifying to the pervasiveness of the concept of spectrality in late twentieth- and early twenty-first-century cultural theory, and the prevailing critical framework—the mode of haunting—is largely that of the uncanny: the emergence of the strange within the familiar. Reason is haunted by its opposite, science by the occult, familiar places by traumatic histories that refuse to lie quietly, and so on. And it is fair to say that, now in the third decade of the twenty-first century, critical and cultural theory continues to emphasize the linked concepts of the ghost and hauntings, albeit often with a more eco-critical orientation.

A case in point is the ambitious two-part collection *Arts of Living on a Damaged Planet* (2017), edited by Anna Tsing, Heather Swanson, Elaine Gan, and Nils Bubandt. Organized around the themes of ghosts and monsters, the essays assert that "entangled histories, situated narratives, and thick descriptions offer urgent 'arts of living' . . . for survival in a more-than-human Anthropocene" (book jacket). In the introduction to the "Ghosts on a Damaged Planet" section, titled "Introduction: Haunted Landscapes of the Anthropocene," the editors emphasize the "Holocene entanglements" of the human and nonhuman as our present is haunted by the past, which in turn directs our possible futures. "Every landscape is haunted by past ways of life," they write. "We see this clearly in the presence of plants whose animal seed-dispersers are no longer with us. Some plants have seeds so big that only big animals can carry them to new places to germinate. When these animals became extinct, their plants could continue without them, but they have been unable to disperse their seeds very well. Their distribution is curtailed; their popular dwindles. This is an example of what we call haunting" (Tsing et al. 2017, G2). The essays that follow in this section then address the consequences of human influence on the environment with emphases ranging from radiation to wetlands to lichens and stones.

"Ghosts on a Damaged Planet" offers a clear illustration of my assertion that our narration of the Anthropocene is as Gothic tale. That the contributors span multiple disciplines from Biology to Ecology to Philosophy to Anthropology suggests the transdisciplinary entrenchment of this narrative. The essays included in the ghosts section, ruminating as they do on the ways that which is not present nevertheless haunts our landscapes and influences our thinking and actions, employ the tropes of spectrality and haunting in familiar ways—although, reflecting contemporary eco-consciousness, the authors' utilize a more capacious framework for thinking spectrality than earlier models rigidly focused on human history. It is now the planet that is haunted by the intermingling of human and nonhuman pasts.

Despite the familiar framework of haunting as uncanny—the strange within the familiar—the "Ghosts on a Damaged Planet" assertions of a haunted planet nevertheless start to exert torque on the spectral turn, twisting it in a different direction away from the uncanny and toward the modes Mark Fisher refers to as the weird and the eerie. Both ghosts and haunting are forms of what Mark Fisher in his final book, *The Weird and the Eerie* (2016), would consider the strange. As opposed to the horrific, the strange has to do with "a fascination for the outside, for that which lies beyond standard perception, cognition, and experience" (8). Fisher then divides the strange into three categories: the uncanny, the weird, and the eerie. The uncanny, as discussed earlier, is "about the strange *within* the familiar, the strangely familiar, the familiar as strange—about the way in which the domestic world does not coincide with itself" (10). The weird and the eerie, in contrast, are not about the familiar but, as Fisher, describes it, the "outside" (10). The weird "brings to the familiar something which ordinarily lies beyond it, and which cannot be reconciled with the 'homely' (even as its negation)" (10–11). The weird is associated with a "sense of *wrongness* . . . the conviction that *this does not belong*" (13). The weird is marked by "the irruption into *this* world of something from outside" (20). The eerie, in contrast, is marked either by a "*failure of absence* or by a *failure of presence*" (61). "The sensation of the eerie," continues Fisher, "occurs either when there is something present where there should be nothing, or [when] there is nothing present when there should be something" (61). The eerie concerns the unknown: "There must be . . . a sense of alterity, a feeling that the enigma might involve forms of knowledge, subjectivity and sensation that lie beyond common experience" (62). Ultimately, Fisher connects eeriness with questions of agency—the "forces that govern our lives and the world" (64). Put concisely, the uncanny, associated with repression, emerges from within, while the weird and the eerie intrude from without. The uncanny is strangely familiar; the weird and eerie are disconcertingly foreign. Our story of the Anthropocene is one in which we are doubly haunted: both by the return of the repressed and by the prospect of "unknown unknowns"—the foreign that resists domestication.

The twenty-first-century twist to the spectral turn, the one perhaps signaled by *The Art of Living on a Damaged Planet*'s roomier articulation of haunting, is one in fact that shifts the spectral turn away from psychoanalysis and deconstruction and instills it instead at the heart of our interactions with objects: in our twenty-first-century narrativization of the Anthropocene, we move from uncanny ghosts to weird spectrality. One place to start to consider this shift is with Graham Harman and the school of philosophy with which he is associated—Object-Oriented Ontology, itself a form of what has come to be called "Speculative Realism." Object-Oriented Ontology or OOO is a twenty-first-century school of thought that rejects "correlationalism," the perspective that, as Ian Bogost explains, "being exists only as a correlate between mind and world" or, put differently, that "if things exist, they do so only *for us*" (Bogost 2012, 4). OOO maintains instead that objects exist independently of human perception and are not exhausted in their interactions with us and other objects. In Harman's 2011 *The Quadruple Object* and elsewhere, he differentiates between "sensual" qualities and objects and "real" objects and qualities. Our perceptions of things are not their truth. The real is that which exists outside of our sensual apprehension of something—it is that which withdraws from knowing. As Harman puts it in *The Quadruple Object*, "When I stare at a river, wolf, government, machine, or army, I do not grasp the whole of their reality. This reality slips from view into a perpetually veiled underworld, leaving me with only the most frivolous simulacra of these entities. In short, the phenomenal reality of things for consciousness does not use up their being" (39).

Already here we have shifted into the language of ghosts, haunting, and radical uncertainty. We never encounter real objects directly, only their sensual qualities; real objects withdraw into a "veiled underworld" (Harman 2011, 39). Instead, we encounter only "frivolous simulacra" (39)—essentially ghosts of real objects. Harman is associated with the philosophical movement known as "Speculative Realism"—a general rubric encompassing a variety of different philosophical perspectives united most immediately by their rejection of correlationalism. As usefully summarized by Steven Shaviro,

> Speculative Realism insists upon the independence of the world, and of things in the world, from our own conceptualizations of them. . . . Reality is far *weirder* than we are able to imagine. Things never conform to the ideas that we have about them; there is always something more to them than what we are able to grasp. The world does not fit into our own cognitive paradigms and narrative modes of explanation. "Man" is *not* the measure of all things. This is why speculation is necessary. We *must* speculate, to escape from our inveterate anthropocentrism and take seriously the existence of a fundamentally alien, nonhuman world. (Shaviro 2015; emphasis on "weirder" mine)

Shaviro's use of the word "weird" in his overview is also Harman's word—and in both cases the use resonates with Fisher's meditations. Harman uses the word several times in *The Quadruple Object* to refer to the strangeness of a universe of things that we don't encounter directly, but then makes it central to his 2012 *Weird Realism: Lovecraft and Philosophy*. For Harman, as I will develop more fully, the fiction of H. P. Lovecraft offers useful illustrations of the principles of Object-Oriented Ontology.

The twenty-first-century twist to more conventional Gothic discourse relating specters to repression and the uncanny is that that Speculative Realism's specters are weird—they are, as Fisher remarks of Lovecraft's gods and monsters, irruptions "*into* this world from outside" (2016, 20). The "outside" for the Speculative Realists is what Quentin Meillassoux in *After Finitude* (2008) refers to as "the Great Outdoors"—*le Grand Dehors* in the French—"the *absolute* outside . . . that outside which [is] not relative to us . . . existing in itself regardless of whether we are thinking of it or not" (7). The specters of Speculative Realism are thus glimpses of another universe—they are, as suggested by the title of Ian Bogost's *Alien Phenomenology, or What It's Like to Be a Thing* (2012)—aliens. The narrative of the Anthropocene as told by the speculative realists is thus a weird one indeed in which we are surrounded by alien ghosts irrupting from the absolute outside and highlighting the limitations on what we can truly know.

Connected to the Speculative Realism school but approaching the hauntedness of the planet from a somewhat different direction is Timothy Morton, whose influential concept of "hyperobjects" has catalyzed a substantial amount of intellectual inquiry since the publication in 2013 of *Hyperobjects: Philosophy and Ecology after the End of the World* (2013a). For the speculative realists, all objects are ultimately unknowable, withdrawing into themselves and hiding their real qualities. Hyperobjects, however, are a special class of unknowable objects defined by their enormous spatial and temporal dimensions. The term "hyperobject" refers to "things that are massively distributed in time and space relative to humans" (Morton 2013a, 1) and encompasses things like black holes, climate change, and the "whirring machinery of capitalism" (1). Importantly, we never encounter these objects directly even when they influence, touch, or penetrate us. The local manifestation of the hyperobject is not the object itself—an unusually hot day or a mega-storm is not global warming, which "cannot be directly seen, but it can be thought and computed" (3, fig. 1). Hyperobjects are, in Morton's terminology, "phased": "they occupy a high-dimensional *phase space* that makes them impossible to see as a whole on a regular three-dimensional human-scale basis" (70). This means "we can only see pieces of hyperobjects at a time" (70).

What hyperobjects do is "humiliate" us (see 17), bring us low, highlighting as they do our physical, temporal, and intellectual limitations as well as our fragility. Where they are massive, we are tiny indeed, and they are weird in every sense. In keeping with Fisher's definition, they intrude from without rather than irrupt from within and, in doing so, reveal our conceptions of things to be inadequate; in keeping with Harman, they highlight the gap between sensual qualities of things and the things themselves and, in keeping with Harman's muse, Lovecraft, hyperobjects excite in us a "profound sense of dread, and of contact with unknown spheres and powers" (Lovecraft, *Supernatural Horror* [1973], 16) as Lovecraft characterizes the weird tale. Our entanglement with them even invokes the older concept of *wyrd*, fate, as they influence human destiny on the planet. Our experience of them is inevitably incomplete—we only ever encounter spectral glimpses of them even as they haunt our experience. Recycling an idea present in Carl Sagan's 1985 science fiction novel *Contact* and its 1997 film adaptation, the third season of the science fiction series *The Expanse* (2018) has an alien intelligence manifesting before a protagonist in the form of a ghost. The alien civilization is the hyperobject, the ghost a local manifestation of it that our minds can grasp—both metonymy (connected to the alien intelligence) and metaphor (intelligible form of expression). What Morton discusses as the spectral nature of hyperobjects in particular corresponds with what Speculative Realists assert as the nature of reality in general. We only ever encounter the piecemeal ghosts of things, not the things themselves. Hyperobjects, one must note, are certainly not all new—planetary forces of course predate the Anthropocene; what is new is our awareness of them and our abilities to chart and calculate and speculate on their qualities—and it is our awareness of them and their implications for the human species that, as we shall see, structures the Gothic Anthropocene master narrative of apocalypse. Knowledge of our own limitations when confronted with deep time and cosmic forces highlights the precarity of the human situation.

My reference to *Contact* and *The Expanse* was an analogy suggested by one final piece that I will briefly consider here before moving on: author and scholar Jeff VanderMeer's 2016 piece "Hauntings in the Anthropocene." In this essay, VanderMeer—the popular author of weird fiction notable in particular for his Southern Reach trilogy and its first novel, *Annihilation* (2014), that was adapted for film in 2018—relates Morton's notion of hyperobjects to his own fiction. Hyperobjects in general and global warming in particular, according to VanderMeer, should be understood as "hauntings" that not only "make a mockery of what our five senses can perceive" but challenge conventional understandings of the fixed laws of nature. In particular, these hyperobject hauntings foreground the entanglement of the human with inhuman forces and time scales. "In the Anthropocene," writes VanderMeer, "hauntings and similar manifestations become emissaries or transition points between the human sense of time and the geologic sense of time." The spectral acts as a kind of hinge, pivoting us toward the inaccessible real. In the Anthropocene, the age of hyperobjects, *"The uncanny has infiltrated the real,"* concludes VanderMeer, *"and in some sense that boundary is forever compromised"* (VanderMeer 2016). Weird fiction's contemporary popularity is explained then, at least in part, by its reflection of weird reality. Its defamiliarizations function as analogies for incomprehensible yet lived experience. The weird gives shape to the amorphous irruptions of the outside that puncture the Anthropocene.

Examples can proliferate here. No doubt there are many other directions one could take and paths to consider when exploring the ubiquity of spectral metaphors within twenty-first-century critical discourse, and, indeed, that is precisely the point: Spectrality, along with, as we shall see, monstrosity and apocalypse, has become an organizing conceit of how we narrate our experience of the Anthropocene. When we tell the story of the Anthropocene, whether it focuses on what the human species has done to the world or on how we interact with it, the story seems "naturally" to become a kind of ghost story, a tale of haunting—haunted selves, haunted landscapes, haunted planet.

Monstrosity (From Monster to "Monster")

If the planet is haunted in twenty-first-century critical and popular culture discourse, it is also overrun by monsters ranging from antagonistic angels to flesh-eating zombies. And, like spectrality, monstrosity has received considerable attention from late twentieth- and early twenty-first-century cultural critics who deploy the term in various ways, often ironically turning it back on itself to challenge the human/nonhuman binary opposition it frequently signifies (see, for example, my *Monster Theory Reader* [Weinstock 2020]). As master trope of Anthropocenic discourse, the monster is frequently rendered as "monster," calling attention to monstrosity as social construction and relational rather than ontological. The concept functions most centrally in twenty-first-century discourse to trouble Humanist understandings of identity as singular and autonomous. This is where the irony of the Anthropocene becomes most obvious: In the Anthropocene, we are all "monsters"—not discrete, independent actors, but things enmeshed with other things in various constantly shifting networks. The human is always entangled with the nonhuman; ironically, what makes us human is that we are not fully human.

If Derrida's *Specters of Marx* (2006) catalyzed the spectral turn, then Jeffrey Jerome Cohen's "Monster Culture (Seven Theses)," the introduction to his 1996 edited collection *Monster Theory: Reading Culture* (1996) arguably touched off the "monster turn" of critical and cultural studies. In this introduction, Cohen develops seven theses concerning what monsters are and how they function: 1. they are "pure culture" (1996, 4) reflecting the culturally specific understandings of normalcy and deviance; 2. They "always escape" both because the anxieties and desires they express are difficult to contain and because the same monster can shift over time to reflect different sets of concerns and desires; 3. They reflect categorical confusion; 4. They give shape to anxieties concerning differences of all types; 5. They warn against transgression of cultural expectations—violate the rules and you are in danger of either being eaten by the monster or becoming one; 6. They reflect tabooed desires as well as anxieties—monsters are powerful and do not concern themselves with being polite and abiding by social expectations; and 7. They can metacritically prompt us to reflect on our own assumptions, biases, and expectations.

Cohen's essay has served as a touchstone essay for "monster theory" because of its generally concise and insightful formulations of what monsters are and what they do, and subsequent cultural criticism related to monsters, directed by Cohen's essay, has followed two main channels: explications of how monsters function as metaphors for particular anxieties and desires in specific contexts, and appropriations/deconstructions of monstrosity in the name of social and, more recently, ecological justice. While individual readings of particular monsters as canny reflections of contemporary anxieties and desires (say, zombies as giving shape to anxieties concerning global pandemics; vampire heroes as reflecting capitalist demands to consume in order to stay youthful) and even more ambitious explications of monsters as overdetermined "meaning machines" that "can represent gender, race, nationality, class, and sexuality in one body" (Halberstam 1995, 22) are certainly useful and often compelling, the more interesting thread of monster theory to pursue here in our articulation of the Anthropocene as Gothic tale is what we could refer to as the "hopeful monster" theme.

What Cohen expresses through his seven theses is that the idea of monstrosity is a social construction dependent on one's perspective, but also that the label of "monster" has functioned as a powerful tool of social control—in this, Cohen channels the work of Michel Foucault, who addresses social constructions of normalcy and deviance throughout his work. This understanding of the political deployment of monstrosity as part of a program to maintain an exclusionary status quo and license abuse and domination has led to attempts first to invert and then to displace the normal/abnormal binary opposition as forms of political resistance. Central to the inversion step in cultural criticism has been Donna Haraway, who, particularly in her 1985 "A Cyborg Manifesto: Science, Technology, and Socialist-Feminism in the Late Twentieth Century" and her 1992 "The Promises of Monsters: A Regenerative Politics for Inappropriate/d Others," offers an ironic reappropriation of the label of monster as a gesture of sociopolitical liberation. Adopting a strategy similar to the reclamation of the word "queer" in the late 1980s, Haraway essentially reclaims the word "monster" as a form of resistance to the discriminatory logic of social expectation: monstrosity as refusal.

Haraway's reclamation of the label "monster" in general and, famously, the cyborg in particular reflects a broad cultural shift wherein the label "monster" is ironically turned back on those who affix the label in the first place as a strategy of control and domination. While there are still zombies that eat brains and giant resurrected dinosaurs that rampage and destroy, in progressive twenty-first-century discourse, both popular and critical, the recurring lessons are: (1) monsters are not intrinsically bad, just misunderstood; and (2) human beings—most often, white men in positions of power—are the *true monsters*. This is the inversion step reflective of a system of values that now privileges diversity and free expression of individuality (the ironic "we're all non-conformists here!"). The monsters are not those who look different or act quirky, but those who attempt to bend others to their will in the pursuit of power and/or profit (typically foiled by a gruff but actually good-hearted ogre or a bunch of meddling kids). The logic often boils down to embracing the term "monster," on the one hand, as a rejection of constraints on the free expression of individuality while, on the other, ironically characterizing those who deploy the rhetoric of monstrosity to further their own designs as the true monsters.

Twenty-first-century cultural theory, however, has taken the next step in the deconstruction of the human/nonhuman (monster) binary, which is to displace the opposition entirely through the notion of the posthuman. The logic here shifts to: "We are all monsters/none of us is a monster." This notion too can be traced back to Haraway and her celebration of the cyborg, which she characterizes as a third term that undoes many of the defining oppositions of Western culture, including nature/culture, organic/inorganic, and man/woman. (In Rosi Braidotti's introduction to posthumanism, she notes that posthumanism as philosophical framework for thinking "rejects dualism, especially the opposition nature-culture" [see Braidotti 2013, 3]). Haraway's cyborg has come to function as iconic avatar of posthumanism, that branch of cultural inquiry critical of Humanist assumptions about "the human" and "human nature" (assumptions that have often been central to determining who is or is not construed as monstrous).

In Haraway's 2015 *Staying with the Trouble: Making Kin in the Chthulucene*, she returns to her hopeful philosophy of monstrosity again, here celebrating "chthonic monsters"—creatures of the earth with wonderous nonhuman morphologies: "replete with tentacles, feelers, digits, cords, whiptails, spider legs, and very unruly hair" (2). Such creatures cannot be tamed and "belong to no one" (2) as they "writhe and luxuriate in manifold forms and manifold names in all the airs, waters, and places of earth" (2). They are with the human without being for the human, with worlds of their own that nevertheless are part of the human world. The challenge of what Haraway refers to as the Chthulucene is to forge "kinship" (2) with such monsters, rather than to seek to tame or eradicate them. In Latour's terms, we must "love" our monsters, which he conceives of as "a process of becoming ever-more attached to, and intimate with, a panoply of nonhuman natures" ("Love Your Monsters" [2012]).

Twenty-first-century cultural theory, taking its cues from Haraway, Latour, and others, utilizes the rhetoric of monstrosity in its narration of the Anthropocene to highlight the ways human beings are not independent and autonomous, but "entangled" or "enmeshed" in networks of human and nonhuman actants. Here again, Tsing, Swanson, Gan, and Bubandt's *Arts of Living on a Damaged Planet* (2017) is instructive. The monsters section, titled "Monsters and the Arts of Living" (which, indeed, includes an essay from Haraway), begins with an introduction titled "Bodies Tumbled into Bodies" that frames monstrosity as multiplicity. The editors essentially agree with Cohen's thesis that monstrosity is associated with "category crisis," but then foreground the fact that categorical confusion is the nature of existence, prompting the need to rethink the idea of discrete categories altogether: "Against the conceit of the Individual, monsters highlight symbiosis, the enfolding of bodies within bodies in evolution and in every ecological niche. In dialectical fashion, ghosts and monsters unsettle *anthropos*, the Greek term for 'human,' from its presumed center stage in the Anthropocene by highlighting the webs of histories and bodies from which all life, including human life, emerges" (Tsing et al. 2017,

M3). From the bacteria in our gut to our influence on the ecosystem, human bodies are entangled with nonhuman bodies, and our present enmeshed with other times. "Monsters," the editors assert, "are bodies tumbled into bodies" (M10). The Anthropocene narrative is that we are all then monsters, everything is monstrous, everything is a monster: "monster."

Both peril and promise exist here. As the editors of *Arts of Living on a Damaged Planet* argue, "Suffering from the ills of another species: this is the condition of the Anthropocene, for humans and nonhumans alike . . . We are mixed up with other species; we cannot live without them" (M4). Humans are not the center of things, but nodes in a decentered network. This highlights our vulnerability as a species—indeed, rather than the futuristic cyborg of science fiction, in some respects a more apropos posthuman avatar for the twenty-first century might be the DC Comics superhero Swamp Thing, a humanoid/plant creature vulnerable to pollution. And there is danger here in another respect: reconstruing human beings as objects among objects as part of a "flat ontology" (see Bryant 2011; Bogost 2012, 17) in which all things are equal in existing can license rather than diminish exploitation—which is why Jane Bennett in *Vibrant Matter: A Political Economy of Things* (2010) suggests "a touch of anthropomorphism" as a strategy to "catalyze a sensibility that finds a world filled not with ontologically distinct categories of beings (subjects and objects) but with variously composed materialities that form confederations" (99). Some sense of human exceptionalism must be retained, suggests Bennett, to avoid treating human beings in the same disastrous way in which human beings have treated the natural world. A "flat ontology" can "elevate" the "shared materiality of all things" (Bennett 2010, 13). The danger, however, is that, in a world in which the nonhuman is often valued for its utility to human beings, a flat ontology could work in the other direction—reducing human beings (many of whom have never enjoyed full status as human to begin with) to the status of nonhuman things to be exploited.

Critics of this New Materialist ontological flattening have also significantly highlighted the fact that not all bodies have historically been regarded as fully human. As Leon Hilton observes in a review of Mel Y. Chen's *Animacies: Biopolitics, Racial Mattering, and Queer Affect* (2012), "Recent attention within the humanities to matters of life and agency beyond the human—from the ongoing invocations of affect to the contemporary philosophical interest in 'Speculative Realism'—have notoriously been less attentive to the racialized, heteronormative, and ableist dimensions of their accounts of materiality" (Hilton 2013). These concerns are echoed by other theorists who explore "racial mattering"—understood as the materialization of beliefs concerning race in the form of physical bodies. Monique Allewaert, for example, in *Ariel's Ecology:*

Plantations, Personhood, and Colonialism in the American Tropics (2013) explores the representation of "African-descended human beings" in colonial texts of the seventeenth, eighteenth, and nineteenth centuries as "parahuman": as "constituting a kind of interstitial life between humans, animals, objects, and sometimes even plants" (6). Echoing Allewaert's consideration of the black body's interstitiality in colonialist discourse, Alexander G. Weheliye, in *Habeas Viscus*, foregrounds the "assemblage of forces that ... articulate nonwhite subjects as not-quite-human" (2014, 19). Zakiyyah Iman Jackson, too, considers how "the black body's fleshiness was aligned with that of animals and set in opposition to European spirit and mind" (Jackson 2013, 6). From the perspective of those who document how the materialization of racial ideologies through a process of "enfleshment" (Weheliye 2014, 2) has worked in concert with racist hierarchization, bracketing off the history and social context of bodies "suppresses different lived experiences of power to ontology, neglects the insights of feminist and queer theory as well as indigenous cosmologies, and stumbles when it comes to race" (Shomura 2017). To say that "all things equally exist" (Bogost 2012, 11) in an ontological sense—including all bodies as things—may be true but ignores "objecthood as a historical category with roots in larger political systems like racial capitalism, biopolitics, or colonialism" (Tompkins 2016). Put differently, New Materialist and related paradigms "committed to thinking through the non-relational autonomy of the object world" (Tompkins 2016) fail to consider sufficiently that, while all things exist equally, they are not equal in existing—and where monstrosity is concerned, it is important to bear in mind that racial difference has often been elaborated into monstrosity, with "parahuman" or "not-quite-human" dark bodies falling precisely into the zone of categorical indeterminacy where monstrosity is situated (see Cohen 1996, 6–7).

Despite these concerns, the discourse of monstrosity as part of the nonhuman turn of twenty-first-century critical theory tends to recuperate the monster as a figure for a possible future more accepting of difference. A case in point is Cohen, who, at the end of his "Seven Theses," foregrounds a kind of hope inherent in the monster for living more justly: "Monsters are our children," he writes. "They ask why we have created them" (Cohen 1996, 20). Reflective consideration of what we consider monstrous can prompt reconsideration of sedimented ways of thinking that participate in forms of political violence and exclusion—no doubt important. But twenty-first-century cultural theory has gone further. The promise of Anthropocenic monstrosity inheres in that catalyzed sensibility that recognizes the human entanglement with the nonhuman. From this perspective, human survival requires shaking off Humanist conceptions of the discrete Individual and instead acknowledging our shared monstrosity. We have always been posthuman "monsters," but current threats to the planet and human survival now require we acknowledge this and take appropriate steps to stave off catastrophe.

Apocalypse

And if we do not acknowledge our precarity, we go the way of the dinosaurs—assuming we are not already too late—and the planet, better off without us, won't mourn our passing. The third master trope of the Gothicized narrative of the Anthropocene is the darkest: apocalypse, associated as well with extinction of the human as a species. From all-too-real global pandemics to climate change to nuclear annihilation, the Anthropocene is the age of apocalypse. To be fair, speculation about the end of the world is nothing new and plays a significant role in many world religions and traditions; however, awareness of the possibility of catastrophe, especially in the wake of Covid-19, now structures our thinking about ourselves, our relations to others, and the (im)possibility of a future.

Popular culture is of course awash with apocalyptic and post-apocalyptic narratives ranging from the bombast of super villains threatening human existence to the horror of hordes of ghouls to the quiet majesty of Emily St. John Mandel's post-apocalyptic *Station Eleven* (2014). The world is constantly ending everywhere we look, including in contemporary cultural theory. Unlike spectrality and monstrosity, however, there is not as far as I am aware a single foundational text catalyzing an "extinctionist turn" of cultural criticism—Susan Sontag's "The Imagination of Disaster" (2004; first published in 1965) seems important, as do Ray Brassier's 2007 *Nihil Unbound: Enlightenment and Extinction*, Claire Colebrook's 2014 collection *Death of the PostHuman: Essays on Extinction, vol. 1*, and Patricia MacCormack's 2020 *The Ahuman Manifesto: Activism for the End of the Anthropocene*, but none of these seems (yet) to have established itself as a kind of touchstone text directing subsequent criticism to the same extent as Freud and Derrida have influenced our thinking about spectrality and Foucault and Cohen have directed theorization about monsters. Instead, apocalypse and extinction seem for the most part to serve as the backdrop against which much contemporary cultural theory is articulated: We need cultural criticism because our way of life is killing us. Indeed, it may well be that all the ghosts and monsters have emerged in popular culture and cultural criticism precisely because we seem poised on the edge of catastrophe—we are haunted by the prospect of apocalypse, we are committing slow (but accelerating) suicide, we are the monsters. *One master trope then to control them all: the Anthropocene as apocalyptic narrative breeding ghosts and monsters.*

This is more or less the conclusion of philosopher Eugene Thacker, whose work is often associated with that of the Speculative Realists and with philosophical nihilists such as Brassier. In *In the Dust of This Planet* (2011), the first of Thacker's "Horror of Philosophy" trilogy, Thacker explores horror narrative as a kind of thought experiment that seeks—like Speculative Realism—to consider what things are like in their unknowable essence. Here Thacker distinguishes among the "world-for-us," which is the world "we interpret and give meaning to" (4), the "world-without-us," which is a depopulated planet that we can still imagine, and the "world-in-itself," the inaccessible real world. Horror, asserts Thacker—and here he has in mind in particular, like Harman, weird fiction and the cosmic horror of Lovecraft—"is a non-philosophical attempt to think about the world-without-us philosophically" (Thacker 2011, 9). Horror is "about the enigmatic thought of the unknown" (8–9). Horror narrative is the natural outgrowth of the Anthropocene thought of as the age of extinction, in which the human species is forced to confront its monstrosity in the sense articulated in *Arts of Living on a Damaged Planet* (Tsing et al. 2017)—that is, as bodies tumbled into other bodies, inflicting and receiving suffering as a consequence of entanglement in human/nonhuman networks and bad decisions.

The questions of how to respond and what to do about being on the brink of apocalypse are those taken up by Matthew J. Wolf-Meyer in his 2019 *Theory for the World to Come: Speculative Fiction and Apocalyptic Anthropology*—an at-times personal and lyrical meditation proposing an approach but no easy answers (because there are no easy answers). According to Wolf-Meyer, speculative fiction and social theory both confront questions about catastrophe, aftermath, ramifications, and response. The true problem, however, is that, as Wolf-Meyer puts it, the "apocalypse is never singular; it is always multiple. In its multiplicity, the apocalypse is unimaginable. What is to be done when the future eludes our capacities for imaginative play and scientific modeling?" (4). How do we prepare for the unimaginable future? How do we grasp the ungraspable hyperobject? How do we know the unknowable real object? How do we negotiate the weirdness of the Anthropocene? "The end of the world," writes Morton, "is correlated with the Anthropocene, its global warming and subsequent dramatic climate change" (2013a, 7). Myra Hird articulates a similar sentiment, correlating Anthropocene with the end of the world, "our vulnerability to planetary forces" (2017, 255), which she sees connected to anxieties about the "consequences of human proliferation" (251). And she agrees with Wolf-Meyer that the future is ungraspable: "At the limits of the Anthropocene, the future cannot be visualized: It is an unknown aesthetic in excess of scientific prediction, human agency, and good will. It is indeterminate" (264).

"Speculative fiction—and social theory—that considers desolation and its aftermath," responds Wolf-Meyer, "helps to point to ways forward, ways to live through the apocalypse, even if living through doesn't manage to keep things the same as they were" (Wolf-Meyer 2019, 15).

This then is a central—perhaps *the* central—story of the Anthropocene thus far as articulated both in twenty-first-century critical and cultural theory and popular culture: a Gothic tale of a haunted planet, filled with monsters, framed against the backdrop of apocalypse. Late twentieth- and twenty-first-century discourse has pivoted around these three master tropes: spectrality, monstrosity, and apocalypse. So much about them seems to "naturally" express our contemporary structure of feeling: the uncanny hauntedness of our present moment, the strategic deployment of monstrosity and the "monster" as a way to refuse destructive philosophical paradigms, the weirdness of a universe in which we are entangled with nonhuman actors we can't fully know, the ever-present specter of catastrophe.

Ominous Matter

Previously, I offered an overview of the Anthropocene as Gothic tale as narrated in twenty-first-century critical discourse. I would now like to focus in more detail on a handful of moments in theoretical texts highlighting the Gothic subtext of Thing Theory. In my introduction to this book, I attended to the assemblage of items Jane Bennett observed one spring morning on a storm drain. Here, I'd like to take a look at another list of items—this one taken from Ian Bogost's introduction to Object-Oriented Ontology, *Alien Phenomenology*. At the end of his second chapter on "ontography," a kind of "inscriptive strategy that uncovers the repleteness of objects and their interobjectivity," Bogost offers the following "ontograph," a list of apparently random objects intended to show "how *much* rather than how *little* exists simultaneously, suspended in the dense meanwhile of being" (2012, 59):

> On August 10, 1973, at a boathouse in Southwest Houston, the shovel of a police forensics investigator struck the femur of one of seventeen corpses excavated that week, victims of serial killer Dean Corll.
>
> Meanwhile, 235 nautical miles above the earth's surface, a radio wave began its course from Skylab to a parabolic radar dish antenna aboard United States Naval Ship Vanguard.
>
> Meanwhile, at Royals Stadium in Kansas City, Lou Piniella's cleat met home plate, kicking up dust as it scored what would become the team's winning run against the Baltimore Orioles.

And meanwhile, at the Trail's End Restaurant in Kanab, Utah, a bowl snuggled a half cantaloupe, and butter seeped into the caramelized surface of a pancake. . . . (59)

Where Bennett's assemblage or "confederation" of materialities simply provided the raw materials for narrative—glove, pollen, rate, cap, stick—and then implicitly demanded that we refrain from narrativizing them, Bogost gives us as his raw materials snippets of preconstituted narrative, bits of stories—and the results are curiously unsettling, beginning as they do with a serial killer and ending, like a scene from the program *Hannibal* about cannibal Hannibal Lecter, with a weirdly eroticized scene at the breakfast table.

Indeed, where Bennett invites us to construct a narrative out of a list of objects (but then implicitly asks that we don't), Bogost's juxtapositions within his ontograph tantalize us in a dark way with the prospect of connection and almost compel us to dig deeper—which we can do by exhuming information about the exhumation. That Object-Oriented Ontology moves us into the affective terrain of the Gothic—OOO as horror story—seems evident even from the first item in Bogost's ontograph: the body part of the victim of a serial killer. Dean Arnold Corll was an American serial killer who (with two young accomplices named David Brooks and Elmer Wayne Henley Jr.) abducted, raped, tortured, and murdered at least twenty-eight boys in a series of killings spanning from 1970 to 1973 in Houston, Texas. Corll was also known as the Candy Man and the Pied Piper because he and his family had owned and operated a candy factory in Houston, and he had been known to give free candy to local children. At the time of their discovery, the Houston Mass Murders were considered the worst example of serial murder in American history (Bovsun 2008). To include the femur from the body of the young victim of a serial killer indiscriminately among a list of other things and tableaus is a curious move indeed, and raises some important ethical questions: What happens when people are treated as things? Can we and should we tell the story of a pedophile serial killer together with a story about modern communication technologies and breakfast foods? If, as OOO theorists assert, all things are equal in the fact of their existence, does that mean we should treat all things as equal? It is precisely the Gothic that explores these questions and the pernicious consequences of treating human beings as objects—which, I would suggest, is part of the reason the Gothic should matter to us today.

For us to enter the affective terrain of the Gothic by way of Object-Oriented Ontology and New Materialism, however, doesn't require a corpse or body part; the fundamental premise of Graham Harman's Object-Oriented Ontology is that all objects possess "real qualities" inaccessible to human perception.

"The object," writes Harman in *The Quadruple Object*, "is a dark crystal veiled in a private vacuum" (2011, 47). Real objects always withdraw from knowing—into the "shadows of the world" or the "shadows of being" (Harman, *Weird Realism* [2012, 31]) or an "underworld" where they remain as veiled dark crystals, inaccessible to human knowledge or mastery. As Timothy Morton summarizes in his 2013 *Realist Magic: Objects, Ontology, Causality*, "object-oriented rhetoric becomes the way objects obscure themselves in fold upon fold of mysterious robes, caverns, fortresses of solitude and octopus ink" (2013b, 85). "Weird realism" is Harman's name for this philosophical perspective asserting that objects recede into themselves and do not simply exist for us; the universe as a result is far stranger—weirder—than human beings like to acknowledge as the correlationalist "human-world circle" in which the world is construed as there for us is revealed to be "indefensibly narrow" (Harman 2012, 62).

It is precisely for this reason that Harman turns explicitly to the Gothic—to the fiction of H. P. Lovecraft in his 2012 book *Weird Realism: Lovecraft and Philosophy*—to illustrate his theory. "No other writer," asserts Harman, "is so perplexed by the gap between objects and the powers of language to describe them, or between objects and the qualities they possess" (Harman 2012, 3). Lovecraft is the preeminent author of "weird realism" because his writing continually gestures toward an unrepresentable other reality beyond sensuous perception—and he does this, according to Harman, in two ways: first, through the gap between the "ungraspable thing and the vaguely relevant descriptions that the narrator is able to attempt" (24) and second, by overloading language with a "gluttonous excess of surfaces and aspects of the thing" (25). The literary world of Lovecraft is thus one in which "real objects are locked in impossible tension with the crippled descriptive powers of language" and "visible objects display unbearable seismic torsion with their own qualities" (27), making Lovecraft the "poet laureate of object-oriented philosophy" (32).

This revelation of the "secret life of objects" rattles our knowledge of the universe in unsettling ways. Timothy Morton speaks of it in *Realist Magic* as "the Rift," an irreducible gap between things and their appearances (26). This undoing of correlationalism for Quentin Meillassoux orients us toward "the great outdoors" (*le Grand Dehors*)—space-time "absolutely indifferent to humanity and even to animal life" (Saldanha 2009)—and it is this indifference that authors of weird and horror fiction such as Lovecraft foreground as a source of anxiety, a rebuke to anthropocentrism. The most unsettling implications from an anthropocentric perspective of the undoing of correlationalism are found in philosophical works advancing a nihilist point of view, such as those of Ray Brassier, Thomas Ligotti, and most especially Eugene Thacker. Indeed, Thacker makes the case in *In the Dust of This Planet: Horror of Philosophy*, *vol. 1*, that "'horror' is a non-philosophical attempt to think about the world-without-us philosophically" (2011, 9). As opposed to the world-for-us—the world in which we live—and the world-in-itself, "the world in some inaccessible already-given state, which we then turn into the world-for-us" (5), the world-without-us is a kind of impossible limit, the attempt to think the unthinkable—to imagine the universe without humans doing the imagining.

Morton's take in *Hyperobjects* is a bit different. Rather than try to think the world without us, he seeks to undo the notions of "world" and "nature," which he considers as counterproductive concepts that prevent a complete engagement with the emergency that is Anthropocene global warming and environmental despoliation. And it is here that Morton's rhetoric takes a decidedly Gothic turn in *Hyperobjects*: "Without a world, there is no Nature. Without a world, there is no life. What exists outside the charmed circles of Nature and life is a *charnal ground*, a place of life and death, of death-in-life and life-in-death, an undead place of zombies, viroids, junk DNA, silicates, cyanide, radiation, demonic forces, and pollution" (2013a, 126). "Haunting a charnal ground," Morton concludes, "is a much better analogy for ecological coexistence than inhabiting a world" (126).

Morton's language throughout *Hyperobjects* in fact tends insistently toward the Gothic, and this may be in part because his whole notion of the hyperobject is as something that unseats human dominance. "Hyperobjects," he explains, "force us into intimacy with our own death (because they are toxic), with others (because everyone is affected by them), and with the future (because they are massively distributed in time)" (139). Our present moment is "the uncanny time of zombies after the end of the world" (160). The aesthetic experience of the hyperobject "can only be detected as a ghostly spectrality that comes in and out of phase with normalized human spacetime" (169). Art in the age of hyperobjects is "an attunement to a demonic force coming from the nonhuman and permeating us" (175). "Ecological coexistence is with ghosts, strangers, and specters" (195). Repeatedly, Morton deploys language appropriated from the Gothic to express the uncanniness of hyperobjects and the undoing of the world our awareness of them precipitates.

Indeed, among the practitioners of the nonhuman turn, it is Morton who comes closest to a full acknowledgment of its Gothic underpinnings. Such rhetoric also suffuses, for example, his consideration of "dark ecology," introduced in his 2007 *Ecology without Nature* and meditated on more fully in his 2016 *Dark Ecology: For a Logic of Future Coexistence*. According to Morton, humans need to jettison romantic notions of "Nature" because they come freighted with deeply entrenched associations regarding the human and its interrelation with the nonhuman, reducing the world to things that correspond to "preformed concepts" (Morton 2016, 7) that hinder comprehension of the urgency of climate change. As Morton puts it in his 2010 book *The Ecological Thought*, "Dark ecology oozes with despair. Being realistic is always refreshing. Depression is the most accurate way of experiencing the current ecological disaster" (Morton 2010, 95). Dark ecology is dark, however, not just because of the crisis that is global warming. As Derrick Harris puts it, "Borrowing from Graham Harman's speculative realist Object-Oriented Ontology, Morton argues also that dark ecology is dark also because every aspect of it, every *real* thing, *especially the human*, is incredibly strange, mysterious, contradictory, unspeakable, deceptive, *weird*, or uncanny—right in front of us, inside us, all around us, it *is* us. Yet it is so alien to us it escapes reduction into language and/or thought" (Harris 2016, 303). The rhetoric of the Gothic that suffuses Morton's writing—darkness, spectrality, monstrosity, the weird, the uncanny, "strange strangers," and so on—is thus consciously adopted by Morton as a way to unsettle familiar paradigms of human autonomy, agency, and mastery.

More characteristic of what I refer to in the introduction as the positive valence of twenty-first-century Thing Theory are Bennett and Bogost. In Bennett's 2001 *The Enchantment of Modern Life: Attachments, Crossings, and Ethics*, her book prior to *Vibrant Things*, the metaphor she uses to frame the beginning point for an ethical engagement with the world is, as signaled by the title, "enchantment." For Bennett, to be enchanted "is to be struck and shaken by the extraordinary that lives amid the familiar and the everyday" (Bennett 2001, 4). A synonym for enchantment that Bennett uses, "wonder," is also used by Bogost in *Alien Phenomenology* as an ideal outcome of our engagement with the world—wonder evoked by "the awesome plenitude of the alien everyday" (Bogost 2012, 134) prompts us to "suspend all trust in one's own logics, be they religion, science, philosophy, custom, or opinion, and to become subsumed entirely in the uniqueness of an object's native logic" (124).

Both Bennett and Bogost acknowledge that these moments, these openings, these spells cast by objects are potentially moments of fear as well as wonder, but then quickly shift away from the dark side. Bennett explains that the mood she is calling enchantment involves "a pleasurable state of being charmed by the novel and as yet unprocessed encounter" as well as "a more *unheimlich* (uncanny) feeling of being disrupted or torn out of one's default sensory-psychic-intellectual disposition" (2001, 5). Fear, however, cannot dominate for enchantment to persist because "fear will not becalm and intensify perception but only shut it down" (5). Later, in a chapter on "cross-species encounters" as evocative of wonder, Bennett briefly observes concerning monsters that "not all crossings, of course, enchant" (30). Contra Cohen's assertions concerning the threatening nature of categorical transgression, however, Bennett suggests that the negative affect elicited by monsters may stem "more from the voracious character of these creatures than from their combo-form" (30). That is, if they weren't trying to eat us, we might not find them quite as "loathsome" (31). And then, having acknowledged that the "momentarily immobilizing encounter" in which one is "transfixed, spellbound" (5) can be evocative of terror, she shifts her focus to the ways "human generosity can be enhanced by an onto-picture of a vibrant, quirky, and overflowing material world" (162). Bogost makes the same move in his discussion of wonder as zombies briefly shamble onto the scene: "In the face of the undead, we exhibit terror. Troubled souls seek relief, silence, release. They operate by broken logic, ones recognizable as neither alive nor dead but striving for one or the other. We fear them because we have no idea what they might do next." "Idealisms," Bogost continues, "amount to undead ontologies" (2012, 133). In contrast, the "return to realism in metaphysics is also a return to wonder, wonder unburdened by pretense or deception. Let's leave rigor to the dead" (133). Paradigms of the nonhuman turn return us to wonder, which is "to respect things as things in themselves" (131).

As noted, aspects of the nonhuman turn have been critiqued in various ways. As Chad Shomura summarizes regarding New Materialism, it can be criticized for the way it "suppresses different lived experiences of power to ontology, neglects the insights of feminist and queer theory as well as indigenous cosmologies, and stumbles when it comes to race" ("Exploring the Promise" [2017]). Thing Theory has been criticized as a kind of backdoor idealism that ironically fetishizes objects at the expense of their material histories (see, for example, DeFazio [2014] for a blistering Marxist critique of New Materialism). The purported undoing of correlationalism central to OOO, too, has been questioned, as even pronouncing "real things" as unknowable is a pronouncement from the human perspective for and about things.

The Gothic, as this study will develop, shares some of these concerns, particularly when it comes to undoing anthropocentrism and refiguring the human as part of a flat ontology in which humans are no more exceptional than paper cups. Nevertheless, Thing Theory is useful as a way to frame this project both because of how directly it reflects the twenty-first-century zeitgeist and the extent to which its pronouncements about objects correspond with what the Gothic has been saying for centuries. Thing Theorists and theorists of the nonhuman turn more generally emphasize enchantment and wonder, respect for and ethical engagement with the world, ecological awareness and human generosity. But, at the same time, their rhetoric is insistently Gothic: ghosts, monsters, apocalypse, the weird and eerie, dead rats, exhumed corpses, mysterious veiled objects, lurking shadows, the uncanny, Lovecraftian cosmic dread, the world as a charnel ground, the world-without-us. This language reflects not just Anthropocene anxiety over the precarious position of the human in the age of hyperobjects but fundamental uncanniness at the core of Thing Theory: Objects have unexplored depths, withdraw, but can become suddenly vibrant; our senses cannot be relied upon to convey accurate information; a rift exists between objects and their qualities; we can suddenly be thrust into the Great Outdoors as the agency of the material world catches us off-guard. What Thing Theory sidesteps the Gothic engages head on: the intense anxiety that results from the upending of the world and the equation of human beings with nonhuman things. Where Bennett sees Vibrant Materialism as elevation of matter, Gothic materialism imagines it instead as debasement: the body made a thing, meat to be confined, tortured, manipulated, investigated, consumed, disposed of. What Thing Theory regards as evocative of wonder or as enchanting, the Gothic presents as evocative of horror or as terrifying. And the Gothic, every bit as much as Thing Theory, addresses the human experience of objects—both of interacting with them and of being one. The Gothic is precisely about embodiment, about having a body that interacts with other bodies. At its core, it is about materiality—and it is to Gothic things that we will now turn.

2
Dark Enchantment and Gothic Materialism

The appeal of the Gothic as an artistic mode that depicts or relates violent or macabre scenes or events is a curious thing—after all, when you think about it, why would anyone care to linger over (much less savor) horrific images or accounts of murder, mutilation, monsters, and mayhem? While this question is a subset of the larger problem of what Steven J. Schneider refers to as the "paradox of fiction"—the question of how we can be moved by what we know does not exist in the first place ("Paradox" [2009])—it has its own particular twist, since the content involved is presumably *distasteful*; the Gothic confronts us with that from which we would normally recoil in fear or disgust. This raises the question of the pleasure of Gothic horror: If being frightened or repulsed is unpleasant, why would anyone actively seek out such experiences? What is there to enjoy in tales of violence, horror, and monstrosity?

There have been numerous attempts to explain the seemingly counterintuitive hold that Gothic horror possesses over the reader or viewer. Philosopher Noël Carroll, on the one hand, narrows it down in his 1990 *The Philosophy of Horror: Or, Paradoxes of the Heart* to a contest between basic curiosity and disgust. Restricting his attention to "art horror" (artistic representations of horror), Carroll proposes that narrative engages the viewer's interest while horror elicits disgust. If our curiosity about how the characters will fare and how things will turn out is stronger than our disgust, we continue to consume the narrative. If disgust prevails, we stop reading or viewing. Kendall Walton, on the other hand, argues that it is only "make-believedly" true that horror narratives frighten us. Appealing to "common sense"—we can't be afraid if we aren't actually in danger—Walton proposes that what we actually feel is what he refers to as a "quasi-emotion." As summarized by Steven J. Schneider,

"Quasi-emotions differ from true emotions primarily in that they are generated *not* by existence beliefs (such as the belief that the monster I am watching on screen really exists), but by 'second-order' beliefs about what is *fictionally* the case according to the work in question (such as the belief that the monster I am watching on screen *make-believedly* exists)" (2009). We thus derive enjoyment from playing along and pretending to be scared.

Shifting the terms of the conversation a bit, I would like to suggest using language indebted to Jane Bennett, Ian Bogost, and Michael Saler that the allure of the Gothic and the fascination it provokes inheres at least in part in its staging of a peculiar sort of *enchanted* world—in particular, a world in which the line between subject and object becomes muddled and obscured. The milieu of the Gothic narrative is one of animate objects—of things that acquire mystery, depth, and often life of a sort—and of de-animated subjects, people who are treated like or become things. This confusion of ontological states is of course at the heart of what Freud famously describes as the uncanny. For Freud, the *frisson* of the uncanny is produced by a sort of upending of the world precipitated by the crumbling of preconceptions. It is experienced when the familiar becomes strange and when strange things seem familiar. What I will refer to as enchantment—or, more properly as concerns the Gothic and its monsters, *dark enchantment*—is a second-order uncanny sensation of extended duration. It is experienced by the reader or viewer captivated by a familiar world made strange and who, knowing it to be a fiction, nevertheless cannot look away.

My contention is that this dark enchantment, this hold of Gothic horror provoked by ontological confusion, goes beyond the curiosity concerning narrative events proposed by Carroll or the fun of pretending to be scared suggested by Walton and derives—as both Victoria Nelson and Michael Saler suggest—from deep-seated desires for and fascination with the prospect of another world governed by different laws. This desire for wonder, which manifests in the affective state underlying the emotional response to the Gothic, is so strong that even dark enchantment—even monsters and murder—becomes satisfying. In fact, dark enchantment with its Gothic aura of dread and despair may be particularly well suited to contemporary sensibilities because it fuses magic with postmodern cynicism. Gothic horror reintroduces a sense of the numinous into an allegedly disenchanted landscape, but in such a way that human hubris is chastened and egotism upbraided. It may be easier and, indeed, both more appealing and convincing to imagine a world of ambient dread and actual horror than a fairytale world of happy endings.

In order to develop this approach to the role of what we may, following Bennett, refer to as "Gothic thing-power," I will first consider the enchantment of fantastic narrative as suggested by Nelson and Saler. I will then offer an overview of the Gothic's empire of uncanny things with a focus on three categories of Gothic objects: cursed, conduits, and inspirited. I will then round out this chapter with case studies focusing on works by two pop Gothic Things Theorists: David Lynch and Stephen King. Gothic things, as we shall see, invert conventional understandings of subject and object, person and thing. In doing so, they reconfigure the universe in a way that both enchants and unsettles.

Dark Enchantment

The topic of enchantment has been the focus of several twenty-first-century studies, including Jane Bennett's 2001 *The Enchantment of Modern Life: Attachments, Crossings, and Ethics*, Victoria Nelson's *The Secret Life of Puppets* (2001), and historian Michael Saler's 2012 *As If: Modern Enchantment and the Literary Prehistory of Virtual Reality*. In Bennett's *Enchantment*, she variously defines enchantment as "a stage of openness to the disturbing-captivating elements in everyday experience," "a window onto the virtual secreted within the actual," a "mood with ethical potential," and a "picture of the world as a web of lively and mobile matter-forms of varying degrees of complexity" (2001, 131). Contra assertions by Max Weber and others that processes of rationalization, secularization, and bureaucratization have drained the world of wonder (Saler 2012, 8), Bennett's point in *Enchantment* is that there is plenty in the world today that still enchants (including technologies and commodities—Bennett does not focus on fiction).

Both Nelson and Saler supplement Bennett by addressing the enchantments of fantasy *literature*, which they see as satisfying the desire for wonder in a secular age. Nelson frames things in religious terms: the "sub-zeitgeist" of popular culture allows "the displaced religious impulse" (2001, 19) to "sneak in the back door" (18). Fantastic narratives thus provide a way that "we as non-believers allow ourselves, unconsciously, to believe" (vii) and reflect a "displaced longing for the transcendental" (84). Saler, too, while eschewing the language of religion and transcendence, asserts that "the vogue for fantastic imaginary worlds from the fin-de-siècle through the twentieth century is best explained in terms of a larger cultural project of the West: that of re-enchanting an allegedly disenchanted world" (Saler 2012, 5). Saler, however, adds a little twist to Nelson, arguing that "modern enchantment" is characterized by a "self-conscious strategy of embracing illusions while acknowledging their artificial status" (13). With provocative, if unexplored, connections to Kendall Walton's notion of quasi-emotions, Saler proposes that what marks modern consumption of fantasy is what he refers to as the "ironic imagination": a "double-minded consciousness that became widespread in Europe and America in the late nineteenth century" and "permits an emotional immersion in, and rational reflection on, imaginary worlds, yielding a form of modern enchantment that delights without deluding" (30). For both Nelson and Saler, fantasy literature enchants the reader who finds the impoverished modern landscape sterile and lifeless. Fantasy restores wonder and, for Nelson, is a poor-man's substitute for religion in secular modern culture.

Where I extend on Nelson and Saler is with the proposition that part of the spell cast by the Gothic is woven with its uncanny things. In the first chapter of Fred Botting's *Gothic* (1996), Botting characterizes the Gothic as "a writing of excess" (1). While Botting foregrounds actions and emotions that "transgress social proprieties and moral laws" (3)—"vice and violence . . . selfish ambitions and sexual desires beyond the prescriptions of law or familial duty" (4)—much of the excessiveness of the Gothic arguably derives from its uncanny subjectification of presumably inert matter and the concomitant objectification of living things. The darkly wondrous world of the Gothic is first and foremost a world of "ominous matter"—of mysterious objects that exceed their intended purposes and, through their interactions with human characters, become drenched with affect and supersaturated with psychic investment. These are things that become more than things—things with depth, hidden qualities, and indeed life of a sort. Privileged categories of Gothic things include representations of the human body, bodies of knowledge, and architecture or landscape inhospitable to human well-being (spaces of confinement, spaces of disorientation, disorienting or liminal Foucaultian "heterotopias")—and I will address body, book, and building respectively in ensuing chapters. Here, however, I would like to focus even more broadly on the ways in which material objects in Gothic narrative acquire uncanny thing-power. While body, book, and building are three insistently recurring categories of ominous matter in Gothic narrative, *any* object can function as a Gothic thing—and it is this realization that marks the Gothic as contemporary Thing Theory's dark reflection—and a reflection of very human anxieties about our interactions with the material world. Like Thing Theory, the Gothic theorizes the human engagement with the nonhuman, complicating the animate/inanimate binary and showing instead how the human is entangled with the nonhuman in Latourean networks and how things themselves have the power to "animate, to act, to produce effects dramatic and subtle" (Bennett 2010, 6). In the Gothic, however, this animacy of matter is ominous, imperiling human safety and sanity by undoing Enlightenment understandings of the universe, making plain our precarious situation, and/or opening us up to malevolent forces.

Cursed

Material objects in Gothic narrative can be grouped into three broad categories: *cursed things*, *conduits* (which are often closely tied to cursed things), and *inspirited things*. Cursed things are magic objects invested with an intrinsic power to bring misfortune and tragedy to those who handle or possess them, and such narratives often revolve around location and ownership—cursed objects are often ones removed from their "proper" place by an unauthorized wielder. Frequently framed as morality tales about the consequences of greed, such narratives interestingly have also often functioned as rebukes of colonialist exploitation—albeit in problematic ways that ultimately reaffirm stereotypes of colonized and/or indigenous peoples as mystical and less advanced than Western white populations. Such things have an intrinsic magical power, but a power that is also frequently a kind of congealed history of graft and abuse.

There have, of course, been actual objects reputed to be cursed and with either real or invented backstories linking them to theft, exploitation, and/or tragedy. Probably the most famous is the Hope Diamond, an extremely large blue diamond weighing over 45 carats, the history of which is gleefully summarized on many websites and in popular press publications fascinated by the purported curse. Karl Shuker, for example, writes of the Hope Diamond in his 1996 *The Unexplained: An Illustrated Guide to the World's Paranormal Mysteries* (a popular press title addressing everything from the yeti to crop circles) that "it sparkled in the brow of an Indian temple idol—until it was impiously plucked out by a thieving Hindu priest, whose punishment for this unholy act was a slow and agonizing death" (123). The story has the diamond then making its way to France and being sold to King Louis XVI—the merchant who sold it subsequently being "mauled to death by a pack of wild dogs" (123). After Louis XVI and Marie Antoinette lost their heads, the diamond was recut into a smaller gem and was subsequently acquired by Henry Thomas Hope. As playfully summarized by Benjamin Radford, "The misfortune attributed to the diamond would strain the imagination of soap opera writers: Owners committed suicide, were murdered, and left penniless through bad investments. Those who came in contact with the diamond suffered failed marriages, dead children, drug addiction, insanity, and probably bad hair days and paper cuts as well" (Radford 2014). Radford goes on to note that the Hope Diamond curse is "in some ways a morality fable about the cardinal sin of greed" (Radford 2014). The diamond in these accounts brings bad fortune to those who own it; linking curse to conduit, however, its power is an expression of divine displeasure.

Cursed objects are often central to Gothic works as well as fantasy narratives with Gothic themes in literature and film. For example, the Orientalist conceit of the revenge of the colonized via cursed object is at the center of the blockbuster *Pirates of the Caribbean: The Curse of the Black Pearl* (Gore Verbinski, 2003). Within the film, *The Black Pearl* is a ship with contested ownership rather than an actual gem. The curse, however, pertains to pilfered Aztec gold. The audience learns that, when pirate Captain Barbossa (Geoffrey Rush) stole Hernán Cortés's treasure, he and his crew were condemned by an Aztec curse to become undead skeletal creatures under moonlight until the gold is returned and atonement made in blood. In a more immediately Gothic register, Sam Raimi's *Drag Me to Hell* (2009) features a cursed button rather than a doubloon, and the curser is a Romani woman denied an extension on her mortgage by a loan officer angling for promotion by attempting to prove her toughness. The situation, however, is essentially the same: The cursed object exerts power over its possessor, transforming the owner or bringing bad luck.

In works such as *Pirates of the Caribbean* and *Drag Me to Hell*, "Aztec curse" or "gypsy curse" functions as shorthand for the familiar narrative pitting white greed against native or folk belief, variants of which include the "Curse of the Pharaohs" and desecration of an "Ancient Indian Burial Ground." The cursed object—gold, button, idol, weapon, any object at all taken from a sacred site—then functions as the focal point for a contest between Enlightenment rationalism and another belief system that affirms what rationalism dismisses as superstition. While these other belief systems are often non-Western or indigenous ones, this doesn't necessarily have to be the case—the cursed object could just as easily be associated with Judaism or Catholicism. Such narratives inevitably send mixed messages to audiences. On the one hand, within the context of the narrative, they critique greed and colonialist exploitation and often affirm what might be called "indigenous ways of knowing"—that is, those who pilfer Aztec gold, invade Egyptian tombs, or desecrate sacred burial sites are punished for their transgressions in narratives affirming indigenous belief systems as reflecting an external reality. For audiences, however, the enchantment of such narratives inheres precisely in their fictive nature. Following Nelson and particularly Saler, the fun of such works involves pretending to believe in a universe in which magic functions. To actually believe in magic, however, marks one as naïve. So, while such works may indeed critique colonialist exploitation of indigenous populations and insist on respect for other traditions, at the same time they caricature those other traditions as backward and irrational.

A variant on the cursed object as punishment for greed is the cursed object that illustrates the consequences of attempting to evade fate or to tamper with the "natural order of things." Among the most famous examples is W. W. Jacobs's short story, "The Monkey's Paw," first published in 1902. Within the story, a mummified monkey's paw, having been enchanted by an old Indian fakir in India and brought to England, possesses the power to grant the bearer three wishes; however, the wishes are always accompanied by unintended—and tragic—consequences. When Mr. White wishes for £200 to pay off his mortgage, his son Herbert is killed in an accident at the factory where he works, and his employer makes a goodwill payment to the family of £200. When Mr. White, at his wife's insistence, wishes for his son back (an early version of Stephen King's 1983 *Pet Sematary*) (1983), he has a vision of his son returning as a kind of zombie with a mutilated and decomposing corpse . . . and then there is a knock on the door. Terrified, he uses his last wish to wish away the thing outside the door as his wife cries out in misery.

The ostensible moral of "The Monkey's Paw" is stated clearly in the story by Sergeant-Major Morris, the British soldier who brought the paw back from India: "It had a spell put on it by an old Fakir . . . a very holy man. He wanted to show that fate ruled people's lives, and that those who interfered with it did so to their sorrow" (Jacobs 1902). Translation: be careful what you wish for and be content with your lot. But one doesn't need a monkey's paw from India to make this point, and the cursed material object around which the entire story pivots—the monkey's paw—has much broader significance, as it is a dark nexus of British colonialism, racism, and industrial capitalism. Enchanted by an Indian fakir and given to British colonizers to whom it brings sorrow, the paw is a variant of the "revenge of the oppressed" narrative. Combining Egyptian mummification, Muslim mysticism, an exotic animal from the Orient, and magic, the paw is congealed Otherness and participates in the Enlightenment rationalism/other belief systems opposition discussed earlier. That it is a monkey's paw in the context of British imperialism and early twentieth-century debates over evolution—a paw taken possession by a Mr. *White* no less—amplifies the racial subtext that contrasts white colonizers with the darker-skinned indigenous population. Indeed, the story arguably pivots on a bit of "sleight of hand"—there is already something ghoulish about the idea of an amputated and shriveled monkey's paw, and that this is the object the Indian fakir chooses to enchant participates in the Orientalist logic of India as backward and barbaric. But the present monkey's paw arguably substitutes for the absent Indian human hand, itself a synecdoche for the violence of British imperialism in India. The paw/hand brings bad luck to the colonizers who seek to profit without labor. The Indian fakir's gesture then is profoundly ironic as the severed paw/hand inverts the initial civilized/savage opposition: The savagery belongs to the colonizer, not the colonized.

The story then takes this critique of imperialism and capitalist exploitation one step further by revealing the same mercenary logic at play in the heart of the empire. Herbert dies after he is "caught in the machinery" (Jacobs 1902) at an ambiguous business called Maw and Meggins that disclaims all responsibility for the accident. The same Maw that swallowed India abroad devours Herbert at home, leaving a mangled corpse. Whether in India or England, the story seems to say, the machinery of capitalism mangles limbs and swallows bodies. The monkey's paw at the center of the story is finally a literalization of Marx's notion of commodity fetishism. The belief that it has inherent value and power obscures its role in mediating social relationships among human beings. Sleight of hand indeed: The severed, bloodless paw obscures the bloody connections that in fact structure its existence.

Narratives involving cursed objects not only foreground the material object as a materialization of a belief system, but also make clear that objects have lives in a sense—that is, that they have histories that shape their meanings and the affect they evoke. The spells they weave are products of their qualities that have been shaped over time. In many cases, cursed objects (both real objects like the Hope Diamond and objects in fictional narrative) are associated with tragedy, and that tragedy "sticks" to them, infecting those who handle them. A poignant illustration of this is François Girard's film *The Red Violin* (1998), which tells the story of a mysterious red-colored violin and the unfortunate fates of its many owners from the seventeenth century to the twentieth. Tests on the violin's varnish reveal its tragic backstory: The seventeenth-century violin maker, distraught over the death of his wife and child during childbirth, infused his wife's blood into the varnish, which explains its unique color. The red violin literally carries its mournful history with it, "coloring" its reception and incorporating its owners into a tragic cycle of repetition. It is a cursed instrument of death, born of sorrow and precipitating tragedy for those who own it. Indeed, inverting the commonplace understanding of the opposition, Gothic objects—particularly cursed and inspired ones—themselves do the possessing. They own their owners.

Whether pilfered gold, a severed paw, or a violin painted in blood, the thing-power of the cursed object is thus often invested in its history and constitutes part of its allure. In these cases, it holds within itself a tragic backstory that acts like a battery, powering a kind of dark aura of enchantment that doesn't just glow, but infects those who come in contact with it—the cursed object has become, in a sense, radioactive. Such objects in narrative are captivating in part, however, because they are hyperbolic reflections of commonly held attitudes toward things. Antiques, souvenirs, and objects of "sentimental value" are valued, at least in part, for their histories and are to various extents affect generators that can influence our mood. All objects are—or at least have the potential to become—radioactive in this way, "contaminating" our dispositions.

The amplified agency of cursed objects in Gothic narrative thus reflects in an exaggerated way the thing-power we already afford to many objects in our day-to-day existence.

Conduits

Cursed objects possess an intrinsic power to bring about change through a kind of invisible agency. While in some cases explanations have been proposed for the apparently pernicious effects ownership of the cursed object brings—for example, radiation or bacteria as explanations for the "Curse of the Pharaohs" (see Edwards 2009)—the curse within fictional narrative generally operates by magic, which is part of the dark enchantment of such stories: They engage us in a universe that operates according to non-rationalist principles, even as they emphasize our awareness that objects have hidden depths and histories. A second category of Gothic object consists of those that, rather than having an intrinsic power, instead serve as conduits—channels or portals to another dimension or plane of existence. These objects are often, although not always, ones conventionally used for communication purposes—a letter, radio, phone, television, walkie talkie, and so on. Whatever their form, they permit access to what is generally considered a fictional or non-rationalist realm, in some cases allowing something from the "out-side" to enter into our familiar reality. Like cursed objects, conduits in Gothic narrative have an uncanny aura about them as they permit a violation of the rules of reality as we conventionally understand them. Conduits do not directly affect or harm their bearers—they are not themselves cursed; however, they do facilitate harm—physical, mental, or both—by summoning or mediating contact with supernatural forces.

The most familiar supernatural conduit object is the Ouija Board. Patented as a commercial parlor game in 1891, although having a much longer history as "talking boards," the Ouija Board purports to mediate communication between the living and the dead by way of a planchette—a small piece of wood that on the modern Ouija Board moves over letters printed on the board, spelling out words in response to questions asked (see McRobbie 2013). As a means to facilitate communication with the spirit world, the Ouija Board has frequently been featured in Gothic narrative, where its powers to contact the dead are confirmed. In literature, for example, Shirley Jackson's 1959 *The Haunting of Hill House* has a Ouija Board that targets the story's main character, spelling out the message "Help Eleanor come home" (155). In Stephen King's postapocalyptic novel *The Stand* from 1978, the villainous Randall Flagg twice contacts character Nadine Cross via Ouija Board. Ouija Boards are frequently featured in horror film—*The Uninvited* (Lewis Allen, 1944), *13 Ghosts*

(William Castle, 1960), *The Exorcist* (William Friedkin, 1973), *Paranormal Activity* (Oren Peli, 2007), and a film simply called *Ouija* (Stiles White, 2014) all include scenes of supernatural messages being conveyed via Ouija Board.

Not surprisingly, forms of communication typically used by the living are frequently repurposed in Gothic narrative as means to contact the dead and sometimes as conduits allowing supernatural forces to enter the "real world." For example, Edith Wharton's 1931 short story "Pomegranate Seed" plays with the premise that a widower is receiving letters from his deceased first wife. The 2014 film *Unfriended* (Leo Gabriadze) is an updated version of this narrative in which a ghost communicates through and then materializes by way of social media. In the film *Poltergeist* (Toby Hooper, 1982), the television set is invested with dread as it becomes a conduit for a supernatural entity to invade a middle-class home and kidnap a child. In *Ringu / The Ring* (Hideo Nakata, 1998 / Gore Verbinski, 2002), rather than it being the TV, it is instead the screening of a particular videotape that summons the malevolent supernatural entity—watch the disturbing video and you have seven days to live. In *Poltergeist II: The Other Side* (Brian Gibson, 1986), updating a classic *Twilight Zone* episode ("Long Distance Call," 1961), a toy telephone permits communication with the spirit world, while in the first season of the television series *Stranger Things* (2016–), walkie talkies allow contact between our familiar world and another dimension referred to as the Upside Down.

Such narratives play on and amplify the uncanny qualities already associated with these technologies. As Jeffrey Sconce has developed in his 2000 study *Haunted Media*, "In media folklore past and present, telephones, radios, and computers have been . . . 'possessed' by such 'ghosts in the machine,' the technologies serving as either uncanny electronic agents or as gateways to electronic otherworlds" (4). Sconce's study deals with the occult powers of electronic media going back to the telegraph, which "held the tantalizing promises of contacting the dead in the afterlife and aliens on other planets" (10). He notes how the telegraph and radio were imagined to allow spirits to speak through them, while spirits in fact seemed to inhabit later forms such as television (127). As philosopher Jacques Derrida developed extensively, however, writing in general has a long history of being associated with absence and ghosts (see, for example, *Of Grammatology* [2016] and "Signature, Event, Context" [1988]). The letter one receives is from someone not present, possibly someone dead, and inscribed within the mark is the inevitability of one's future disappearance.

In some Gothic works, conduit objects do not just open up a channel or portal to another dimension; they invoke or summon a particular entity. This is certainly the case in M. R. James's unsettling "Oh, Whistle, and I'll Come to You, My Lad" from 1904. In this story, the conduit object is the titular whistle, discovered by a skeptical Cambridge professor named Parkins on holiday in a seaside town on the southern coast of England. While investigating the ruins of a Templar preceptory, he comes across a whistle with Latin inscriptions on top and bottom. Parkins is able to translate one of the inscriptions as, "Who is this who is coming?" and quickly concludes that, "Well, the best way to find out is evidently to whistle for him" (James 1904b). Parkins blows, and the sound provokes a vision: "It had a quality of infinite distance in it, and, soft as it was, he somehow felt it must be audible for miles round. It was a sound, too, that seemed to have the power (which many scents possess) of forming pictures in the brain. He saw quite clearly for a moment a vision of a wide, dark expanse at night, with a fresh wind blowing, and in the midst a lonely figure—how employed, he could not tell" (James 1904b). While the second inscription, "FLA FUR BIS FLE," defeats Parkins, it can be translated roughly as "thief, blow, weep." Alas for Parkins—not attending to the ominous warning of the second inscription, his blowing of the whistle summons a supernatural entity,

Figure 1. James McBryde's 1904 illustration of the looming bed sheets for "Oh, Whistle, and I'll Come to You, My Lad," included in *Ghost Stories of an Antiquary* published by Edward Arnold

presumably the "lonely figure" of his vision, that rises from an unused bed beneath the bedsheets with "an intensely horrible . . . face of crumpled linen" (James 1904b). Parkins survives the encounter, but with his worldview and equanimity shaken.

While I will be addressing the human form in Chapter 3, it is worth pointing out here that "Oh, Whistle" in fact has two uncanny material objects: the whistle and the linen of the extra bed in Parkins's room that rises up and assumes human form. Indeed, the peculiar horror of the story is that the supernatural entity summoned by the whistle lacks any visible corporeal form of its own and, to manifest, it enlivens inanimate matter. When interrupted in its assault upon Parkins, the entity disappears, leaving "a tumbled heap of bedclothes" on the floor (James 1904b). The linen in this way offers a curious parallel to Jane Bennett's notion "strangely vital things" (2010, 3) at one moment "dead stuff and at the next live presence" (5), but recast as horror. This is the dark enchantment of ominous matter—the suspicion that dead stuff is indeed harboring occult and possibly malicious life.

A less intuitive but far more dangerous Gothic conduit object is the famous puzzle box referred to as the Lament Configuration from Clive Barker's *Hellraiser* books and films. One of several boxes designed by French toymaker Phillip Lemarchand, we learn in *Hellraiser: Bloodline* (Kevin Yagher and Joe Chappelle, 1996) that the Lament Configuration was commissioned by a wealthy aristocrat obsessed with dark magic. Solving a Lemarchand Box creates a bridge to another dimension, with beings able to travel in either direction. The Lament Configuration, when solved, summons demonic entities called Cenobites, chief among them being the iconic Pinhead, whose head is crisscrossed with a lattice of needles. The Cenobites then subject the summoner to excruciating pain as a form of cult-like ritual.

The prominent role of conduit objects in Gothic narrative is foregrounded in Drew Goddard's 2012 *The Cabin in the Woods*. As mentioned in the preface to this book, the cabin's basement is filled with ominous objects—many intended as conscious allusions to horror films. When manipulated in the correct way, the objects then summon an associated monster. Some of the allusions are very specific, such as the puzzle sphere that summons "Fornicus, Lord of Bondage and Pain"—an obvious allusion to the puzzle box in the Hellraiser films and to Pinhead. A necklace atop a wedding dress summons The Bride, presumably a reference to 1972's *The Blood Spattered Bride* (Vincente Aranda). Doll masks seem to allude to the antagonists of the 2008 film *The Strangers* (Bryan Bertino). And the "zombie redneck family" summoned by the diary of Patience Buckner certainly derives its inspiration from *The Texas Chainsaw Massacre* (Tobe Hooper, 1974)—with a George Romero twist.

Figure 2. The famous puzzlebox from the *Hellraiser* films

In contrast to the specificity of these monsters and references, some of the objects and the creatures with which they correlate in the film are more generic. A conch shell summons Merman, a *Creature from the Black Lagoon*–type monster. A music box apparently summons the Sugarplum Fairy, a monstrosity seemingly inspired by the Guillermo del Toro's creations as filtered through *Black Swan* (Darren Aronofsky, 2010). An amulet summons a werewolf, a fortune-teller summons machine evil clowns, a unicorn tapestry summons a peculiarly violent unicorn, and so on.

Whether specific or generic, however, the artifacts in the basement of the cabin in the woods highlight the prominent role of conduit objects within Gothic narrative. These are objects that, like cursed objects, have a kind of supernatural power or aura associated with them—manipulating them in particular ways causes a shift in the characters' understanding of reality as the rules change. Portals open to other dimensions, and in many cases something from the outside, from that other dimension, is allowed access to our world. Like cursed objects, conduit objects are hyperbolic representations of the thing-power we often attribute to objects in our regular lives. Books—which I will be discussing in Chapter 5—as well as games, films and TV shows, and communications of all kinds, can open a kind of portal to another world, and, indeed, almost any object if looked at from a strange angle or in a different light can elicit a form of ontological vertigo. This is, in essence, the nature of Jane Bennett's contingent tableau in *Vibrant Matter*, which opens a portal to "a strange dimension of matter, an *out-side*" irreducible to the "milieu of human knowledge" (2010, 3). All objects can become portals to a kind of inhuman dimension—but the Gothic already knew that.

One final type of Gothic conduit object—a form that starts to shift us toward "inspirited objects" to be addressed later—are what we might call "imbued objects." These are objects that convey some part of a former owner—spirit or personality—to a new owner. Like other conduit objects, imbued objects do not act with conscious volition. However, once possessed, they transform the owner. This is exemplified by the odd "possessed hands" subgenre of horror in which transplanted hands imbue their new owner with their prior owner's violent inclinations. The template for this was set in 1924 by the German silent film *The Hands of Orlac* (*Orlacs Hände*, director Robert Wiene) in which the hands of a pianist are terribly injured in an accident and replaced with those of an executed murderer. Orlac then seems to be taken over by the transplanted hands, culminating in the murder of his father. *Orlac* has been remade several times—including *Mad Love* (Karl Freund, 1935) with Peter Lorre, *The Hands of Orlac* (Edmond T. Gréville, 1960), and *Hands of a Stranger* (Newt Arnold, 1962). In the last, the transplanted hands want revenge for their past owner's death. Playing with this familiar trope, a Halloween episode of *The Simpsons* titled "Hell Toupée" (S10, E4, 1998) has Homer going on a killing spree after transplanted hair takes control of him.

Articles of clothing within Gothic narrative can similarly be imbued with a prior owner's personality and direct a new owner's actions. The 1962 episode of *The Twilight Zone* called "Dead Man's Shoes" (S3, E18) is a case in point. In the episode, a homeless man steals a pair of shoes off the corpse of a victim of a Mafia hit. The shoes infuse him with the memories and personality of Dane, the man who was murdered, and he goes to confront the mob boss that ordered the hit. He is gunned down again but promises before he dies that "I'll keep coming back . . . again, and again!" The body is dumped, and another homeless man finds the shoes, leading us to surmise that Dane will make good on his promise.

More clearly than other categories of Gothic objects, imbued objects make plain that objects have histories and "personalities," and they foreground in a Gothic register a particular form of "thing-power" objects possess. We tend to think of our possessions as extensions of ourselves. The clothes we wear, the vehicle we choose, the objects we decorate our living spaces with are considered as expressions of our personality. But what Gothic narratives featuring imbued objects highlight is the old expression (here slightly updated) that "the clothes make the person." That is, our tastes may direct our decisions when it comes to material things, but those things then exert a reciprocal influence on our identities. We become the person who wears the vintage hat or daring dress—and part of this transformation is connected to affect elicited by the object's history and associations. We are in a sense "infected" by objects, which in this way exert thing-power, influencing our sense of self. This is true of any object with which we form an affective connection, new or old; however, what I am calling imbued Gothic objects are ones saturated with a violent and/or tragic history that overtakes the owner's present. Narratives pivoting around these objects offer a hyperbolic representation of thing-power that makes clear in an unsettling way how we are controlled by the things we possess.

Inspirited Objects

It is a short step from imbued Gothic things to a third class of Gothic object that is perhaps the most disconcerting of all: inanimate objects that are in some sense "alive" in that they seem to act with conscious volition. These are objects that not only exert a kind of magical influence but will the outcome. While, as I will develop in Chapters 3 and 4, this is most commonly a representation of the human body—a mannequin, doll, puppet, and so on—this doesn't have to be the case. Any object can be infused with uncanny animacy and invested with dread in Gothic narrative, which makes clear the extent to which the Gothic is the dark reflection of contemporary Thing Theory's emphasis on "vibrant materiality."

Because I turn to representations of the human body in Chapter 3, I will limit my discussion here to non-anthropomorphic examples. The most famous one is likely the 1958 Plymouth Fury called Christine in Stephen King's 1983 novel of the same name (King 1983a) (adapted for film the year of its release and directed by John Carpenter). Within both novel and film adaptation, Christine is a vehicle actuated by supernatural forces. Like most Gothic objects, Christine has a violent and tragic backstory—although, in a kind of chicken and egg conundrum, it is never clear whether Christine's malevolence is a result of these events or if it was "born bad." Either way, high school student Arnie Cunningham gets more than he bargained for when he buys Christine from Roland D. LeBay (a name that clearly alludes to occultist Anton LeVay). The car, acting on its own volition, murders several people, and it comes to light that its former owner, LeBay, was an angry and violent man. His daughter choked to death in the back seat of the car on a bite of hamburger, and his wife, depressed over the loss of their child, committed suicide in the front seat by carbon monoxide poisoning. There is speculation within the novel that LeVay may have intentionally sacrificed his wife and child to prepare Christine as a receptacle for his own spirit.

It's never made entirely clear in the novel whether LeVay's spirit is animating Christine (which would introduce some fascinating gender politics into the novel!) or whether Christine possesses a will of her own; however, the uncanniness of the novel derives from the obvious confusion between subject and object: Christine is a thing that acts with conscious volition. Indeed, beyond having been given a name, Christine is persistently anthropomorphized across the novel. Arnie's girlfriend, Leigh, makes clear how we are supposed to regard the car when she tells Arnie's friend Dennis that "It's not [Arnie] I hate. It's that frig—no, it's that *fucking* car. That bitch, Christine" (1983a, 225).

Something similar is the case in "Mr. Steinway," one of the segments of the 1967 British horror film *Torture Garden* (Freddie Francis). Within the film, five people at a fairground sideshow attraction have their futures revealed to them by Dr. Diabolo (Burgess Meredith). In one of the tales, a possessed grand piano named Euterpe (the Greek muse of music) becomes jealous of its owner's new lover. Euterpe manifests her indignation by allowing her top to slam shut and causing the girlfriend's picture to fall and shatter. However, when Leo (John Standing) agrees to forsake a scheduled concert tour and fly off with Dorothy (Barbara Ewing), Euterpe—playing a funeral march on her own—corners Dorothy and forces her through a window, causing her to fall several stories to her death.

It isn't jealousy that animates the malicious mirror in the 2013 horror film *Oculus* (Mike Flanagan), but simply the will to do evil. The plot of the film focuses on two survivors of childhood tragedy attempting to document the supernatural powers of an antique mirror repeatedly associated with violence and murder before destroying it. The mirror, however, which houses a spirit or supernatural force that manifests as a woman named Marisol (Kate Siegel), has powers to manipulate the reality of those within its sphere of influence, causing confusion or hallucinations. The mirror not only acts out of self-preservation but seems to feed on anger and despair as it torments those who come into contact with it. This is not a matter of reflection—the mirror does not simply reflect back the "dark side" of those who peer into it; rather, the mirror itself directs the action.

Examples of inspired objects proliferate rapidly if we step back from Gothic horror in particular and consider fantasy narrative more generally. From the "one ring" of Tolkien's *The Lord of the Rings* series to the sword Stormbringer from Michael Moorcock's *Elric* series, and from the sorting hat and Voldemort's "horcruxes" in the *Harry Potter* books to The Luggage in Terry Pratchett's *Discworld* novels, animate objects are a staple of fantasy fiction, where they are particularly prominent in narratives for children. The difference in such works tends to be proximity to what we regard as the "real world." Gothic thing-power provokes discomfort when it is regarded by characters and the audience as a violation of the "rules" of a reality that reflects a post-Enlightenment rationalist understanding of the universe. Fantasy narratives are less likely to elicit an uncanny response, as Freud explains in his essay "The Uncanny" (see Freud [1919] 2003), 156–57), because their realities are presented as operating according to a different logic—one generally accepted by the denizens of that universe.

Having offered this overview of three general types of Gothic objects and the ways they enchant darkly through the troubling of the active/passive, animate/inanimate, possessor/possession dichotomies, I would now like to introduce two test cases that can help develop our understanding of Gothic narrative as dark reflection of contemporary Thing Theory further. I will start with David Lynch's original *Twin Peaks* series, which, I will argue, offers five different strategies for producing Gothic objects. I will then turn to Stephen King's *Needful Things* (1991), which makes clear that any object can function as a Gothic object. Together, Lynch and King help illustrate the overarching argument that the matter of the Gothic is indeed matter itself as the Gothic persistently emphasizes the human relationship with the nonhuman.

Lynch's Things: The Case of *Twin Peaks*

An early inspiration for this project was David Lynch and Mark Frost's original *Twin Peaks* series, which ran from 1990 to 1991, because much of the strangeness of the world they create inheres in its uncanny representation of matter—things out of place, things saturated with affect, defamiliarized things, inspirited things. It is not just the owls in *Twin Peaks* that are not what they seem—neither are people and ceiling fans, drape runners and cave pictographs, wood ticks and creamed corn. From disorienting buildings to bodies wrapped in plastic to proliferating golf balls and donuts and sticky notes, things in *Twin Peaks*—objects and people and buildings—resist their place in the order of things as they insist on being noticed and at times transgress the boundary between sentient and non-sentient and living and dead. This ontological confusion participates in constructing *Twin Peaks*'s allure, its production of a kind of captivating dark enchantment or what Nigel Thrift refers to as "secular magic" (Thrift 2010, 290).

The matter of *Twin Peaks*, the roles that objects play and the uncanny affect with which they are invested, is clearly central to the series' allure, and part of *Twin Peaks*'s originality—and a primary strategy in the production of its captivating ambient dread—is its persistent thematization of thing-power that is developed through five loose and at times overlapping categories of defamiliarized things in *Twin Peaks*. These uncanny things work in concert to construct Twin

Peaks as a kind of Gothic fantasy space functioning according to a different logic than that governing our familiar reality. These categories are (1) displaced matter; (2) ominous matter; (3) inspirited matter; (4) fragmented or multiplied matter; and (5) objectified matter.

The first category, "displaced matter," refers to matter literally out of place, and such matter takes on several different forms within the series ranging from instances clearly remarked within the diegesis to sorts of confusion that operate on the formal level. In a comic register, Pete Martell (Jack Nance) comes rushing in a step too late to stop Cooper (Kyle McLachlan) and Sheriff Truman (Michael Ontkean) from drinking coffee, explaining, "You'd never guess. There was a fish ... in the percolator!" (episode 2); during an investigatory trip to a vet's office, a llama pushes between Cooper and Truman, looks Cooper in the eye, and snorts derisively (episode 8); Bobby Briggs (Dana Ashbrook) ironically sports a varsity letter on the back of his black leather jacket; and Dr. Hayward (Warren Frost) affords the viewer a close-up view of a squashed wood tick on the end of the bullet that plugged Cooper. Much darker examples of matter out of place include Laura Palmer herself wrapped in plastic by the river, the letter found beneath the fingernail of each of Bob's victims, the part of a poker chip found in Laura's stomach, Maddy Ferguson's (Sheryl Lee) body stuffed into a golf bag, and the pool of scorched engine oil within the ring of Sycamore Trees at Glastonbury Grove that serves as the entrance to the Waiting Room to the spirit world.

In terms of furthering the plot, objects are repeatedly lost or discovered in unexpected places: the magazine *Fleshworld* is uncovered by Cooper hidden in a ceiling light in Jacque Renault's (Walter Olkewicz) apartment; Laura's locket is recovered from its hiding place in the woods and then concealed in a fake coconut by Dr. Jacoby (Russ Tamblyn); cash is stashed in a football; drugs are concealed in Leo's (Eric Da Re) shoe and planted in the gas tank of James Hurley's (James Marshall) motorcycle—later, Cooper himself is set up with planted drugs in a similar way; Audrey Horne's (Sherilyn Fenn) letter to Agent Cooper slips under his bed; Audrey herself ends up at the Canadian brothel, One Eyed Jack's, and, in one of the series' most uncomfortable scenes, conceals herself from her father (Richard Beymer) behind a mask; Laura's secret diary is recovered from a hidden shelf in Harold Smith's (Lenny Von Dohlen) home and her audiotapes are concealed in her bedpost; Windom Earle (Kenneth Welsh) plants a microphone on a bonsai tree delivered to the police station; and almost the entire investigation of Laura Palmer's murder is framed by the giant's taking and returning of Cooper's ring.

At times, matter out of place in *Twin Peaks* is unmistakably insistent in its sheer absurdity: a mounted buck's head on a table at the bank confronts Sheriff Truman and the newly arrived Cooper in the pilot ("oh, it fell down," explains the bank clerk [Jane Jones], with the head on the table in the foreground of the shot), the latter of which then humorously holds in his hand "a small box of chocolate bunnies"; in episode 9, it is creamed corn rather than chocolate bunnies that appears in and then disappears from the hands of Pierre Tremond (Austin Jack Lynch—Creamed corn is revealed in *Twin Peaks: Fire Walk With Me*, the prequel to *Twin Peaks*, to be the physical manifestation of "garmonbozia," the negative spiritual energy of pain and suffering fed off of by the entities of the Black Lodge). Related to the llama in the vet's office and buck's head on the desk is the vision of the white horse in the Palmer living room twice experienced by Sarah (Grace Zabriskie). Then, of course, there are Nadine's (Wendy Robie) cotton balls—the answer to her obsession with creating silent drape runners—and the canister containing Andy's (Harry Goaz) semen sample that slips from his grasp and rolls across the floor. Relatedly, although functioning on a different level, one could include here the out-of-place music, dramatic and dreamy, that bizarrely entertains biker bar and diner patrons.

These instances of matter out of place, rife within the series, create moments of incongruity that fold together into the construction of a different order of things, a world that operates by a different epistemic logic—a kind of "cryptic totality," to borrow from Graham Harman (2005, 122). As part of this process, certain objects within the series are enlivened and invested with affect—primarily dread (although also pleasure where food is concerned). What we may refer to as ominous matter within *Twin Peaks* consists particularly of those objects associated with circular or stationary movement. Into this category we may place the ceiling fan and record player at the Palmer house, the swaying traffic light and blowing trees, as well as Cooper's ring and Hank Jennings's (Chris Mulkey) domino. In each instance, the affective charge associated with these objects is thickened and catalyzed by framing, sound, and narrative context.

The fan is first introduced in the pilot when Sarah Palmer goes upstairs with the intention of waking Laura for school. The camera remains fixed at the bottom of the stairs pointing upward as ominous music plays and Sarah disappears from the top left of the frame into Laura's room, only to find it empty. After Sarah comes back down distraught, a curious close-up of the spinning fan is introduced. The fan in this way is associated with Laura's absence and her mother's anxiety. The ominous quality of the ceiling fan is then reinforced at various points throughout the series and particularly in episode 14—the episode in which Maddy is killed and Leland is revealed to be Bob's host—where it is also connected with the skipping record player and with spinning more generally. In a scene divided into three parts, we first see and hear a record player skipping, undergirded by an ominous wash of noise. The camera tracks across the rug at floor level to the stairs, where Sarah Palmer

Figure 3. *Twin Peaks*'s ominous ceiling fan

comes into view, her hand entering the scene at the top right as she crawls down, moaning as if sick or injured and speaking Leland's name once before appearing to lose consciousness. Sarah comes down the stairs just as she did in the pilot when she has discovered Laura missing, only this time her distress is greatly magnified by her inability to walk. The scene then cuts to the ceiling fan, connecting it with Sarah's anguish, before shifting to the police station, where Ben Horne is being brought in for questioning. The action jumps back to the Palmer house, where the camera again highlights the skipping record player prior to focusing on Sarah, who continues to crawl across the carpet before having a vision of a white horse in a spotlight in her living room and again passing out. The camera tracks from her prostrate form to the record player and across the room to Leland, who is fixing his tie in front of a mirror. From here, the episode cuts to the Roadhouse, where the Giant tells Cooper, "It is happening again," before returning a third and final time to the Palmer house, again starting with a shot of the skipping record player. The scene finally erupts into violence as Leland/Bob attacks Maddy and, like the record player and fan, spins with her in his arms in a dizzying conflation of agony and ecstasy.

Like the fan and record player, shots of the traffic light at Sparkwood and Twenty-first and the image of trees blowing in the wind are also introduced in the pilot, concern circular movement or movement in place, and are connected by association to Laura Palmer and her death. The traffic light, which sways gently in the wind and cycles from green to red, marks the intersection where Laura jumped off James's motorcycle and ran into the woods on the night she died. Following Cooper's address in the town hall in which he cautions residents to consider a curfew for those under eighteen and reminds them that the crimes occurred at night, the scene cuts to the traffic light, brilliantly illuminated against a pitch-black background. Undergirded by a low wash of spooky noise, the light changes from green to yellow to red as the scene fades out. As with the fan, the traffic light is then introduced at various other points in the series and infused with an ominous sense of dread, such as at the very end of episode 3, where it shines red against the darkness. As the episode's last image, it seems to insist on some deeper meaning, even as it scrupulously withholds what exactly that significance is. It is one more ominous puzzle among many.

Similarly, in both the pilot and episode 3, the woods into which Laura disappeared are linked directly to her: Following the identification of Laura in the morgue by Leland in the pilot, the camera lingers on Laura's pale face and purple lips before dissolving into a shot of agitated trees being tossed in the wind, signifying the restlessness of nature in the face of evil or perhaps even their inhabitation by Laura's spirit, which has now joined the other restless entities that reside in the suggestively named *Ghostwood* Forest. "I just know I'm going to *get lost* in those *woods* again tonight," Laura prophetically dictated to Dr. Jacoby—a wood that "holds many spirits," according to Deputy Hawk (Michael Horse). The trees are again associated with Laura as a shot of them blowing in the wind dissolves into the minister's (Royce D. Applegate) prayer at Laura's funeral in episode 3. Like Laura, the woods—wondrous and strange, as Judge Stern*wood* notes—are "full of secrets." The trees blowing in the wind, agitated by something unseen, are not only another puzzle box within the series, but particularly animate, moving as though possessing intentionality of their own. As I will discuss, trees in *Twin Peaks* are in this way presented as inspirited objects, objects possessing a kind of sentience.

From the spinning fan and record player to the sharpening of the saw of the opening credits to the circular pool within the ring of Sycamores that swallows up Cooper in the finale, rings and circles assume symbolic significance throughout the series. The fan/record player/Bob assemblage highlights the association of circles and circular movement with violence and the spirit world. This connection is reinforced both through the symbolism of Cooper's ring—taken and returned by the giant when Cooper finally understands who the killer is—and by what Mike/Phillip Gerard (Al Strobel) refers to as a "golden circle" of appetite and satisfaction experienced by him and Bob when they were killing together.

The menacing duplication of circles is also affectively reflected in another prominent ominous object: Hank Jennings's domino. Hank's domino, consisting in season 1 of six dots divided into two sets of three (reflecting the number of people he has killed, according to the online Glastonberrygrove.net site), is first introduced in episode 4 as he fiddles with it during his parole board hearing. According to the actor Chris Mulkey, "the number three represented 'magic' and doubling it represented 'mysticism'" (twinspeaksexplained.com). That we should associate this object with Hank is then made clear at the end of episode 4 when Josie Packard (Joan Chen) opens a letter to find a pencil drawing of the domino. The phone immediately rings, and it is Hank on the line, shown sucking on the domino like a lollipop, and asking if she received his "message." As with other apparent symbols in the series, the significance of the object is hinted at, but never confirmed—the message it conveys to Josie, however, is clearly an intimidating one.

The objects assume a kind of quasi-life by virtue of their investment with affect. They are things that become more than things, puzzles that suggest receding depths of meaning. Call it the domino effect—an object is introduced and, although its significance is unclear, it nevertheless precipitates a range of responses and effects. By virtue of their associations with Laura's disappearance and Bob, the ceiling fan, record player, and the traffic light transform into what, borrowing from Ayers, we may consider as "demonic" objects (see Ayers 2004). The buffeting of the trees seems to connote nature's agitation over the active presence of evil in Twin Peaks and/or the agency of Ghostwood forest's ghosts. Accentuating this quasi-life of objects still further are objects that we may consider as inspirited—that seem within the context of the program to possess a kind of sentience. This is undoubtedly most evident in the case of the Log Lady's log (Catherine E. Coulson), as well as with the owls that are famously—but in keeping with the series' approach to objects more generally—"not what they seem."

The Log Lady Margaret Lanterman acts as Twin Peak's resident sibyl, dispensing cryptic advice and prognostications that she claims are conveyed to her by the log she carries as one would a child. "Can I ask her about her log?" queries Cooper of Truman in the pilot, reflecting the viewer's curiosity. "Many have," replies the Sheriff, intimating that no satisfactory answer will be forthcoming. The log, we are told, "saw something" the night Laura Palmer was murdered, and later Margaret, serving as medium, conveys the log's message to Major Briggs (Don S. Davis) that he should "deliver the message" to Cooper. Online "explanations" of *Twin Peaks'* symbolism hold that the log contains the spirit of her dead husband (see, for example, the Log Lady entry at glastonberrygrove.net). While this theory—of course—is never confirmed by the series, the capacity of inanimate objects to be "strangely vital" (Bennett 2010, 5) is everywhere affirmed by the series. The Log Lady foregrounds this most explicitly in her introduction to the penultimate episode (introductions were created by Lynch for each episode when the series was syndicated to the Bravo network) when, speaking directly to the viewer, she explains that each ring of a crosscut tree (note the emphasis on rings again) indicates a year of the tree's life and then tells the viewer, "My log hears things I cannot hear. But my log tells me about the sounds, about the new words. Even though it has stopped growing larger, my log is aware." The inspiriting of her log synecdochally connects to the spiritual inhabitation of Ghostwood Forest and more generally to the trees everywhere present in Twin Peaks that so captivate Cooper ("Sheriff, what kind of fantastic trees have you got growing around here?" asks Cooper in the pilot).

Connected to the forest and the trees are of course the owls that inhabit them and that are linked to the spirit world. As Cooper lies on the floor after having been shot in episode 8, the giant appears to him with three clues, one of which is that "the owls are not what they seem." What the owls actually are, predictably, is never confirmed, but owls appear throughout the series with increasingly ominous associations. An owl is watching, for example, at the end of episode 4 when Donna Hayward (Lara Flynn Boyle) and James seek to reclaim Laura's necklace from its hiding place in the woods and find it missing; in episode 17, an owl appears in the woods while Cooper is urinating, and Major Briggs disappears—when the Major reappears in episode 20, the only thing he recalls clearly is a giant owl; an owl is also watching when Leo wakes up and attacks Shelly (Mädchen Amick) with an axe in episode 21, and Cooper sees an owl in the trees before he enters the circle of sycamore trees in the finale. More darkly, in Cooper's dream in episode 9, an owl's face appears superimposed over Bob's; in episode 14, the Log Lady translates for Cooper what the Log saw—as part of her narration, she notes that owls first were flying, then near, then finally silent; later in the same episode, preceding the death of Maddy, the Log Lady tells Cooper, "We don't know what will happen or when. But there are owls are the Roadhouse." Connecting owls even more fully with the spirit world, at the end of episode 16, after Leland's death, Sheriff Truman wonders where Bob is now, and the scene cuts to woods at night with the camera moving close to the ground. The scene freezes, and the episode ends with the sudden appearance of the owl, again metonymically connecting the owl with Bob. A pictograph of an owl in the aptly named Owl Cave is a piece to the puzzle of how to access the spirit world, and, in episode 26, an owl is shown flying around the night sky within the silhouette of a hooded figure.

Beyond being simply birds of ill omen, the owls in *Twin Peaks*, like the Log Lady's log, hold within them a kind of alien sentience. Whether they are spies, gathering information for the spirit world, vessels containing inhabiting spirits, or forms taken by the spirits themselves is uncertain; what is clear, however, is that the owls are more than birds. The series insists that we look at trees and birds as inspirited objects gathering within them unanswerable riddles.

A fourth technique used to defamiliarize objects in the series is either to present them in pieces or to multiple them. Two striking examples of fragmentation are Jacques Renault's mouth in episode 7 and the wall tile in episode 11. As I will discuss, human beings within *Twin Peaks* are frequently presented as or confused with objects, and one way *Twin Peaks* performs this conflation is through characters and shots that fragment the body. This, of course, is the case with Phillip Gerard, the one-armed man, and Nadine, the one-eyed lady—as well as perhaps with the wheelchair-bound Eileen Hayward (Mary Jo Deschanel)—but it is rendered much more viscerally in extreme close-ups of body parts that metonymically accentuate a particular affect. In episode 7, this is first the state of affairs with Dr. Jacoby, who, having been assaulted by Hank, loses consciousness as the camera zooms in for an extreme close-up on his left eye before dissolving into a spinning roulette wheel (yet another spinning circle) at the appropriately named *One Eyed Jack's*, where Cooper—posing as a drug financier—hires Jacque Renault to move drugs across the border. As Jacques lasciviously recalls the night at the cabin when Laura died, the camera moves in for an extreme close-up of his mouth, the shot echoing and accentuating the repulsiveness of both the story told and the teller.

Fragmentation is used as an especially disorienting defamiliarizing technique most dramatically at the start of episode 11, which is introduced by a crash of scream-like noise and darkness. The camera pulls back within what appears to be a dark tunnel as a distorted childlike voice intones "daddy" and we hear what seems to be a beeping heart monitor indicate cardiac arrest. As it pulls further back, now spinning, the camera emerges from a hole subsequently revealed to be one among many. As it continues to pull back, the holes at last resolve themselves into sound-dampening wall tiles. Sheriff Truman steps into the scene, repeating "Leland Leland," and then the camera focuses on Leland's sideways head before rotating 90 degrees so that Leland's image is upright. The effect here is clearly one of disorientation as the camera expressionistically renders—and interpellates the viewer into—Leland's confusion.

A similar sort of disorienting effect is created by uncanny multiplication, rendered in the series for both comedic and dramatic effect. Multiplication in

Figure 4. A policeman's dream

space is used in an absurd and light-hearted way in the series, such as in the pilot when Cooper and Sheriff Truman are greeted in the station by rows upon rows of stacked donuts ("a policeman's dream!" enthuses Cooper), and a similarly comedic effect is evoked by a row of six cigar-smoking police officers all adopting the same posture when Donna meets James at Wallies Hideout in episode 22. More portentously, in episode 15, when James comes looking for Maddy at the Palmer house, Leland's living room is shown filled with hundreds of golf balls, which reflects the mania the possessed Leland experiences following the murder of Maddy.

Connected to fragmented images of human beings and their duplication and the inverse of the inspiriting of objects is a fifth and final technique of defamiliarization: the objectification of human beings (which I will discuss more fully in Chapter 3). While things in *Twin Peaks* assume a kind of quasi-life, living creatures become thing-like. This effect is achieved through fragmentation of the body, as indicated previously, and the prominent placement of taxidermied animals, as well as through death and severe injury, duplication, and possession.

Through death, severe injury, and duplication, the ontological privileging of the human subject as special is undercut. Wrapped in plastic or stuffed into a golf bag, the bodies of Laura and Maddy become things to be investigated or tossed into the boot of the auto. (Indeed, the conflict in the pilot between Albert Rosenfeld [Miguel Ferrer] and the town as represented by Sheriff Truman is over the ontological status of Laura's dead body, with Albert asserting its status as essentially a thing to be fragmented and probed for evidence and Sheriff Truman resisting this position and asserting that the corpse possesses a greater social significance.) Leo, after being shot by Hank, becomes a "vegetable" for a time, partially recovering his cognitive abilities only to become a shock-collar-wearing slave to Windom Earle. Combining the inspiriting of objects with the objectification of human subjects is the bizarre fate of Josie Packard in episode 23. Discovered at the Great Northern, Josie kills Thomas Eckhardt and then collapses. Following this, the viewer is treated to the image of Josie—presumably her soul—trapped within the knob of a night table drawer. The objectification of human beings, however, is rendered most literally at the end of episode 26 when Windom Earl murders a hapless drifter (Rusty, played by Ted Raimi) and transforms him into a human chess piece.

Doppelgängers and, most dramatically, possessed individuals within the series similarly undercut the uniqueness of human subjects and force a consideration of human beings as merely things to be copied or inhabited. Doppelgängers are apparent in the cases of Laura and Maddy, Laura and the "cousin" of the Man from Another Place in Cooper's dream ("She's my cousin . . . but doesn't she look almost exactly like Laura Palmer?" [episode 2]), and Cooper in the series finale ("doppelgänger!" exclaims the Man from Another Place as Cooper flees, pursued by a copy of himself). The possession of Leland by Bob is, of course, central to the series—as is the possession of Gerard by Mike. In episode 6, Mike explains to Cooper that, having cut his connection with Bob by severing Gerard's arm, Mike nevertheless "remained close to this vessel, inhabiting him from time to time." In episode 16, Bob, speaking through Leland, refers to Leland as "a good vehicle." In each instance, the autonomy and indeed personhood of the subject is negated. People, like owls or logs, hotels or percolators, are simply things to be filled and inhabited—vessels and vehicles.

Twin Peaks charms viewers by inviting them into a world of spellbinding objects around which the narrative is constructed and that brings together the characters as they blur the lines between person and thing, sentient and nonsentient, and living and dead. The various forms of defamiliarized objects summarized previously—displaced, ominous matter, inspirited matter, fragmented or multiplied matter, and objectified—combine to create a world marked by the gothicized insistence of commonplace things: objects in *Twin Peaks* demand to be noticed and present themselves in ways that chasten fantasies of human mastery. Matter throughout the series—like the flickering morgue light or the fish in the percolator or the buck's head that won't stay on the wall—repeatedly is presented as unruly, recalcitrant, even whimsical. Things in *Twin Peaks* invariably rebound, introduce mysteries rather than solve them—and insist that we see them again precisely as mysterious things.

It is precisely this strangeness of objects—and indeed of the world in which they exist—that *Twin Peaks* repeatedly insists we acknowledge. This is a fundamental component of the program's allure, a method through which it captivates the viewer and one exemplifying what Jane Bennett refers to as the "vitality" of objects: the "capacity of things . . . not only to impede or block the will and designs of humans but also to act as quasi agents or forces with trajectories, propensities, or tendencies of their own" (2010, viii). For theorists of things such as Bennett and Ian Bogost, recognition of the intermeshing of human beings in networks or assemblages of things is a starting point for a reconceived ethical program that undercuts anthropocentric arrogance. With Peter Stallybrass, Thing Theorists ask, "What have we done to things to have such contempt for them?" (Stallybrass 1998, 203), and attempt to envision a new, more harmonious relation between human beings and the world that "denies the human subject the sovereign central position" (Alaimo 2010, 16). What *Twin Peaks* reveals, however, is the Gothic underside to such a reconceptualization. What the program renders prominent in its process of worlding is the anxiety that underlies the decentering of the human. When things come alive and human beings are reduced to things, we enter the affective terrain of horror. Nothing in *Twin Peaks* is what it seems; what things are, however, is never clear—and it is this provocation of objects, anticipating theories of things developed decades later, that participates in fostering the program's allure, captivating viewers seeking to make sense of the matter of *Twin Peaks*.

King's Things

Among the themes that Stephen King has repeatedly turned to in his horror fiction for over half a century is the uncanniness of animate objects. In *Christine*, as addressed earlier, he gives us a sentient killer car—a theme King had introduced in his earlier story "Trucks," first published in 1973. In "Trucks," large vehicles, including semis, are mysteriously brought to life and turn on humans. "Trucks" was then adapted for film in 1986 as *Maximum Overdrive*, directed by King himself, where the animacy of objects is extended to lawnmowers, chainsaws, and even hair dryers. In King's later *From a Buick 8* (2002), the titular car—in addition to being at least somewhat sentient—acts as a portal to another dimension. In King's *The Shining* (1977), child protagonist Danny is threatened by a variety of uncanny objects, including moving hedge animals and a firehose. King's story "The Monkey," first published in 1980, features a cursed cymbal-clanging monkey toy—every time the cymbals bang, someone close to the protagonist dies. In King's "The Mangler" (1972), an industrial laundry press becomes possessed by a demon resulting in a number of deaths. Indeed, King's catalog of Gothic things is so extensive that it was parodied on the animated program *Family Guy* where King, forced to quickly come up with a pitch for a new novel, resorts to a lamp monster ("A Picture Is Worth 1,000 Bucks," S2, E11).

Nowhere in King's oeuvre, however, is the thing-power of Gothic objects emphasized more fully than in his 1991 novel *Needful Things*. Set in King's fictitious town of Castle Rock, Maine, the novel's focus is on the opening of an unusual curio store and its mysterious proprietor, Leland Gaunt. Gaunt's shop always seems to have the precise object of each customer's desire, from a rare Sandy Koufax baseball card to a fragment of wood believed to be from Noah's ark to Elvis's sunglasses (King takes a certain amount of glee in playing on references to "the King" throughout), and Gaunt sells them at absurdly low prices, provided that customers then play some kind of prank on someone else in Castle Rock. Supernaturally cognizant of the town's feuds, grudges, and animosities, Gaunt revels in chaos and successfully sows discord until the town erupts in violence. In the end, Gaunt is defeated by the town's sheriff, Alan Pangborn, who realizes that Gaunt is a demonic shyster who tempts the town's citizens into surrendering their souls—but not before his machinations result in the destruction of the town.

Through its emphasis on thing-power, *Needful Things* is not only very much in keeping with King's body of work but exemplary of the Gothic tradition as a whole. This emphasis on the agency of the material is signaled right from the start through the name of the store from which the novel takes its name: "Needful Things." Part of King's playfulness in the novel is the dual meaning of the word "needful," which signifies both necessary and needy. In the first sense, the things are objects needed by someone or something; in the second, the things are the subjects, themselves full of need. The novel thus takes as its focus the uncanny life that material objects assume and foregrounds the rift between their perceived and real qualities. At the core of the novel, as of the Gothic more generally, are objects with unexplored depths that act in ways surprising and uncanny.

Of the commentators on King's novel, John Sears, in his 2011 *Stephen King's Gothic*, appreciates this most fully, although his emphasis is not on the things themselves, but rather on their roles in capitalist transactions. *Needful Things* is in Sears's estimation "King's most extended and forceful allegory of consumerism as the misdirection and corruption of desire" (Sears 2011, 217). Sears sees the novel as critiquing Leland Gaunt's "conventional capitalist philosophy" that "everything's for sale" (218). As part of this analysis, Sears observes how the "language of transaction and exchange permeates the novel's rhetoric" (218) and notes how the word "thing" "circulates through this economy, accruing . . . a range of uncanny significances. 'Things' variously names objects and actions and people, so that 'Needful Things' names both Gaunt's shop . . . and its customers, as well as the 'things' they buy and the 'lousy things' . . . they must do to pay for them" (220).

I agree with Sears that the novel functions, at least to a certain extent, as a critique of consumerism. What, however, is truly central to the novel and the affect it elicits is not just the role of objects in various transactions, but *the uncanny potency of the objects themselves*. Needful Things presents the Gothic's fascination with uncanny objects writ large. It focuses on and magnifies the allure of Gothicized things—things that one needs and things that have needs of their own.

Indeed, a large part of the novel's early sections is devoted to detailing the odd assortment of things available in the shop. For example, when a central character, Polly Chalmers, first stops at the store, King writes:

> The items which had been placed out when Brian [another important character] stopped in the afternoon before—geode, Polaroid camera, picture of Elvis Presley, the few others—were still there, but perhaps four dozen more had been added. A small rug probably worth a small fortune hung on one of the off-white walls—it was Turkish, and old. There was a collection of lead soldiers in one of the cases, possibly antiques, but Polly knew that all lead soldiers, even those cast in Hong Kong a week ago last Monday, have an antique-y look.
>
> The goods were wildly varied. Between the picture of Elvis, which looked to her like the sort of thing that would retail on any carnival midway in America for $4.99, and a singularly uninteresting American eagle weathervane, was a carnival glass lampshade which was certainly worth eight hundred dollars and might be worth as much as five thousand. A battered and charmless teapot stood flanked by a pair of gorgeous *poupees*, and she could not even begin to guess what those beautiful French dollies with their rouged cheeks and gartered gams might be worth.
>
> There was a selection of baseball and tobacco cards, a fan of pulp magazines from the thirties (*Weird Tales, Astounding Tales, Thrilling Wonder Stories*), a table-radio from the fifties which was that disgusting

shade of pale pink which the people of that time had seemed to approve of when it came to appliances, if not to politics.

Most—although not all—of the items had small plaques standing in front of them: TRI-CRYSTAL GEODE, ARIZONA, read one. CUSTOM SOCKET-WRENCH KIT, read another. The one in front of the splinter which had so amazed Brian announced it was PETRIFIED WOOD FROM THE HOLY LAND. The plaques in front of the trading cards and the pulp magazines read: OTHERS AVAILABLE UPON REQUEST.

All the items, whether trash or treasure, had one thing in common, she observed: there were no price-tags on any of them. (King 1991, 43, all capitalizations in original).

Rocks, cameras, pictures, rugs, lampshades, baseball cards, and so on. While this scene—and the others like it that parade before the viewer Mr. Gaunt's miscellaneous wares—occurs in a curio store in Castle Rock, Maine, we nevertheless are back again in the cellar of *The Cabin in the Woods*. The objects are all cursed, patrons are manipulated by malevolent external forces, and the price for all the items ends up being the same: one's soul. The objects thus become part of a cosmic battle between good and evil as they speak to human needs and desires. The uncanny potency of the material world undermines human agency and thrusts us into the great outdoors.

What King also proposes in *Needful Things* is that the "real qualities" of things always escape us, withdraw into the shadows. Speaking with his conscripted lackey, Ace Merrill, Mr. Gaunt muses, "Perhaps all the really special things I sell aren't what they appear to be. Perhaps they are actually gray things with only one remarkable property—the ability to take the shapes of those things which haunt the dreams of men and women" (King 1991, 370). Mr. Gaunt here is an Object-Oriented Ontologist discussing the difference between perceived qualities—objects for us—and real qualities, qualities that escape knowing and recede into the shadows. What *Needful Things* makes abundantly clear are the ways we invest objects with affect and meaning, transforming them into objects of nostalgia and desire for us; at the same time, however, those objects go beyond the meanings and narratives we overlay onto them. They possess the capacity to resist us, to surprise us, to act—thing-power—even as they ultimately exceed and escape explanatory paradigms.

What Bennett calls thing-power or Vibrant Materialism, the Gothic figures finally as dark magic. There is in fact a strange inversion of Marxist economic theory at work here as the fantastic materials of the Gothic are literally invested with magical properties. They are fetishes in the original sense of objects believed to be invested with supernatural powers. And unlike Marxian commodity fetishism that obscures the labor and social relations invested in commodity production, these fetishes, these magic objects, working in reverse are then used to stimulate social relations—albeit in an antagonistic way.

In the end, it all comes back to the things—what matters in the Gothic is the ominous matter itself. Whether in the cellar of the Cabin in the Woods or the forest of Twin Peaks or Mr. Gaunt's curio shop, the fantastic materials of the Gothic uncover fully what is barely concealed by Thing Theory: cosmic dread in the face of human decentering. And Gothic things provoke the philosophical and ethical questions Thing Theory, in the name of sustainability or eco-consciousness or posthumanism, tends to sidestep: what good are qualities that can never be known? And, centrally, can we and should we consider human beings as part of a democracy of things all equal in existing? Should the exhumed femur of the victim of a serial killer be lumped together with a parabolic satellite dish and a bowl of cantaloupe? How should we respond when an assemblage containing a corpse becomes "vibratory"? Through these questions derived from its insistent focus on matter, the Gothic asks difficult questions about how human beings should regard and relate to the nonhuman and to each other. If forms of New Materialism, Speculative Realism, and Object-Oriented Ontology have a tendency to "theorize object life in its most radically non-relational forms" (Tompkins 2016), Gothic materialism forces our attention back onto issues of mattering, "enfleshment," and objectification. This is most particularly the case with the object most central to Gothic narrative, the human body, to which we now turn.

3
Body-as-Thing

Because of the centrality of the body to our own identity and lived experiences, the Gothic thing par excellence is the human body. Gothic narratives insistently emphasize the fragility of the body by putting characters into situations of danger where bodily harm is possible or likely; however, the body as uncanny Gothic object is produced through an inversion of animacy in which, on the one hand, the body is reduced to the status of a thing and, on the other, the thing-as-body is endowed with uncanny life. The first category, body-as-thing, consists of narratives in which human bodies are treated as assemblages of pieces, tools, vessels, and "meat"—that is, the body is foregrounded as *matter* and given no special ontological status in the "democracy of objects" (see Bryant [2011]); it is simply an object existing with other objects, often to be utilized without particular care or sensitivity. This is the realm of mad scientists, serial killers, and cannibals—and, in a different context, slave narratives—and these tales are generally framed in such a way that readers and audiences are asked to reject the equation of body = object among other objects. The other category, thing-as-body endowed with uncanny life, includes animate corpses and body parts, as well as animate dolls, puppets, mannequins, statutes, robots, idols, masks, portraits, photographs, reflections, and other representations of the human form that not only challenge understandings of the line between living and dead, but frequently seem *more alive* than the human beings who encounter them. Put differently, representations of the body-as-thing endowed with uncanny life often stage inversions in which the inanimate thing assumes life at the expense of the living thing, which is frozen or vitiated. Both types of inversion within Gothic narrative—body-as-thing and thing-as-body come to life—evoke negative affect from characters as well as audiences because they are invested with dread about the fragility of the body, emphasize the abject, and undo human exceptionalism in troubling ways. The affective dread elicited by such scenarios in these ways underscores the dark side to Thing Theory and the constellation of approaches grouped under the rubric of the nonhuman turn as narratives involving Gothic bodies foreground just how difficult—and possibly dangerous—it is to construe human bodies as objects numbered among other objects. The Gothic in this way raises concerns about how easily the "nonhuman turn" can exert an *inhuman* torque as bodies are construed as objects subject to manipulation and exploitation.

As I have developed in earlier chapters, for most Thing Theorists and critics associated with the nonhuman turn, the elevation of objects and concomitant critique of anthropocentrism have ethical underpinnings as the critics seek "to counter the narcissism of humans in charge of the world" (Bennett 2010, xvi) in the hope of fostering more ethical, fulfilling, and sustainable ways of existing. According to Timothy Morton in *Hyperobjects*, Object-Oriented Ontology, for example, "radically displaces the human by insisting that my being is not everything it's cracked up to be—or rather that the being of a paper cup is as profound as mine" (2013a, 17). This "humiliation" (17) of the human is for Morton a necessary prerequisite toward engaging in a substantive way with the prospect of ecological disaster. Bennett's word in *Vibrant Matter* isn't humiliation, but rather "chasten": "I believe that encounters with lively matter," she writes, "can chasten my fantasies of human mastery, highlight the common materiality of all that is, expose a wider distribution of agency, and reshape the self and its interests" (2010, 122). Similarly, for Stacey Alaimo, recognition of the "trans-corporeality" of the human—that is, the intermeshing of the human with the "dynamic, material world, which crosses through them, transforms them, and is transformed by them" (Alaimo 2018, 435)—"allows us to forge ethical and political positions that can contend with numerous late twentieth- and early twenty-first-century realities in which 'human' and 'environment' can by no means be considered separate" (Alaimo 2010, 2). For these critics, living ethically and addressing the crises of the Anthropocene necessitate the undoing of human exceptionalism.

Of particular note here in relation to the Gothic as dark underside to contemporary Thing Theory is the concept of a "flat ontology" promulgated by Object-Oriented Ontologists such as Ian Bogost, Graham Harman, and Levi R. Bryant. As Bogost explains in "What Is Object-Oriented Ontology?," a 2009 blogpost, "Object-oriented ontology . . . puts *things* at the center of this study. Its proponents contend that nothing has special status, but that everything exists equally—plumbers, cotton, bonobos, DVD players, and sandstone, for example" (Bogost 2009). Bryant points out in his discussion of what he refers to as the "democracy of objects" that this is not a political stance but rather an "*ontological* thesis" (2011, 19), a statement about the beingness of things outside of their particular utility for or perceptions of by humans. Bogost does clarify in *Alien Phenomenology* that by flat ontology OOO-theorists mean that "*all things equally exist, yet they do not exist equally.* The funeral pyre is not the same as an aardvark; the porceletta shell is not equivalent to the rugby ball" (2012, 11). All things existing equally does not mean that all things are the same.

The Gothic, however—much like some critics of New Materialism, Thing Theory, and related paradigms—is deeply suspicious of the notion of a flat ontology, and it has dwelt since its origins as a genre in the eighteenth century on the consequences for human happiness of thinking of human beings as objects whose being is no more profound than that of a paper cup. In contrast to critical positions asserting the necessity of the decentering of the human subject as an ethical imperative toward living in more generous, authentic, and/or sustainable ways is the whole history of the Gothic emphasizing the terror associated with being "humiliated," being "chastened," and treating humans as objects without special status—as things, meat, or matter to be confined, utilized in mechanical ways, or consumed literally or metaphorically. Bennett suggests in *Vibrant Matter* that "if matter itself is lively, then not only is the difference between subject and objects minimized, but the status of the shared materiality of all things is elevated" (2010, 13). To this, the Gothic replies, "but what if it goes the other way and the shared materiality of all things, including the human, is diminished?"

This is the Gothic underpinning to all forms of bigotry and slavery: When human beings are treated as things, they are then available for exploitation. Indeed, what is called the female Gothic, as well as the American slave narrative, uses Gothic devices as a means to contest the abuse of particular types of bodies.[1] In Kari J. Winter's *Subjects of Slavery, Agents of Change: Women and Power in Gothic Novels and Slave Narratives, 1790–1865* (1992), she considers Gothic novels and American slave narratives by women in tandem, emphasizing their kinship in addressing the "horrifying aspects of patriarchal culture" (53). According to Winter, female-authored Gothic novels and slave narratives overlap in their representations of parasitical (white) patriarchs, societal power inequities, and the control of knowledge in the service of subjugation (55). Addressing the interrelations of New World slavery and the Gothic directly, Teresa A. Goddu notes that "the Gothic as a genre emerged simultaneous to and in dialogue with the rise of new World slavery and the construction of racial categories" (Goddu, "The African Slave Narrative" [2014], 71). "As many critics have noted," continues Goddu, "there is a structural affinity between the discourse of slavery and the conventions of the Gothic" that cluster around suffering, tyranny, and violence (72). Sarah Gilbreath Ford is even more specific in her 2020 study *Haunted Property: Slavery and the Gothic*, in which she focuses on slavery's transformation of people into property (6): "From early slave narratives to contemporary postmodern novels, authors have chosen to use the gothic as a tool to demonstrate how the conflation of people and property results in nightmares of haunting" (8). What Winter, Goddu, and Ford make clear in their analyses of the Gothic conventions of slave narratives is that the Gothic coalesces around the distinction between human and thing—and frequently seeks to contest the confusion between the two where women (the Female Gothic) and black bodies (the slave narrative) are concerned. Contemporary Thing Theory in general seeks to decenter the human, emphasizing the shared materiality of all things. Skeptics of this move argue that it "sidestep[s] the analytical challenges posed by the categories of race, colonialism, and slavery" (Jackson, "Animal" [2013], 671), adding in some cases that it is easier for those whose humanity is already presumed to dispense with humanism than for those whose humanity has always been in question (672). The Gothic, too, sounds a cautionary note through its representations of abused, debased, deformed, parahuman, and "abhuman" bodies that are treated as things available for manipulation, consumption, and exploitation.[2] The Gothic, in short, particularly when it focuses on bodies as things, gives us Thing Theory gone wrong.

Body-as-Object

The Gothic is at its core a corpse-producing machine, emphasizing the thingness of the body as it opens them up, breaks them into pieces, and sometimes reassembles them in new configurations. Its matter is insistently the matter of the body, the body as matter: Gothic mattering. The milieu of the Gothic is therefore abjection, the reaction elicited by the threatening breakdown of meaning caused by the loss of the distinction between subject and object or between self and other. As developed by Julia Kristeva, the "utmost of abjection" (1982, 4) is the corpse, that which was once a person but is now a thing, and which cannot help but remind us not only of our own mortality, but our materiality. At the heart of the Gothic is the transformation—threatened or accomplished—of person into thing, of body into object or sometimes objects. The most gruesome moments in Gothic works invariably foreground the materiality of the body: Victor Frankenstein, whose materials are furnished by "the dissecting room and the slaughter-house" and who assembles body parts in his "workshop of filthy creation" (Shelley [1818] 1993, 36); Agnes in her cell holding her deceased and decaying worm-ridden infant in Matthew Lewis's *The Monk* (1796); the disintegration of Helen Vaughn at the end of Arthur Machen's *The Great God Pan* (1894). Cinematic horror in particular has elaborated this sensibility present in the Gothic from the start through a fixation on the materiality of the body in over-the-top scenes of murder, mutilation, and dismemberment: the alien exploding from Kane's (John Hurt) chest in Ridley Scott's *Alien* (1979), the transformation of Jeff Goldblum into "Brundlefly" in David Cronenberg's *The Fly* (1986), cannibal zombies in George Romero's *Night of the Living Dead* (1968), cannibal rednecks in *The Texas Chainsaw Massacre* (Tobe Hooper, 1974), the chest defibrillator scene in John Carpenter's *The Thing* (1982)—the horror subgenres of torture porn and body horror are in fact built around evoking intense affect through graphic displays of bodily harm and torture.[3]

It must be acknowledged that the apparent "bad taste" of such scenes within Gothic narrative has often been recuperated by cultural and film critics as canny forms of social commentary. This is certainly the case with Female Gothic works read as subversive critiques of patriarchal control of women and slave narratives that use Gothic devices to contest slavery and racialized capitalism. Even brutally gruesome films have been explained as reflections of or commentaries on political issues and their historical moment. One can interpret *The Texas Chainsaw Massacre*, for example, as a critique of industrial capitalism, analyze *Night of the Living Dead* as a racial allegory, or consider Eli Roth's 2006 *Hostel* as a response to the American war in Iraq and American anxieties about its "chickens coming home to roost."[4] Such readings may well be persuasive and offer insight into the works. Nevertheless, to explore these films as allegories and political critique, we have to move past what initially arrests our attention: the spectacle and affect evoked via representations of the body transformed into and treated as an object to be abused and abased. It begins with the body and the affect—surprise, horror, disgust, fascination, possibly even amusement—elicited by the body poised to become or in fact transformed into a thing. Indeed, the centrality of the body-as-object theme in Gothic narrative is so ubiquitous as arguably to define the genre. I have therefore selected two texts for closer scrutiny that emphasize the anxieties attendant on the notion of the body as part of the "democracy of objects" in striking ways: Edgar Allan Poe's short story "Berenice" ([1835] 1996) and Clive Barker's "The Midnight Meat Train" ([1984] 1988). Separated by almost 150 years, Poe's and Barker's stories are nevertheless variants on the same Gothic theme: the human body treated as a thing available for fragmentation and even consumption.

Berenice's Teeth

Edgar Allan Poe's "Berenice," first published in March of 1835 in the Richmond, Virginia–based *Southern Literary Messenger*, is a gruesome tale of the fetishization of particular body parts and of bodily "thing-power." At its center is the "monomania" of the tale's narrator, Egaeus, who has a disorder that causes him to become mesmerized by commonplace things. "This monomania, if I must so term it," explains Egaeus, "consisted in a morbid irritability of the nerves immediately affecting those properties of the mind, in metaphysical science termed the *attentive*" (227). He continues, "I fear that it is indeed in no manner possible to convey to the mind of the merely general reader, an adequate idea of that nervous *intensity of interest* with which, in my case, the powers of meditation . . . busied, and, as it were, buried themselves in the contemplation of even the most ordinary objects of the universe" (227). The objects of Egaeus's "undue, intense, and morbid attention" were invariably, in his words, "frivolous."

> To muse for long unwearied hours with my attention rivetted to some frivolous device upon the margin, or in the typography of a book; to become absorbed for the better part of a summer's day in a quaint shadow falling aslant upon the tapestry, or upon the floor; to lose myself for an entire night in watching the steady flame of a lamp, or the embers of a fire; to dream away whole days over the perfume of a flower; to repeat monotonously some common word, until the sound, by dint of frequent repetition, ceased to convey any idea whatever to the mind; to lose all sense of motion or physical existence in a state of absolute bodily quiescence long and obstinately persevered in:—Such were a few of the most common and least pernicious vagaries induced by a condition of the mental faculties, not, indeed, altogether unparalleled, but certainly bidding defiance to anything like analysis or explanation. (227)

Egaeus, in sum, is a sort of precocious Object-Oriented Ontologist, seized by the thing-power of material objects numbered among a kind of flat ontology that finds equally riveting the details of floors and tapestries, books and flowers. Egaeus's obsessive gaze begins and ends with the materiality of the thing. "Few deductions, if any, were made," he tells us, "and those few pertinaciously returning in, so to speak, upon the original object as a centre" (228). "Berenice" is a story insistently about the devious and defiant materiality of things—with a particular set of things at its center.

The ghoulish course taken by the story is set firmly on its path when Egaeus's attention fixates on the teeth of his cousin Berenice, a once-beautiful girl afflicted by a kind of wasting disease—and, since this is a Poe story, Berenice's disease is one that also manifests in the form of death-like trances. Egaeus tells us that he had paid little attention to this cousin while she was healthy; however, she becomes an object of his attention in her decline. Surveying the once beautiful girl, he shifts his attention from the "glassy stare" of her "lifeless . . . lustreless" eyes to her "thin and shrunken lips," which then part to reveal her teeth (230). After Berenice's departure from his chamber, Egaeus ruminates at length upon her teeth:

> But from the disordered chamber of my brain, had not, alas! departed, and would not be driven away, the white and ghastly *spectrum* of the teeth. Not a speck upon their surface—not a shade on their enamel—not a line in their configuration—not an indenture in their edges—but what that period of her smile had sufficed to brand in upon my memory. I saw them *now* even more unequivocally than I beheld them *then*. The teeth!—the teeth!—they were here, and there, and every where, and visibly, and palpably before me; long, narrow, and excessively white, with the pale lips writhing about them, as in the very moment of their first terrible development. Then came the full fury of my *monomania*, and I struggled in vain against its strange and irresistible influence. In the multiplied objects of the external world I had no thoughts but for the teeth. All other matters and all different interests became absorbed in their single contemplation. They—they alone were present to the mental eye, and they, in their sole individuality, became the essence of my mental life. I held them in every light. I turned them in every attitude. I surveyed their characteristics. I dwelt upon their peculiarities. I pondered upon their conformation. I mused upon the alteration in their nature. I shuddered as I assigned to them in imagination a sensitive and sentient power, and even when unassisted by the lips, a capability of moral expression. Of Mad'selle Sallé it has been said, "*que tous ses pas etaient des sentiments,*" and of Berenice I more seriously believed *que touts ses dents etaient des ideés*. (231)

I will return to Egaeus's concluding proposition that Berenice's teeth are "ideas." What I wish to emphasize for the moment is the story's intense insistence on a kind of psychic dismemberment of Berenice. She fades into the background as a person—and, indeed, as a complete body—until all that is left of her, like the Cheshire cat, is her teeth.[5]

The gruesome conclusion to the story seems as inevitable as that of the Greek tragedy suggested by Egaeus's name. Berenice has died, and Egaeus now finds himself in his library. On the table beside his chair burns a lamp, and near it sits a mysterious ebony box—one that Egaeus recognizes as that of the family physician. Egaeus feels he has done something terrible, but of what he has no recollection. A servant enters with the distressing news that Berenice's grave has been disturbed, the body "disfigured" (232) but that she has been found alive! The servant then calls Egaeus's attention to his clothing, "muddy and clotted with gore," as well as to a spade propped up against the wall. Memory flooding back, Egaeus snatches up the ebony box and attempts to force it open. It slips from his grasp and bursts into pieces on the floor, revealing "some instruments of dental surgery, intermingled with many white and glistening substances that were scattered to and fro about the floor" (233). The story ends here, leaving the reader to make the horrible connections: The teeth are Berenice's. Berenice had been prematurely interred, and Egaeus, having violated her grave in a trance-like state, has wrenched the teeth—presumably all of them, one by one—from her still-living body. His fantasied dismemberment of her has become literal.[6]

Poe himself, it is worth mentioning, seems to have had some reservations about the gruesomeness of this story. In a letter written to Thomas W. White, principal editor of the *Southern Literary Messenger*, defending the story against the charge of "bad taste," Poe acknowledges that the subject is "far too horrible" before going on to assert famously that "to be appreciated you must be read, and these things are invariably sought after with avidity" (Poe, "Letter to White" [1835]). It is however useful to consider in this story of teeth where the bad taste inheres. Presumably, it has to do with the violence executed against the human body in the extraction of the teeth—and it is horrible indeed to picture to oneself the scene of Egaeus having disinterred the still-living Berenice from her grave only then to wrench the teeth from her mouth—a mouth, one might add, that, in keeping with female characters in Poe more generally, utters not a single word in the course of the narrative. Since the scene of extraction is absent from the narrative, it is the reader who, seized by the "many white and glistening substances that were scattered to and fro about the floor," seeks meaning in them and conjures into being the gruesome tableau. It is we who extract Berenice's teeth.

More generally, however, Poe's "Berenice" foregrounds the Gothic underside to Object-Oriented Ontology and Thing Theory. As I discuss in the Introduction to this book, in the first chapter of Jane Bennett's *Vibrant Matter*, she introduces the notion of "thing-power" by describing her own experience of considering debris on a grate over a storm drain on a street in Baltimore, Maryland, that vacillates between being "dead stuff" and "live presence." There is a similar kind of "contingent tableau" (Bennett 2010, 5) introduced at the end of "Berenice," consisting of a lamp, a box, and a spade—an assemblage that, together with muddy and gore-clotted clothing, first arrests thought then precipitates action in the form of a conscious repetition of a prior disinterment. The lamp illuminates the scene as another box is opened and the teeth extracted a third time (having been extracted previously first in fancy and then in fact) as the "many white and glistening substances," together with the ominous "tools of dental surgery," scatter across the floor. The box becomes a mouth spilling teeth; Berenice's mouth becomes a box, an object housing other objects. The body is thus foregrounded as an assemblage of parts.

This, of course, is the realization upon which "Berenice" insists as it illustrates both the "thing-power" of Berenice's teeth and their inscrutability. While Egaeus concludes that Berenice's teeth "were ideas," the story counters this tendency toward abstraction by insistently emphasizing their materiality: long, narrow, excessively white, glistening. In correspondence with the description of objects given by Harman, Morton, Bryant, and other Object-Oriented Ontologists, the sensual qualities of the teeth are conveyed while their "real qualities" withdraw "into the shadows of being, untranslatable into any sort of human access" (Harman, *Weird Realism* [2012], 31). What Poe depicts for us through the meditation on teeth is what Harman refers to as the "gaps at the heart of objects" (44) or what Morton calls the "rift" between the appearance and the essence of a thing (*Hyperobjects* [2013a], 63). While Egaeus contemplates things obsessively, as noted earlier, he tells us, "Few deductions, if any, were made; and those few pertinaciously returning in, so to speak, upon the original object as a centre." Things can be exhaustively described and yet still unknown.[7]

What "Berenice" illustrates finally is the anxiety underlying the idea of a flat ontology that elides the difference between organic and inorganic, that numbers human beings among things, and that sees all things as equal in existing. Poe's Gothic narrative showcases the all-too-human anxieties associated with the elevation of the object and the objectification of the human as the story stages a kind of chiasmus in which humans surrender autonomy to things.[8] The unknowable teeth obsess Egaeus, who, acting in a trance, surrenders to unconscious compulsion. Egaeus, in this story of people who approximate corpses and move in trances, is less lively and more thing-like than the objects that seize him.

In its own way then, "Berenice" is a fantastic narrative of the living dead—one character who, zombie-like, moves in a trance while controlled by forces of which he is not aware and who seeks not brains but teeth; another character who, seemingly having died, literally then returns from the grave bloody and disfigured. "Berenice" is also, however, an uncanny tale of the mesmerizing inscrutability of material things and the power they possess—and foremost among their thing-power is their resistance to correlationalist abstraction. Egaeus refers to Berenice's teeth as ideas—but of what he does not know. In place of words (knowledge), Berenice's mouth yields teeth (things): hard kernels of inscrutable meaning that resist and exceed interpretation. Indeed, if the teeth are ideas, the idea represented is precisely the Object-Oriented Ontologist's conclusion of the inscrutability of the material. The teeth may be extracted from the body, but all attempts to extract meaning from the teeth fail. They are, finally, not even teeth but "thirty-two small, white, and ivory-looking substances" that scatter across the floor. Through their metonymic connection to Berenice, they compel the disconcerting realization that the body is an assemblage of detachable or extractable parts. Their extraction highlights the kinds of violence to which the body is liable when it is treated as a thing among other things. Egaeus is in a sense chewed up by Berenice's teeth, and, as we too are swallowed by Poe's gruesome narrative, the affect evoked is generated by the horrific transformation of a person into pieces.

"Berenice" is instructive because it offers a clear illustration of the uncanny thing-power common to material objects in Gothic narrative. The world of the Gothic is filled with material objects that act in accordance with the ways that Thing Theorists say that they do—that are both strangely vibrant and inscrutable. In the Gothic, however, this is a source of anxiety rather than hope as this uncanny animacy precipitates the realization of human insufficiency: We do not know the world or our place in it. Further, the elevation or animation of things within the Gothic is frequently offset by the objectification or "thingification" of the human. Vampire-like, the objects siphon off life from the living. Inverting the conventional hierarchy that places humans above things and undercutting anthropocentrism, Gothic things are finally more lively than people—people seemingly reduced to the status of lesser things—or, in the case of Clive Barker's "The Midnight Meat Train" to which we will now turn: meat.

Body as Meat

In Poe's story, a woman is taken apart by her supposed lover; the focus of the story is her body, which Egaeus first figuratively then literally disassembles as he abstracts and then extracts her teeth. While one could pursue the psychoanalytic implications of Egaeus's fixation and unconscious actions (particularly in relation to the ideas of the fetish, necrophilia, and the vagina dentata), such interpretation follows in the wake of our digestion, so to speak, of the *ghoulish* nature of the story in which a man disinters what he presumes to be the corpse of a woman and wrenches the teeth from her mouth—if the story leaves a "bad taste" in ours, it results from the violence performed on Berenice's body, which is treated as a thing to be manipulated and mutilated. Almost 150 years later, Clive Barker's "The Midnight Meat Train" elaborates the same theme even more explicitly, revealing the hidden cannibalistic subtext of Poe's "Berenice," a story about mouths, teeth, and bodies. In Barker's story, the anxiety rendered clearly is the reduction of the body to *meat*, flesh to be consumed.

Clive Barker's *Books of Blood* series, volume 1 of which was released in 1984 and that includes his short story "The Midnight Meat Train," was a turning point for literary horror, combining the gruesome with the mundane and fantasy with horror in original ways. "The Midnight Meat Train" is a story that itself enacts an interesting transition, taking the reader on a journey along with its protagonist Leon Kaufman from body horror to cosmic horror. Central to the story, however, is another transition—the Gothic transformation of body into object signaled by the story's title. The story is insistent all the way through that the human body is *meat*, flesh, matter to manipulated and consumed.[9]

The context for the story is anxiety in New York City over a serial killer dubbed "the subway slaughterer." "Bodies had been discovered," explains the narrative, "in one of the subway cars on the Avenue of the Americas, hacked open and partially disemboweled, as though an efficient abattoir operative had been interrupted in his work" (29). The killings were "so thoroughly professional" (29) that meat-packing plants and slaughterhouses were surveilled and "every man . . . who had some past connection with the butchery trade" (29) was interviewed. The victims had all been "swiftly and efficiently dispatched" as though they were pieces of "meat" (30).

It's in the midst of these killings that the story's protagonist, Kaufman, is making his way home one evening by subway when he discovers a scene of butchery going on in the next car and realizes that he is riding the titular "Midnight Meat Train" (39) and that the killer is colluding with the subway driver. The details of the story are gruesome, but because they are central to the argument being made here, I will provide one representative example: Kaufman, finding himself among dangling corpses in a subway car-turned-abattoir, glimpses the back of one of the victims. "The meat of her back had been entirely cleft open from neck to buttock and the muscle had been peeled back to expose the glistening vertebrae. It was the final triumph of the Butcher's craft. Here they hung, these shaved, bled, slit stabs of humanity, opened up like fish, and ripe for devouring" (42).

This is contemporary Thing Theory turned back upon itself and soaked in blood and gore. Like Bennett's contingent tableau on a storm drain grate one summer morning in Baltimore of dead rat, glove, stick, and so on that becomes vibratory, the contingent tableau here of bodies cleft and glistening with their clothes neatly piled on the seats next to them one night in New York City beneath the streets is similarly hypnotic but pulsing with dread. And Barker's aestheticization of the scene is a provocation, a challenge to the reader: Can we divorce ourselves from deeply engrained anthropocentric ethics and admire the tableau and the butcher's artistry? Can we respond to human corpses dangling in a subway car like a meat locker as anything other than abject?

The story's conclusion at least is, no, we cannot, and we should not. Guided by the responses of Kaufman, we are intended to witness the scene with dismay and revulsion—this, of course, is the affective orientation of Gothic horror writ large. We are supposed to reject the equation of body = thing among other things. Yes, the Gothic confronts us with the specter of death and plays on our worst fears and anxieties. But Barker's story, from the title to its final sentence, lays bare the affective machinery of the genre as it confronts audiences with the challenge to think the body as *meat*, a thing among other things. This is not the elevation of objects or a celebration of the "shared materiality of all things" (Bennett 2010, 13) but rather a decentering of the human that recoils from the idea of treating human bodies in the same way animal bodies raised for meat are utilized.[10]

Barker's story, it should be pointed out, ends up as a caustic and compelling allegory of American history as horror. The Midnight Meat Train on the Avenue of the Americas in New York City takes fresh corpses as food to the City Fathers, disfigured and repulsive ghouls whose cannibalism affords them a kind of debased immortality. Kaufman, who has killed the Subway Slaughterer and survived the trip, confronts one of them, which offers this explanation: "'We are the City fathers,' the thing said. 'And mothers, and daughters and sons. The builders, the lawmakers. We made this city'" (Barker [1984] 1998, 47). Kaufman is appalled but comprehends the truth of it on some deep level: "Kaufman thought of the city he'd loved. Were these really its ancients, its philosophers, its creators? He had to believe it. Perhaps there were people on the surface—bureaucrats, politicians, authorities of every kind who knew this horrible secret and whose lives were dedicated to preserving these abominations, feeding them, as savages feed lambs to their gods" (48). And presiding over all is the even more monstrous Father of Fathers, "the precursor to man. The original American, whose homeland this was before Passamaquoddy or Cheyenne" (48). In the end, Kaufman, rendered mute by the severing of his tongue, is conscripted to take over procuring meat for the monsters, a job he now embraces, and the city will continue going "about its business in ignorance: never knowing what it was built upon, or what it owed its life to" (51).

America, concludes "The Midnight Meat Train," is built on cannibalism, the chewing up of human bodies treated as nonhuman objects. Within the story, the City Fathers, animated by the presiding spirit of America itself—what we could call the Founding Father—continue to govern, subsisting on the flesh of the city's citizens. Figuratively, the story foregrounds the history of America as one soaked in blood and gore—not just the racist horrors of slavery and removal, but the grinding up of working-class bodies demanded by industrial capitalism. Is there any more apt analogy for capitalism than a "meat train"? And, crucially, that history is not dead and gone but persists into the present, organizing our experience and understanding of America: the Avenue of the Americas subway line continues to run, carrying bodies as meat to the masters. After his ordeal, Kaufman is awakened on the floor of the subway train by the driver. "The face that was looking down at him was black, and not unfriendly. It grinned. . . . 'You've got a job to do, my man: they're very pleased with you. . . . Lots to learn before tomorrow night" (50). Grinning faces of the subaltern prepared to do their master's bidding, ready to do their part in the rendering up of the bodies that the system, built on racist and classicist ideology, needs to perpetuate itself.

In the service of capitalist critique, the story in fact sidesteps a consideration of specifically racial disparity. Mahogany, the story's original Subway Slaughterer, despite his name, is white; Kaufman, who takes his place, is referred to by Mahogany as a "dirty little Jew" (34); the subway driver is black. The victims aboard the train consist of two white women and a Puerto Rican man. The ghoulish City Fathers themselves are presumably white, but they insist that Kaufman must service them as well as "those born before the city was thought of, when America was a timberland and desert" (38), and the monstrous Father of Fathers is the original native American, associated with but preceding indigenous tribes. The animating spirit of America, suggests the story, is cannibalism. Ignoring entrenched histories of racial disparity and racist ideology that figured certain ethnicities as less than human and, therefore, more available for exploitation, "The Midnight Meat Train" suggests America is indeed democratic in its consideration of people as animals regarded as available to be yoked to the machine or butchered and consumed: a democracy of people-as-objects—Thing Theory as nightmare.

The transition within the story from the Subway Slaughterer to the Father of Fathers is a shift from body horror, the abjection of the corpse, to Lovecraftian cosmic dread, terror over alien gods and irresistible forces that threaten sanity. That same movement from corpses in a subway car to the original

American is a transition from literal to figurative, from the specific story of Kaufman confronting a killer in a subway car to a consideration of all America as that subway train. Both literal and figurative interpretations of the story, however, pivot over the status of the body itself, foregrounding its materiality and recoiling at the reduction of the body to the status of meat. Whether literally butchered and strung up as meat or "consumed" by the machinery of capitalism, the butchered body of Barker's story is emblematic of Gothic materiality as Thing Theory, raising the question of whether we are ready and able to think of the body as a thing among other things, and of the consequences of that form of democracy of objects.

Possession

While the body treated as an assemblage of pieces or meat to be manipulated is central to Gothic horror and the dread it evokes, another way in which the body is reframed as a thing is through narratives of loss of control in which the body becomes a kind of shell manipulated by some other force. In some cases, this is a result of supernatural possession; in others, it results from some form of mind control; still in others, the compelling force is madness. In each situation, however, the body becomes a kind of puppet or tool at the disposal of what is—or is perceived to be—someone or something else. These Gothic narratives ask us what happens when we cease to be ourselves—that is, when our actions and agency are subsumed by some other power and we become tools and vessels—objects—motivated by some force outside our control.

In Gothic tales of demonic possession, the body is invaded and taken over by a malevolent spirit that then controls that body, forcing it to act and even to manifest in particular ways. The obvious reference point here is of course William Friedkin's *The Exorcist* (1973), based on William Peter Blatty's 1971 novel of the same name. Within the film, a young girl, Regan (Linda Blair), becomes possessed by a demon known as Pazuzu, which forces her to speak and act in unsettling ways. What perhaps is most disconcerting about *The Exorcist*—generally regarded as an effective horror movie in the sense of evoking intense affect (tension, repulsion, fright, and so on)—is what happens to Regan's *body*. Early on in the film, she urinates on the carpet during a party at her mother's house. She is then subjected to a brutal sequence of medical tests. Her skin deteriorates, becoming wrinkled and sore-ridden; she vomits prolifically, levitates, masturbates brutally with a crucifix, and, impossibly, turns her head all the way around. Her identity displaced by the demon, Regan's body becomes Pazuzu's plaything, an object subjected to various violent manipulations. Regan—her identity—is essentially gone. All that remains is her body, a thing manipulated by an alien presence. To exorcise the demon then is to restore her subjectivity—to transform her back from object to subject able to exert agency over her body and actions.[11]

A variant on the demonic possession narrative in Gothic horror is the tale of the displacement of the subject's will via mind control of some sort. This is sometimes the result of supernatural telepathy—Dracula, for example, in Stoker's famous novel from 1897 and many of its film adaptations, has a hypnotic gaze and can even exert his will over a distance, compelling those with weaker minds or whom he has bitten to bend to his will. In what many regard as the original zombie film, *White Zombie* (Victor Halperin, 1932), the zombies aren't reanimated corpses (the "living dead") but rather individuals controlled by the evil Murder Legendre (Bela Lugosi), who compels them either via magic or drugs to do his bidding. In films such as David Cronenberg's *Videodrome* (1983) and John Carpenter's *They Live* (1988), evil organizations and entities use the media to control people's minds. Although the controlling force in these narratives originates from without rather than within the subject, the outcome is nevertheless a form of psychic possession that subordinates the will of the subject transforming them into what we might consider "quasi-objects" to be used as tools to facilitate their master's agenda.[12]

Madness as well, as depicted in Gothic narrative, often is represented as a form of psychic possession in which the subject's agency is overridden by psychic compulsion—the madness manifesting as controlling demon. In some instances, the narratives make a distinction between the characters and their madness, framing the madness as a force that takes control or possession of the characters, displacing a particular character's "normal" identity. This is generally the case in cinematic (and, one must acknowledge, usually very problematic) representations of multiple personality disorder. Norman Bates, as Dr. Fred Richmond (Simon Oakland) explains at the end of Hitchcock's *Psycho* (1960), converses with and, at times, "becomes" his mother: "At times he could be both personalities, carry on conversations. At other times, the mother half took over completely. Now he was never all Norman, but he was often only mother. And because he was so pathologically jealous of her, he assumed that she was jealous of him. Therefore, if he felt a strong attraction to any other woman, the mother side of him would go wild." As I'll address more fully later, Dr. Decker in Clive Barker's *Cabal* (1988; Decker is played by David Cronenberg in the 1990 movie adaptation, *Nightbreed*, directed by Barker) essentially becomes his mask when he puts it on and it compels him to kill. Complicating the mental illness narrative, both Brad Anderson's *Session 9* (2001) and M. Night Shyamalan's *Split* (2016) concern characters with multiple personality disorder who may or may not also be compelled by a supernatural force—they may be both mad *and* possessed.

In works such as *Psycho, Cabal, Session 9,* and *Split,* madness congeals into a kind of identity that subjugates the subject's "normal" sense of self and takes possession of the character, compelling him or her to perform monstrous acts. It is presented as being akin to demonic possession, only the demon is one that is conjured into being by the subject's psyche rather than an independently existing entity that invades from without. The result, however, is essentially the same: The body becomes a vessel inhabited by what is perceived to be an alien controlling presence—the body becomes a thing, and the subject's physical appearance acts as a façade or mask for the alien presence within.

The Mask Makes the Monster

While the body acts as a figurative mask in Gothic narratives of madness in which parts of the self are at odds with each other, literal masks have also often played important roles in Gothic tales.[13] Masks within Gothic narrative amplify the uncanny agency associated with masks on the whole and function in the discussion here as a convenient lynchpin between considerations of body-as-thing and thing-as-body endowed with uncanny life because the mask enacts *both* transformations. Masks in general tend to license a kind of role playing that permits wearers to explore what they perceive as risqué or off-limits identities. To the extent that the mask affords anonymity, the temptation toward the taboo is amplified. Masks further have the potential to evoke a variety of affective responses from spectators, ranging from the uncanny to amusement to disgust.

In science fiction, fantasy, and horror, these qualities of masks are foregrounded as donning the mask transforms the wearer into a kind of "quasi-thing" that is at the same time somehow more than human. Masks are de rigueur, for example, in superhero narratives, in which the mask allows both crime fighters and criminals to disguise themselves while simultaneously expressing their "true" selves. In some cases, such as the Jim Carrey fantasy film *The Mask* (Chuck Russell, 1994), masks exert true agency, transforming their wearers into different people with enhanced abilities. In *V for Vendetta* (both Alan Moore's 1982 graphic novel and James McTeigue's 2006 film), the depersonalization afforded by the Guy Fawkes mask allows V to function as an allegorical figure—a spirit of liberation—and thus to be a transferable identify. It is the mask that makes one V, and whoever takes up the mask can serve in that capacity, as Evie does in the end.

In Gothic narrative in general and the slasher subgenre of Gothic horror cinema in particular, it is the uncanny and grotesque qualities of masks that are emphasized as the masks depersonalize their wearers, seem to license or facilitate their transgressions, and in some cases to endow their wearers with magical abilities. The two most iconic masks in horror film are Jason Voorhees's hockey mask and Michael Myer's mask in the *Halloween* franchise.[14] The generic quality of the masks accentuates the lack of affect exhibited by their wearers as they ruthlessly pursue their murderous designs, and the effect is to transform Jason and Michael into something less than human beings—quasi-things—but things unencumbered by human scruples or constraints and endowed with more than human abilities. The mask simultaneously makes them both less and more than human. The almost magical qualities of the mask receive particular emphasis in David Gordon Green's 2018 reboot of the Halloween franchise in which two true-crime podcasters visit Michael Myer (James Jude Courtney) in the sanitarium where he is housed, teasing him with the mask in the attempt to goad him into speaking with them. While this has no apparent effect, the first thing Michael does after the inevitable escape is to kill the two podcasters and recover the mask.[15]

The transformation enacted by the mask of its wearer into a kind of quasi-object is exemplified in particular by the prominence of the burlap sack mask within horror narrative. The burlap sack functions in two main capacities: First, it creates an association with scarecrows—an inanimate anthropomorphic figure that itself is often included in horror stories; second, the texture of burlap suggests discomfort and abuse. The association of the burlap mask with the scarecrow is obviously played on in grotesque ways by the character Scarecrow in Christopher Nolan's dark fantasy film *Batman Begins* (2005). Within the film, villainous Dr. Jonathan Crane (Cillian Murphy) wears the mask as a sadistic form of torture for those who have inhaled a fear-inducing hallucinogen. In a similarly sadistic vein, one of the primary antagonists in Bryan Bertino's 2008 *The Strangers* wears a burlap mask to accentuate the fear of those he terrorizes. Two horror films from 2007, Michael Dougherty's *Trick 'r Treat* and J. A. Bayona's *The Orphanage*, share the conceit of children whose disfigurement is concealed by a burlap sack. In the former, Sam (a reference to Samhain, played by Quinn Lord) is a sort of supernatural creature—very much associated with a scarecrow—who enforces the "rules" of Halloween; there is a particular poignancy to the masked child in Bayona's *The Orphanage*, as he is a ghost with a very sad backstory—the burlap sack in his case horrifies as a form of abuse meant to conceal his deformities from those who do not wish to see them.

Especially disconcerting within Gothic horror are human masks, which often evoke the sensation of the uncanny as described by Japanese roboticist Masahiro Mori in his discussion of the "uncanny valley" ([1970] 2012). Mori's proposition is straightforward: The more human an artificial being looks, the more favorably we respond to it, but only up to a point. When something looks almost human, but not quite, it evokes a sensation of the eerie or uncanny, and we recoil. Horror films featuring human masks can trigger this response by making human figures look slightly less than human. As explained by Heller-Nicholas, "Masks are uncanny because they are faces-that-are-not-faces" (2019, 15). The exemplar here is the character Christiane (Édith Scob) in Georges Franju's 1960 *Eyes without a Face* (*Les Yeux sans visage*) who spends most of the film behind an unsettling face-like mask that has the effect of making her look like a mannequin or doll.

Some masks in Gothic horror do not just depersonalize and objectify their wearer but express the antagonist's perversity and fundamental lack of humanity—masks as revelation rather than concealment. This is the case with the character Leatherface, who wears a mask made of poorly stitched together human skin in Tobe Hooper's 1974 *The Texas Chainsaw Massacre*. Almost as

Figure 5. Decker's mask in *Nightbreed*

unsettling is the mask Dr. Decker wears in Barker's *Nightbreed*. Made of leather, with buttons for eyes, an off-center jagged zipper for a mouth, and stitching up the back, the mask manages to combine SM bondage, scarecrow, doll, and zombie associations in order to reflect Dr. Decker's sadism. Indeed, in *Cabal*, Barker's 1988 novel adapted as *Nightbreed*, it is the mask that actually directs Decker and takes over his personality, talking to him and compelling him to murder. " *'I'm not Decker,'* the Mask replied," writes Barker when Decker is addressed by the story's main protagonist, Boone (81).

Masks in Gothic narrative are thus Gothic things that exert a special kind of thing-power. On the one hand, they obscure the specific features and facial expressions of their wearers, making them more thing-like and uncanny. Often the mask creates the impression that the wearer, rather than a human being, is an animate scarecrow, mannequin, or doll of some kind. Certain kinds of masks—notably the burlap sack—also trigger associations with torture and abuse. At the same time, the depersonalized Gothic antagonist, transformed by the mask into a kind of quasi-thing, often exhibits extreme or supernatural powers and abilities that seem in some way connected to the mask. Donning the masks allows the antagonist to terrorize, maim, and kill with seeming impunity and to survive retaliation that would disable or kill a "normal" human being. If the clothes make the person, then what Gothic narrative tells us is that the mask makes the monster.

4
Thing-as-Body

The potential transformation of body into a thing in Gothic narrative may well be the central anxiety galvanizing the entire genre. While not every Gothic tale turns on the opposition between body and thing—in some tales, for example, the threat is to sanity rather than anatomy—the foregrounding of the body as matter is nevertheless so pervasive as arguably to define the genre. The Gothic is at base a bodily genre, not just in seeking to evoke an affective response from those who consume it, but in its representations of bodies in various states of danger, distress, and decay. This tendency to emphasize the body as thing, however, is then often countered by its inverse: the animation of things that become bodies exercising agency. As I develop in Chapter 2, anything at all, from cars to toys to pianos, can "come to life" in Gothic narrative and act with malevolent desire or intention. Gothic narrative, however, privileges two types of things in particular: reanimated corpses and representations of the human form that come to life or exhibit uncanny agency, including dolls, puppets, mannequins, statutes, idols, masks, portraits, photographs, and reflections. Reanimated corpses (i.e., zombies) are alarming for several reasons: They violate our conventional understanding of the distinction between alive and dead, they seem compelled by some kind of irresistible force that deprives them of agency, and they confront us with the materiality of the body through their physical decay—indeed, as deteriorating mobile cannibalistic corpses, zombies take abjection to new levels. Animate representations of the body tend to be less abject, but more uncanny, unsettling distinctions between living and dead in the way that all animate objects do. However, animate representations of the body also "feed" on human bodies in their own ways, draining them of life and energy. The irony of Gothic tales featuring animate representations of the human body is that the representations frequently seem *more alive* than the human beings who encounter them.

The Living Dead

Zombies are animate things—objects, corpses, that have been endowed with uncanny life. They are distinct from other Gothic objects, however, in that they are produced by a two-step process, with each step evocative of horror in its own way. Step one is unique to the reanimated human corpse, and that is the transformation from living body to dead matter. Before there can be the oxymoronic living dead, a living body must become a dead one, and corpses on their own are endowed with thing-power. The corpse, according to Kristeva, is the "utmost of abjection" (1982, 4). The specter of death made present, we recoil in disgust from that which was once a subject but is now an object. Step two is then the reanimation of that object. The dead thing revives, confounding the line between life and death. But, importantly, the reanimated corpse remains a corpse, matter subject to a visible process of decay—indeed, what the cinematic zombie genre relishes most is the abject physicality of the decaying zombie body and the expression of its cannibalistic appetite. The zombie is then abject thing, albeit one infused with uncanny animacy, and its deteriorating physical condition becomes the focal point of zombie narrative.[1]

There are in fact arguably two primary variants of the modern zombie narrative. Most commonly, the reanimated dead possess limited sentience and are compelled solely by their hunger for human flesh. In George Romero's *Night of the Living Dead* (1968), for example, the zombies are described as "ghouls" that "[eat] the flesh of the people they kill." While they do possess limited intelligence—they are able to use rocks as tools, for example—they are deprived of speech, rendering them animalistic as they shamble about seeking victims. Some of the zombies are disfigured, while others look sickly but close to normal; all, however, are deprived of emotion and personality—and their lack of affect, which renders them akin to sleepwalkers, is part of what makes them so disconcerting. More recent variants, such as Dan O'Bannon's campy *Return of the Living Dead* (1985)—the film that introduced the idea that zombies seek human brains in particular—grant some of the zombies greater intelligence and a limited capacity for speech, particularly newly "born" zombies, but they remain defined by their hunger, an irresistible compulsion that defines the zombies as zombies and overwhelms any bonds with the living. Rather than human beings, reanimated corpses in Gothic narrative come back as cannibalistic *machines*, programmed to consume.

The less common variant is the sentient zombie. These are animate corpses that can think and talk and possess a range of emotions. As in Jonathan Levine's *Warm Bodies* (2013), for example, based on Isaac Marion's novel of the same name (2010), they may be sympathetic, retain something of a moral compass, and express a range of emotions. More often than not, sentient zombies introduce a comic element because of an incongruity between their intelligence, on the one hand, and both their physical decay and compulsion toward cannibalism, on the other. Along these lines, Taika Waititi and Jemaine Clement's vampire comedy *What We Do in the Shadows* (2015) introduces zombies among the supernatural creatures present at an "Undead Masquerade." They act and speak in a polite and civilized way until they sense that one of the attendees is among the living, and then their hunger takes over, introducing an ironic contrast between their seemingly pleasant and polite demeanors and their irresistible hunger for human flesh. Such narratives are unsettling in their suggestion that even seemingly sentient and civil people might nevertheless be compelled by irresistible tabooed desire, which feeds the twenty-first-century anxiety that monsters may not be visually distinct but lurk among us (see Weinstock, "Invisible Monsters" [2020]).

In both versions of the contemporary zombie narrative, the thing-like nature of the zombie is emphasized through the compulsion to feed and the spectacle of physical decay. On the one hand, undeterred by any threat to their continued existence, they are eating machines. Frequently depersonalized and defined by large numbers, they no longer exhibit the attributes we associate with "being human"—personality, a range of emotional responses, the ability to communicate. And, notably, driven by their hunger, they are not active but instead acted upon. They cannot choose but only respond. On the other hand, they are defined by an intense, and often abject, physicality as their bodies are presented in various states of decay. This indeed may be the hallmark of the cinematic zombie, as filmmakers and special effects artists have gone to exuberant lengths to craft the most physically repulsive zombies possible. We cannot look upon these zombies and not be reminded that they are flesh, they are matter, they are *things*. Within the context of Gothic narrative, they typically want to eat us; within the context of our lives, they—decaying corpses—are our destiny. Quasi-things, zombies, perhaps more so than any other Gothic object, raise troubling questions about where the line between human and object is drawn.

With this in mind, the racial history of the zombie then becomes especially important. As Sarah Juliet Lauro explains in *Zombie Theory: A Reader*, "The zombie myth was, in its first incarnation, an analogy for the slave's ambivalent status as expendable life, as a subhuman commodity" (2017, 184). Tracing the lineage of the zombie to African soul capture myths imported into the Caribbean via slave ships, the modern zombie is intimately connected to a "history of colonialism, enslavement, exploitation, and appropriation" (ix). Imported to the United States via Haiti, the zombie's origins in black slavery cannot be effaced from the monster, argues Lauro (xi). Zombie narratives thus have the potential, on the one hand, to reinforce racist stereotypes of people of color as what Allewaert calls "parahuman" in *Ariel's Ecology* (see 2013, 6)—a kind of "interstitial life" (6). On the other hand, zombie narratives can also critique that same thinking. The ending to George Romero's famous *Night of the Living Dead* (1968), in which the assertive and heroic black protagonist, Ben (Duane Jones), survives the horrific night only to be ironically mistaken for a zombie and casually shot by a white posse, would seem to function in this capacity. More generally, Annalee Newitz proposes in her analysis of zombie narratives that stories of the undead, regardless of time period, "share a common

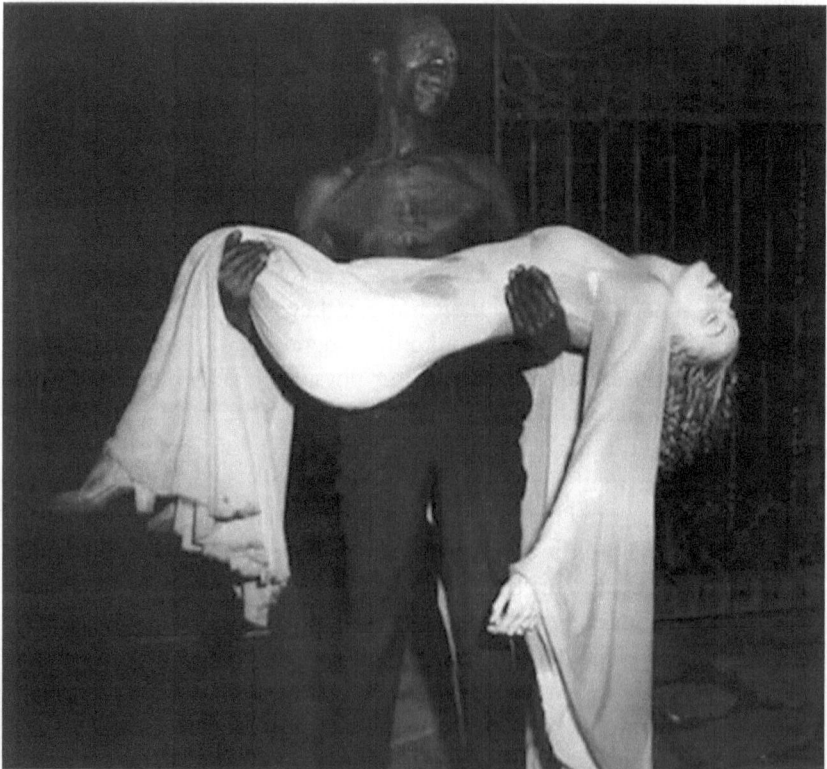

Figure 6. The black body as zombie playing on white fears in Jacques Tourneur's *I Walked with a Zombie* (1943)

investment in the idea that communities murdered by colonialism can linger on, half-alive, and refuse to leave the living remainder alone" (2006, 91)— undead bodies, including for Newitz that of the zombie, bear "the signs of great social injustice whose effects cannot ever be entirely extinguished" (91). Highlighting the Afro-Caribbean origins of the zombie reminds us that both Gothic narratives and New Materialist theorizing questioning or eroding the line between human and thing must bear in mind deeply entrenched racist thinking that has withheld full humanity from non-white populations, facilitating their exploitation. It is indeed for this reason, as Lauro notes, that twenty-first-century political theory has often had recourse to the language of living death (2017, 183).[2]

Animate Representations

While narratives of reanimated corpses constitute a very specific subgenre of the Gothic, a much broader category consists of uncanny representations of the human form imbued with life. Encompassing animate dolls, puppets, mannequins, statues, robots, idols, masks, portraits, photographs, and reflections, this category can itself be divided into two categories based on the extent of agency exhibited: In some cases, the representations are what we may refer to as influencers; in other cases, the representations become active agents in their own right, threatening the safety and well-being of those they stalk or encounter.

Horror in Two Dimensions A: Portraits—The Past Made Present

The most ubiquitous representation of the human form in Gothic narrative is arguably the portrait. Indeed, to establish the significance of uncanny portraits to the Gothic tradition, one need look no further than the compendium of Gothic tropes that is Walt Disney's Haunted Mansion attraction. Spectators first encounter portraits in the "Stretching Room," an octagonal room featuring paintings of a bearded gentleman, a young woman with a parasol, an old woman holding a rose, and a man in a bowler hat. Introduced by the attraction's "Ghost Host" as "guests as they appeared in their corruptible mortal states," the pictures all transform as the room appears to stretch. The bearded man is revealed below the waist to be only in his undergarments and poised atop a lit keg of dynamite; the young woman with the parasol is balancing on a tightrope over a hungry alligator; the old woman is perched on a gravestone at the bottom of which is a bust of her husband with a hatchet in its head; and the man in the bowler hat is revealed to be the third in the sequence of men

Figure 7. The Haunted Mansion's Stretching Portraits Revealed

on each other's shoulders sinking into quicksand. Spectators subsequently encounter six more portraits that transform when lightning flashes. In one, a young woman transforms into a decrepit hag, in another a handsome nobleman changes into a skeleton in a rotting suit. Similarly, in a third, horseman and rider morph into skeletons. Two feature young woman changing into either Medusa or a tiger, and the last features a clipper ship that becomes a ghost ship with tattered sails.

The Haunted Mansion's foregrounding of portraits indexes their prominence and highlights their functions within Gothic narrative. As Kamilla Elliott observes in her 2012 *Portraiture and British Gothic Fiction*, the Gothic is the "mother ship" of what she refers to as "literary picture identification" (6), a process that, to be extremely reductive, matches an image with a person. Elliott notes that, of the 208 texts surveyed in Ann B. Tracy's *The Gothic Novel, 1790–1830: Plot Summaries and Index to Motifs* (1981), "portraits and miniatures are motifs in 80" and appear as social objects in many of the remaining 128. Elliott's own study spanning 1764–1835 considers picture identification in more than 100 Gothic texts, making the motif more common than many of the others associated with the Gothic, including ghosts, convents, rape, seduction, and so on (2012, 6–7). Portraits, of course, continue to play a significant role in Gothic narrative post-1835.

Portraits in Gothic narrative in a sense are always "haunted."[3] As with the portraits in the Stretching Room of the Haunted Mansion, Gothic portraits typically reveal or gesture toward an untold story of tragedy or usurpation, and, as with the portraits that change "in a different light," Gothic portraits are often connected with the revelation of a character's "true character" as someone esteemed is revealed to be a villain or someone maligned is proven to have been virtuous. Whenever they are featured, there is a materialization of the past in the present that exerts uncanny effects, influencing the course of the narrative. As discussed by Elliott, picture identification—the process of matching face with social identity—in Gothic literature is both "empirically formidable and psychologically fraught, inculcating it with terror, horror, mystery, suspense, lust, danger, violence, and fatality" (2012, 8). Gothic fiction uses picture identification to "rework social legitimacy and entitlement" (8).

Gothic portraits are exemplary of thing-power as both influencers and agents as they inevitably act on their viewers in various ways, surprising them, entrancing them, interacting with them, directing them, even, vampire-like, draining them. In some cases, obsessive attention to a portrait reveals a character's melancholic fixation on the past—Melville's eponymous Pierre (1852) obsesses over a portrait of his father secreted in his closet, while Mrs. Danvers in Daphne du Maurier's *Rebecca* (1938) moons over the portrait of her lost matron. In Nathaniel Hawthorne's *The House of the Seven Gables* (1851), the portrait of Colonel Pyncheon acts as a straightforward symbol of the persistence of the past and, the reader is told, seems to shake its head or frown when something happens of which it doesn't approve. In other cases, as in Charles Maturin's *Melmoth the Wanderer* (1820) and Sheridan LeFanu's *Carmilla* (1872), the uncanny resemblance between a portrait of someone presumed long dead and a living character indexes the supernatural longevity of the latter.

But the Gothic portrait par excellence is one that does not just influence the course of events by raising questions about social legitimacy and entitlement, but also comes to life or exerts a kind of magical spell over the viewer. The conceit of the living portrait within Gothic narrative goes all the way back to the genre's founding with Horace Walpole's *The Castle of Otranto* ([1764] 2014). Within the narrative, the tyrant Manfred seeks to hold on to his usurped power as lord of the Castle of Otranto. When he impiously proclaims, "Heaven nor hell shall impede my designs," a portrait of his grandfather "utter[s] a deep sigh, and heave[s] its breast" (25). The figure then steps down from its frame, descending "to the floor with a grave and melancholy air" and signaling to Manfred to follow it (25). In keeping with Elliott's claims, the ghostly portrait in *Otranto*, together with other ghostly manifestations in the narrative, "rework[s] social legitimacy and entitlement" (8) by rejecting Manfred's lawfulness as ruler. The haunted portrait indeed is a constant conceit of the Gothic genre as demonstrated by *Ghostbusters II* (Ivan Reitman, 1989) and the 1999 remake of *The Haunting* (Jan de Bont). In *Ghostbusters II*, a museum portrait contains the spirit of a sixteenth-century tyrant, Vigo the Carpathian. The spirit seeks to defy death and return to the world of the living by transferring from the portrait to a living body. In *The Haunting*, the spirit is tyrannical patriarch Hugh Crain, who manifests through his portrait. In a nod to Disney's Haunted Mansion, the portrait in *The Haunting* at one point morphs into a skeletal face.

In the cases of *Otranto*, *Ghostbusters II*, and *The Haunting*, the inspirited portrait allows for a literal irruption of the past into the present as a figure from the past emerges and attempts to wrest control of the present from the living. The uncanny living portrait quickly slips into metaphor, making manifest the "hauntological" nature of the present as described by Jacques Derrida (see *Specters of Marx [2006]*)—that is, the ways in which the present is in fact never fully present but rather haunted by both the past that shapes it and the future yet to come. Nevertheless, within the context of Gothic narrative, the literal thing-power of the portrait is arresting; it is a moment of violation of "the natural order," and the consequence is an inversion of power as the portrait overflows with vitality while the living are vitiated.

This inversion is made even more evident by Gothic narratives in which a portrait, rather than reflecting the past, is linked to the life or marks the present of a living character. This is the case in Edgar Allan Poe's short story "The Oval Portrait" ([1842] 1996), as well as famously in Oscar Wilde's *The Picture of Dorian Gray* ([1890] 2008). In Poe's story—interpreted by James Twitchell as a variant on the vampire tale (see Twitchell 1977)—a traveler seeking refuge in a strangely deserted mansion in the Italian Apennines scrutinizes the artwork, which is described in a kind of catalog. He becomes enthralled in particular by the "absolute *life-likeliness* of expression" (482) depicted in the portrait of a young woman—an expression that, at first, startled him, and then "finally confounded, subdued, and appalled" him (482). The story of the portrait described in the catalog reveals a tale of magical vampire-like inversion. The painter of the portrait—the husband of the young woman—sought to capture her through his art. As he painted, she "grew daily more dispirited and weak." He could not see that "the tints which he spread upon the canvas were drawn from the cheeks of her who sate beside him" (483). Upon completion of the portrait, the painter exclaimed, "This is indeed *Life* itself!" only then ironically to discover that his bride was dead, her vitality seemingly transferred to the painting.

Drawing inspiration from Poe's tale, Wilde's *The Picture of Dorian Gray* develops the concept of the symbiotic or parasitic portrait more fully. Having made a kind of Faustian bargain, Dorian Gray's portrait ages and becomes increasingly disfigured as Dorian sins, while Dorian remains ever youthful and beautiful in appearance. In essence, Dorian and his portrait exchange places—Dorian becomes a painting, a static object, while the painting becomes

Figure 8. Dorian Gray, played by Hurd Hatfield, with his portrait in the 1945 film adaptation directed by Albert Lewin

mutable and reflects Dorian's experiences and moral character—the subject. In metaphysical terms, the portrait houses Dorian's soul, while Dorian's physical body is a shell. In another Gothic inversion, the portrait in the novel represents *truth*—it is Dorian's "true face" manifesting the debasement of his soul. When in the end, Dorian, seeking to destroy the evidence of his debauchery, stabs his portrait (another nod toward Poe, this time to his "William Wilson" [1839]), he breaks the spell by killing himself. The police entering the room find a withered and decrepit old man with a knife through his heart and a pristine portrait magically restored to its original state.

Like Gothic tales involving portraits of the dead, Gothic tales of vampiric or symbiotic portraits can be interpreted allegorically—Poe's "The Oval Portrait" can be interpreted as an allegory of the artistic process and of the uncanniness of art writ large. The portrait is inevitably a kind of memento mori, a reminder that the subject will age and eventually pass away while the portrait will remain static.[4] To look at one's portrait is unavoidably to be reminded of one's future disappearance. There is also, of course, something fundamentally uncanny in viewing oneself from without and through the eyes of another. It is to see oneself as object. Wilde's tale, in contrast, can be interpreted as a commentary on the perfidy of appearances. The face that we present to the world is inevitably a distortion as we seek to hide our faults, flaws, and misdeeds—a kind of mask. The "true portrait" of ourselves is one we keep carefully concealed. Despite these entirely reasonable interpretations, however, tales of symbiotic or vampiric portraits, as with tales of inspirited ones, arguably derive their affective power from the uncanny inversion of animacy in which humans become objects and objects—portraits—become subjects. In such tales, this inversion is effected via magic of some kind; however, the frequency of the conceit within Gothic tales resonates with contemporary Thing Theory's insistence on vibrant materiality and thing-power. Gothic portraits become exemplary of Thing Theory rather than anomalies. As such, they give shape to deep-seated human anxieties about the fragility of the ego amid an animate world that circumscribes human agency. What am I if my portrait is more alive than I am?

Horror in Two Dimensions B: Photographs—the Truth of the Present

What haunts portraits in Gothic narrative finally is *truth*—that is, the portrait reveals or in some way points up that appearances are deceptive. In some cases, as with Manfred in *Otranto*, the portrait gestures toward the concealed truth that the present state of affairs is illegitimate, founded on falsehood; in other cases, as in Daphne du Maurier's 1938 Gothic novel *Rebecca*, what is revealed by or in association with the portrait is that the subject of the painting has been misremembered or misrepresented; in still other cases, as in *Dorian Gray*, the portrait reveals the "literal" truth of the subject. Photographs of human figures similarly reveal an occulted reality within Gothic narrative, although interestingly with a more expansive temporal orientation. In some cases, photographs, like portraits, uncover a different or obscured narrative of the past; in other cases, they index an alternate reality of the present; and, differentiating them from portraits most fully, Gothic photographs in some instances reveal the future. Examples of each category respectively are M. R. James's short story, "The Mezzotint" (1904a); Stephen King's *IT* (1986) and its 2017 film adaptation by Andrés Muschietti; and James Wong's 2006 film *Final Destination 3*.

Photographs, of course, like portraits, capture a moment in time and, outside of magical scenarios where they somehow offer glimpses of what is to come, are by definition depictions of the past. This can be moments ago, as when we take a photo and then look at our phone to see how it came out, or more than a century. Looking at photographs can "make the past come alive" in the sense of providing steppingstones or supplements to recollection or offering visual depictions of times and places outside of our personal experience. As it does with portraiture, Gothic narrative enhances and literalizes the metaphor of the past coming alive by presenting photographs not as static snapshots, but rather as active agents that transform to reveal a concealed truth. A case in point is M. R. James's ghost story "The Mezzotint," from his 1904 collection *Ghost Stories of An Antiquary*.[5] The story concerns an early nineteenth-century mezzotint of a British manor house obtained by a Cambridge scholar named Williams. Williams doesn't consider the mezzotint particularly interesting until he—and others he conscripts to verify his observations—notices its transformations. Attention to the mezzotint first reveals a muffled figure that intrudes upon the scene of the house: "It was indubitable—rankly impossible, no doubt, but absolutely certain. In the middle of the lawn in front of the unknown house there was a figure where no figure had been at five o'clock that afternoon. It was crawling on all fours towards the house, and it was muffled in a strange black garment with a white cross on the back" (James 1904). When surveyed later, the figure has ominously disappeared into the house through a now-open window. "It looks very much as if we were assisting at the working out of a tragedy somewhere," comments William's associate Nesbit. When the figure subsequently emerges from the house, it carries a child in its arms:

> There was the house, as before under the waning moon and the drifting clouds. The window that had been open was shut, and the figure was once more on the lawn: but not this time crawling cautiously on

hands and knees. Now it was erect and stepping swiftly, with long strides, towards the front of the picture. The moon was behind it, and the black drapery hung down over its face so that only hints of that could be seen, and what was visible made the spectators profoundly thankful that they could see no more than a white dome-like forehead and a few straggling hairs. The head was bent down, and the arms were tightly clasped over an object which could be dimly seen and identified as a child, whether dead or living it was not possible to say. The legs of the appearance alone could be plainly discerned, and they were horribly thin. (James 1904)

When the mezzotint is next surveyed, no trace of the figure remains. It subsequently comes to light that the manor house represented had been the scene of a tragedy in 1802 when an infant—the last heir to the estate—had mysteriously disappeared following the execution of a man for poaching on the property. Subsequent scrutiny of the mezzotint reveals no further changes.

Figure 9. The mezzotint as rendered in the 1986 dramatization for the BBC's *Classic Ghost Stories*

One can, of course, conjecture a variety of explanations for the transformation of the mezzotint. It could be human agency: Williams or one of the other men could in some way—consciously or unconsciously—be altering the mezzotint. It could be the men's perception of some kind of natural alteration to the mezzotint: shadows cast on it by virtue of its position and the lighting on it or a natural transformation of it through exposure to some catalyst being connected by the men as a narrative. Or there could even be multiple mezzotints that are being swapped by someone across the story. Were it a Sherlock Holmes tale, no doubt a natural explanation—however unlikely—would be reached. The story, however, fails to even gesture in this direction. Williams's observations are confirmed by other observers who never doubt that the mezzotint is indeed changing and at no point try to explain it away. That a figure is creeping into the picture "was indubitable," thinks Williams. "Rankly impossible, no doubt, but absolutely certain" (James 1904)—and this is the conclusion of the story as a whole.

As a consequence of this position vis-à-vis the impossible, the story sets up the mezzotint as a nexus of uncanniness that undoes conventional rationalist understandings of the nature of things, the linearity of time, and the line between life and death. The simple fact of the transformation of the mezzotint challenges assumptions about the static nature of objects. While we know that objects can be affected by outside forces and that these transformations can be fast or slow depending on the nature of the force applied, the kind of change exhibited by the mezzotint seems to require some type of conscious agency: Either the mezzotint is inspirited, housing a supernatural presence that can manifest itself within the world represented in the mezzotint, or the mezzotint is itself in some way "alive," able to reconfigure itself to tell a story. The "vibrancy" of the mezzotint then manifests as a form of time travel—a sequence of images that shows in the present what happened in the past. James here in a story from 1904 almost seems to be tapping into the possibilities of the then-new form of cinema, telling a story through the projection of shifting images on the same screen. And, as if the changing mezzotint and replay of a tragic tale from times gone by weren't enough, James amplifies the uncanniness of the tale by suggesting that the perpetrator of the kidnapping and presumed murderer of the infant is in fact a supernatural assailant—an executed poacher named Gawdy. This possibility of revenge from beyond the grave is introduced by a character named Green, a senior member of the Cambridge faculty whose travels in Essex and Sussex allow him to identify the house represented in the mezzotint. According to Green, the theory regarding the missing infant was that the deed was carried out by some friend of Gawdy's. But the ghoulish appearance of the muffled figure in the mezzotint and the "strange black garment with a white cross on the back"—arguably a funeral pall—lead Green to suggest that, rather than some friend or connection, "I should say now it looks more as if old Gawdy had managed the job himself" (James 1904).

In the end, no explanation for the changing mezzotint is proffered by the story. The reader, like the characters in the story, is challenged to accept the mezzotint's transformations as violations of rationalist understandings of how objects function: Through some kind of magical means, the mezzotint becomes a window into the past, answering the question of what happened to the manor lord's son, but in such a way that more questions are raised about the nature of things, spirits, and the universe in general.

Other Gothic narratives featuring uncanny photographs not only inflect or alter our understanding of the past, but also reveal a more truthful—and uncanny—version of reality in the present, showing us what our senses fail to perceive. In Alejandro Amenábar's 2001 film *The Others*, protagonist Grace (Nicole Kidman) discovers nineteenth-century mourning photographs of her servants suggesting they have been dead for fifty years (this presages a similarly disconcerting realization about herself and her children). Something similar is the case in the Stanley Kubrick film version of *The Shining* (1980), in which Jack Nicholson's character is at the center of photograph from 1921, suggesting that, in some way, he is reincarnated and tied to the Overlook Hotel; in M. Night Shyamalan's 2001 *The Sixth Sense*, every picture of main character Cole (Haley Joel Osment) has an orb of light in it, which we can conclude are the ghosts he can see but others can't. Something similar is the case in Masayuki Ochiai's 2008 film *Shutter*, in which photographs reveal otherwise imperceptible ghosts. In these examples, uncanny images of the human form index a reality different from the one perceived by our senses. Through the technological prosthetic of the camera's lens, spirits are revealed, surrounding and menacing us. These uncanny photographs act as influencers, indexing an alternate reality.

Much more active, though, are the photographs in Stephen King's *IT*. In the book version, Bill Denbrough, who has lost his younger brother Georgie to the murderous Pennywise the Clown (the form IT prefers), looks at pictures of his brother in a photo album: "George's eyes rolled in the picture. They turned to meet Bill's own. George's artificial say-cheese smile turned into a horrid leer. His right eye drooped closed in a wink: *See you soon, Bill. In my closet. Maybe tonight*" (1986, 316). Terrified, Bill tosses the book across the room, where it falls open to the same page, and then blood begins to flow from the photograph. Later, Bill and his friend Richie impossibly see themselves in an antique photo of their town, Derry, Maine. The scene then animates, and Bill and Richie watch the representations of themselves being stalked by

Pennywise. When Bill touches the picture, he reaches *into* the picture, and his fingers are badly cut (439–40). Andrés Muschietti's 2017 film adaptation takes this animation of photographs to the next step. Within the film, as Bill (Jaeden Lieberher) is explaining to his group of friends his theory concerning where IT can be found, the slide projector he is using starts to project images of Bill's parents and his brother Georgie (Jackson Robert Scott), seemingly of its own volition. As the sequence of images progresses like a flipbook, Bill's mother (Pip Dwyer) transforms into Pennywise (Bill Skarsgård) the clown, and finally the monster emerges from the screen itself, threatening the children until dispelled by the light of the opening garage door.

Through the animacy of photographs in King's *IT*, both book and 2017 film, the past is revealed as that which actively cuts, bleeds, and threatens in the present. In Walpole's *Otranto*, Manfred's grandfather sighs and steps down from his portrait, signaling his disapproval of Manfred's usurpation and of the disordered state of affairs following in its wake. In *IT*, the children are not just haunted by the past but threatened by its persistence into their present. The research done by character Ben Hanscom (Jeremy Ray Taylor)—also involving gruesome photographs, although static ones—reveals the town's ongoing cyclical history of tragedy and violence. When the photos come alive, linear time is disordered—and it is up to the children to create a future for themselves by confronting the present threat to their existence.

Predictive photos in Gothic narrative are less common. The faces of anyone who has seen the cursed video in Hideo Nakata's *Ringu* (1998) and its American remake, *The Ring*, by Gore Verbinski (2002) appear blurred in photographs, indicating that they are soon going to die. Something similar is the case in the third entry in the *Final Destination* franchise, imaginatively titled *Final Destination 3* (James Wong, 2006). The franchise as a whole is built around the premise of death as a willful force that refuses to be thwarted. When individuals somehow miss their appointment with death, death seeks them out, but the conceit of the series is that certain clues or signs will presage their intended demise. In *Final Destination 3*, a premonition about a malfunctioning rollercoaster allows for ten survivors to avoid their intended deaths. However, riffing on a detail of *The Omen* (Richard Donner, 1976) in which shadows in photographs seem to presage the deaths of characters, the future deaths of the errant living characters are foreshadowed by details in photographs taken at the amusement park. This is photography as prophecy.

Photographs in Gothic narrative, particularly those of human beings, are inevitably active agents in indexing an alternate, occulted reality. In some cases, the technological prosthesis of the camera's lens extends the human sensorium by revealing spirits and supernatural forces, thus compelling a reconfigured

Figure 10. Blurred predictive photographs in *Ringu*

conception of the universe. In other cases, uncanny photographs function in a hauntological capacity, undoing any naïve faith in the linearity of history by revealing the non-presence of the present—that is, uncanny photographs of the past reveal the past's persistence and its role in structuring the present, even as the introduction of an alternate history—a reconfigured past—presents possibilities for the reordering of the future. Predictive photos, in contrast, suggest the opposite: that the future flows directly from the past by way of the present and cannot be altered. What haunts here is the inescapable future, which inevitably culminates in death. Whether finally meditations on the limitations of human perception or complicated negotiations with temporality, photographs in Gothic narrative highlight in disconcerting ways how circumscribed human agency is, as we just can't see what is always right before our eyes.

Horror in 3D—Living Dolls

As discussed earlier, portraits and photographs are most commonly tied to the past and, in Gothic narrative, typically represent an irruption of the past into the present that disorders the status quo by suggesting or revealing an occulted truth of some kind. The thing-power of the Gothic portrait also commonly inverts our understanding of agency: The portrait or picture comes alive, while the corresponding subject of the representation or in some cases the spectator is vitiated or objectified. The subject becomes an object, while an object becomes the subject.

Because three-dimensional representations of the human form—dolls, puppets, marionettes, ventriloquist dummies, statues, robots, and so on—tend not to be iconic of a specific individual, they often function in a different capacity in Gothic narrative than photographs. Instead of circumscribed narratives reordering the past, 3D representations of the human form independent of any tie to a particular individual—what I will refer to as "living dolls"—tend to precipitate broader crises of comprehension in the present as they undo the distinction between living and dead in a more immediate way than portraits. Animate three-dimensional representations of the human form are especially evocative of the "fear and dread" Freud associates with the uncanny ([1919] 2003, 123). Indeed, there is a type of living doll—an automaton—at the very heart of the notion of the uncanny itself—a concept first addressed psychologically by Ernest Jentsch in his 1906 essay "On the Psychology of the Uncanny." Focusing on the German author E. T. A. Hoffmann and his story "The Sandman" (1816), which involves the automaton Olimpia, Jentsch proposes that the feeling of the uncanny is evoked by intellectual "uncertainty," particularly over whether something is alive or not: "Among all the psychical uncertainties that can become an original cause of the uncanny feeling," writes Jentsch, "there is one in particular that is able to develop a fairly regular, powerful and very general effect: namely, *doubt as to whether an apparently living being really is animate and, conversely, doubt as to whether a lifeless object may not in fact be animate*" (Jentsch [1906] 1997, 11).

Sigmund Freud, in developing his notion of the uncanny, also focuses on Hoffman's "The Sandman"; however, he shifts the focus away from intellectual uncertainty to the return of the repressed. For Freud, this includes not just repressed infantile material but "surmounted" ([1919] 2003, 154) primitive beliefs such as witchcraft and telepathy. Freud's focus on Hoffman's Olimpia has to do with the threat to one's eyes as a displaced form of castration anxiety. Animate representations of the human form, however, are easily accommodated by Freud's conception of the uncanny. Freud explains that with "animism, magic, sorcery, the omnipotence of thoughts, unintended repetition and the castration complex, we have covered virtually all the factors that turn the frightening into the uncanny" (149). The living doll, in the first place, seems to confirm an animistic conception of the world, attributing a kind of agency to an inanimate object; second, narratives involving living dolls often involve magic and witchcraft, validating these surmounted beliefs. As Sandra Mills puts it, the living doll is an "atavistic figure that defies rationality, an uncontrolled, ostensibly monstrous 'other'" (2018, 250); third, and perhaps most important, the strangeness of the almost human living doll leads back to something intimately familiar and yet repressed: death and the fact of our own mortality.

The living doll, I would suggest, is not just almost human, but in some ways (to riff on the Tyrell Corporation's slogan for its replicants in Ridley Scott's *Blade Runner* [1982]), "more human than human." Like the living dead, the living doll—as philosopher Slavoj Žižek has said of vampires—is ironically "*far more alive* than us, mortified by the symbolic network . . . the real 'living dead' are we, common mortals, condemned to vegetate in the Symbolic" (2008, 221). Put differently, living dolls pursue their desire without constraint or regard for social expectation. From a psychoanalytic perspective—as Donna Haraway has said of cyborgs in her "Cyborg Manifesto," another variant of the living doll (1991)—they are unhobbled by Oedipal psychosexual development. They do not progress through a Lacanian mirror stage introducing lack at their core and, in many cases, not being alive in the traditional sense, they do not fear death. The uncanniness of the living doll is then that its excessiveness reminds us of our own inadequacy. Its coming to life reminds us of our being-toward-death. Its "unnatural body" reminds us of our own bodies that will one day become an inanimate object—and, as Freud notes, "To many people the acme of the uncanny is represented by anything to do with death, dead bodies, revenants, spirits and ghosts" ([1919] 2003, 148) because we fear and fail to comprehend death.

Then, as if intellectual uncertainty, affirmation of surmounted beliefs, and the foregrounding of human mortality were not enough, living dolls frequently evoke uncanniness in one more respect, trespassing as they do on the terrain described by Mori as the "uncanny valley." As discussed earlier, Mori proposes that the more human an artificial being looks, the more favorably we respond to it, but only up to a point. When something looks almost human, but not quite, it evokes a sensation of the eerie or uncanny, and we recoil. Mori refers to this point of negative association as the "uncanny valley," which he in fact associates with zombies and corpses—reminders of human mortality ([1970] 2012.).

For all these reasons then, living dolls—the whole class of human-like animate things—are privileged Gothic tropes that can be grouped into two categories based on animating force: inspirited dolls and magical/technological dolls. Inspirited living dolls are a particular type of inspirited object (see Chapter 2) animated by some kind of ghost, demon, or supernatural agent that uses the doll as a home or manipulates it. This is famously the case with the doll Chucky in the *Child's Play* franchise and reboots, as well as with the doll Annabelle in *The Conjuring/Annabelle* franchises. In the *Child's Play* series, Chucky is animated by the spirit of a notorious serial killer who seeks to transfer his soul from the doll to a living body. In *The Conjuring/Annabelle* films, the Annabelle doll is inhabited by a demon. In both cases, the thing-power of the inanimate object originates from some kind of supernatural presence that affirms the transcendental. Such narratives thus seem to reflect what Victoria Nelson has described as repressed religious desire. In our post-Enlightenment moment, argues Nelson, a materialist worldview prevails. However, the desire for a link to the transcendent persists and "the repressed religious is . . . visible in representations of puppets, robots, cyborgs, and other artificial humans in literature and film. It endures as a fascination with the spiritualizing of matter and the demiurgic infusion of soul into human simulacra" (2001, 20). Narratives about living dolls feed a repressed desire to believe in a universe larger than the one our senses perceive; however, Nelson asserts that, "because the religious impulse is profoundly unacceptable in the dominant Western intellectual culture" (18), it finds expression in debased form through narratives of demons, devils, ghosts, animate dolls, and so forth.

This desire to believe in the transcendental is also arguably reflected by narratives of living dolls not directly inspired by a particular supernatural presence but rather animated by magic. This category would accommodate the golem from Jewish folklore as well as, to a certain extent, voodoo dolls. In the golem story, the golem is a creature created from clay or mud and magically

Figure 11. The Golem from Paul Wegener and Carl Boese's 1920 *The Golem: How He Came into the World*

given life. The most famous version of the tale has Rabbi Judah Loew ben Bezalel of Prague creating a golem out of clay to defend the Jewish population from pogroms. The golem's body does not house a particular demon or spirit; rather, it is magically given life through Hebrew rituals and incantations. Voodoo dolls in Gothic narrative function in a somewhat different capacity in that they do not exert independent agency; however, through magic they are tethered to a particular individual, and manipulation of the doll by a witch or sorcerer elicits physical responses (usually painful) in the represented subject. What links the thing-power of the golem and the voodoo doll is that the animacy of each is connected to a spiritual tradition—the spells and rituals that bring the golem to life and tether the voodoo doll to its subject reflect a larger belief system including spiritual forces. The golem and the voodoo doll are in this sense materializations of the transcendental.

This emphasis on the spiritual, however, elides the centrality of the body to Gothic narratives of animate human forms. It may certainly be the case that popular culture narratives of the supernatural reflect a deeply engrained human desire for a more enchanted world and an afterlife. However, as I have argued, the Gothic and particularly cinematic Gothic horror is first and foremost a bodily genre: one that manipulates bodies in order to evoke a bodily response from readers and viewers. In living doll narratives in particular, the uncanniness inheres in the materialization of the transcendental that gives "life" to "dead" matter. This is the sacred experienced through the profane—a ghost or demon animating a human-like object and, as discussed earlier, calling to mind the limitations of the human body and the repressed specter of mortality. In Gothic horror, the animate body of the inspirited doll seeks—often successfully—to transform living humans into corpses, or the animating force seeks to occupy a human body in the same way that it occupies the doll, forcing upon us the disconcerting realization that *humans are things among other things*.

Gothic tales of inspirited dolls such as Chucky and Annabelle, as well as magically animated human forms such as golems and voodoo dolls, participate in a well-established narrative familiar to many from religious traditions in which the material world is only a part of a larger reality that also includes the transcendental world—the realm of divinity, spirits, demons, and supernatural beings. The materialization of the transcendental in the doll corresponds in this way with the functioning of religious icons, idols, and even blessed or cursed artifacts such as relics that are presumed to have some intrinsic, magical power by virtue of their connection to a transcendental power. The thing-power of such objects is disconcerting but can be accommodated by a familiar ideological framework or "master narrative" in which human existence is part of a broader cosmic conflict between larger powers.

The counterpart to narratives of living human forms animated by magic are those endowed with life by "science" that ends up approximating magic. The important difference between "sciencey" tales and magic ones, however, is that sciencey ones substitute a mechanistic vision of the universe for a religious one. It is not God, the devil, or some supernatural creature animating the human form; rather, animacy is achieved through the harnessing of so-called "natural forces." The Gothic Ur-text here is certainly Mary Shelley's *Frankenstein*, first published in 1818. Within the novel, the means of reanimating dead matter remain obscure. What we do know, however, is that Victor Frankenstein is a scientist of sorts (in the language of the time, a "natural philosopher"), and his creature's quickening is not effected by bell, book, and candle. That it has something to do with electricity seems likely (as film adaptations have elaborated)—Victor is remarkably impressed as a boy by the power of lightning, as was Mary Shelley by the experiments with electricity of Luigi Galvani and others during her time. And then, as I have noted elsewhere, the novel carefully eschews religious questions of soul and spirit (see my "The Soul of the Matter" [Weinstock 2018]). While the creature is called "devil" and "demonical" by Victor, there is never any suggestion in the novel or the cinematic tradition that follows that it is in fact animated by any supernatural force. The creature in Shelley's novel is literally bigger than life and *inescapably material*. Indeed, Shelley's monstrous creature arguably may be considered the paradigmatic Gothic thing and exemplar of Gothic thing-power: reanimate dead flesh—an assemblage of parts in fact—that exerts its influence on all it touches and calls into question human exceptionalism in the process.

Taking cues from Shelley, science fiction and Gothic horror are filled with uncanny variants of the living doll crafted by mad, naïve, or evil scientists—robots, replicants, androids, cyborgs (which fuse human and nonhuman parts), and so on—that in many cases act of their own volition. The difficulty in such works often is determining—as per Hoffman's Olimpia—whether and at what point a living doll should be construed as "alive" and "human"—conscious, able to make decisions, to feel emotions, to learn, and so on. In *Blade Runner*, what distinguishes humans from replicants is empathy, which the replicants lack (until they don't). In *Alien* (Ridley Scott, 1979), the traitorous Ash (Ian Holm) is revealed as an android; in *Aliens* (James Cameron, 1986), the android Bishop (Lance Henriksen) is far more human than the villain Burke (Paul Reiser). And, while the terminators in the film franchise, whether cast as heroes or villains, seem defined by their programming, what of *RoboCop* (Paul

Verhoeven, 1987), the human/machine cyborg that overcomes its programming? The question of whether a human form is in fact human is the defining question of Alex Garland's 2014 *Ex Machina*.

The other variant here is the "killer robot" narrative, in which *programming* substitutes for spiritual possession. Compelled by its program, the terminator in James Cameron's 1984 film *The Terminator*, for example, pursues its objective—to prevent the birth of humanity's future savior, John Connor, by killing his mother, Sarah (Linda Hamilton), before she gets pregnant—without wavering up to the point of its complete destruction. There is no arguing with Yul Brenner's robot Gunslinger in Michael Crichton's 1973 *Westworld* or the fembot doubles in Bryan Forbes *The Stepford Wives* (1975). What is uncanny about killer robot narratives is the discrepancy between appearance and action: We expect figures that look human to "act" human—that is, to display a range of emotions, including empathy and compassion. The fixity of purpose of the killer robot—like the zombie—is what makes it inhuman and an object of fear.

The killer robot narrative is not just a specific subset of the larger category of Gothic tales of living dolls, however; it is in fact the counterpart or flipside to human possession narratives. In possession narratives, human beings act as though they are robots—that is, humans are "programmed" by some force that is or feels "foreign." As a consequence of possession, thought control of some kind by an external power, or madness, human subjects become, in a sense, "objects"—marionettes manipulated by some other force. Possessed humans pursue some malevolent objective not of their own volition, but because of a kind of control exerted by something "not them." In both cases—killer robots and possessed humans—a human-like façade belies a lack of interiority in the sense of volition and emotional range.

Finally, there are Gothic narratives of living dolls that avoid ascribing the animation of the human form to any specific ideological metanarrative. There are two groups for what we might call "inexplicable animacy": first, what we could call wishing makes it so and, second, the wholly unexplained. In the "wishing makes it so" narrative, intense and prolonged desire on the part of the protagonist finally results in the desired outcome, although the transformation remains divorced from any specific metaphysical or religious tradition. For example, in director Lucky McKee's updating of the *Frankenstein* narrative, *May* (2002), the protagonist, May Dove Canady (Angela Bettis), builds a "friend" out of body parts harvested from acquaintances. At the end of the film, the creation apparently comes alive, wished into existence by May, who dies, possibly transferring her life force to her creation (but not possessing the body as far as we can tell). To the extent that we can confirm that the creation does indeed achieve animacy, it does so based on the strength of May's will rather than her drawing upon religious or occult forces. She has wished it into being. It is magic, but a kind of general magic rather than one connected to any particular tradition.

And then there are Gothic narratives that offer no explanation whatsoever for the unsettling of the line between inanimate thing and animate subject. This is the case in the "Living Doll" episode of *The Twilight Zone*, which first aired in 1963. At the center of the episode is Talky Tina, a talking wind-up doll presented to a young girl named Christie (Tracy Stratford) by her hostile stepfather, Erich (Telly Savalas). (Amusingly, the mother in this famous episode involving an evil, sentient doll is named Annabelle [Mary LaRoche]). When Erich winds up the doll, its phrases morph from the anticipated "I love you" to "I hate you," "you'll be sorry," and "I'm going to kill you." Erich unsuccessfully attempts to destroy the doll in various ways and finally meets his own demise when he trips over the doll, which is inexplicably lying on the stairs. When his wife, Annabelle, rushes to his aid, she discovers the doll on the stairs and it then speaks to her, confirming her husband's story.

What differentiates "Living Doll" from other narratives of evil, sentient dolls like Chucky or Annabelle is that no explanation whatsoever is proffered by the show for Talky Tina's animacy. As far as we know, she is not possessed by an evil spirit, animated by voodoo, or following a program. She is just somehow a thing that is alive. As Rod Serling's closing narration to the episode makes clear, this murky zone between living and dead is the province of *The Twilight Zone*: "Of course, we all know dolls can't really talk, and they certainly can't commit murder. But to a child caught in the middle of turmoil and conflict,

Figure 12. The *Twilight Zone*'s Talky Tina doll

a doll can become many things: friend, defender, guardian. Especially a doll like Talky Tina, who did talk and did commit murder—in the misty region of the Twilight Zone." But as I have attempted to sketch out in this chapter and the project as a whole so far, Gothic narrative in general is just such a twilight zone, a space of ontological confusion where subjects become objects and vice versa, and where the fraught relationship of human beings with the material world, including our own bodies, is the central theme. What brings together narratives in which human beings are transformed into objects and narratives in which objects are endowed with uncanny life is the vitiation of human subjects. Human agency becomes displaced by thing-power, making clear just how potentially unsettling the notion of thing-power actually is in the popular imagination.

5
Book
How to Do Things with Words

This study has made the case so far that any object in Gothic narrative can, by expressing thing-power, transform into an ominous quasi-subject—something alive that shouldn't be but nevertheless is. Gothic narrative fixates on things, developing its own Thing Theory in the process as it explores what things are, how they function, and how they relate to the human. It focuses obsessively on the hidden depths of objects, their uncanny animacy, and the ways that the human and nonhuman are caught up in networks of reciprocal interaction and effect: the human and nonhuman as actants in Latourean networks. And the result in Gothic narrative is often a curious inversion of animacy in which, as things become more like subjects, human subjects become more like things: frozen, vitiated, unconscious, or dead. While any object can function in this capacity, certain classes of objects are privileged, foregrounding particular emphases of Gothic narrative. The body, as I argued in Chapters 3 and 4, is central in this respect as Gothic narrative achieves its uncanny and horrific effects through insistently foregrounding the body's materiality. The Gothic chews up and spits out bodies, forcing readers to acknowledge on some level that bodies are fragile things subject to damage, decay, and death.

A second privileged class of object within Gothic narrative is the book, which here will serve as a broad rubric signifying all forms of written communication: found manuscripts, spell books, letters, scrolls, and written messages of various sorts. The subtitle to this chapter, "How to Do Things with Words," alludes to speech-act theorist J. L. Austin's 1962 study *How to Do Things With Words*, in which he outlines his concept of performative utterances—sentences that, rather than describing something, actually perform a kind of action.

Performatives cause something to take place. I will argue that, in one way or another, all written messages within Gothic narratives end up as performatives causing something to take place, and these "books" can be grouped into five sometimes-overlapping categories of escalating agency, starting with the recovered history or archive and then including four forms of what I will call *accursed books*: the corrupting book, the grimoire, the portal, and the living book. What these forms of Gothic books have in common is that they all literalize and amplify commonplace clichés and understandings of how written language functions, highlighting in the process the unsettling aspects of these associations. What if one really could "get lost" in a book or be "transported" into another world? What if books really could "cast a spell" over the reader, "speak" to the reader, or let "history come alive"? The language we often use to describe the experience of reading already affords written language a kind of thing-power. Gothic narrative capitalizes on this and uses it to uncanny effect. In Gothic narrative, words can break your bones every bit as much as sticks and stones, and books can bite, scratch, and maul.

Books in Gothic narrative, as they do in other genres, also inevitably foreground knowledge and understanding—much of their performative thing-power inheres in unsettling sedimented understandings of the past, the present, and sometimes the universe. Often in Gothic narrative this has to do with an occulted history, the revelation of which reorders the protagonist's understanding of the present, thereby inflecting the course of the narrative and shifting future possibilities. In keeping with Kamilla Elliott's claim concerning portraits in Gothic narrative (see Chapter 4), books, too, in this way possess the potential to "rework social legitimacy and entitlement" (2012, 8). After reading the recovered history contained in the found manuscript, the protagonist and reader see the narrative world in a new light, understanding that what they had thought was the truth is incomplete or false. In a more uncanny register, increasingly active books in Gothic narrative often substitute a magical or animistic universe for a rationalist one. They literally do things with words—and often not just in the relatively narrow performative sense outlined by Austin. Performatives, as explained by Austin, inevitably have a social dimension: They depend on the context and the speaker's authority and cause something to occur, either by changing something's status according to established rules or evoking a response from someone. If I'm your boss and I tell you that you're fired, then I have changed your status from employed to unemployed. And if a drill sergeant orders his troops to march in the context of a training exercise at boot camp, his position and the consent of the troops (who acknowledge his authority to make this demand and are aware of the consequences for disobeying) make marching the likely outcome. Gothic books do things with words in a more direct and uncanny way and without requiring that social dimension. Your boss can fire you, but in a world where magic prevails, the right spell can literally set you aflame. When—in a narrative universe that resembles our own—spells summon demons, manuscripts open portals to other dimensions, or books bite the hand that holds them, the rules that govern our reality have been violated and thus must be reformulated to reflect a new understanding of just how reality works: one that accommodates the animacy of objects and the power of words to literally shape matter and transform the world.

The Recovered Archive: Found Manuscripts

The most familiar and, for that reason perhaps, least surprising interpolation of the book into Gothic narrative is the found manuscript, by which I mean a story within a story accessed and shared by a character with the reader. (This is, therefore, distinct from books, such as Walpole's *Otranto*, marketed in their entirety as recovered medieval tales.) In some cases, the recovered narrative constitutes almost the entire work, usually with only a thin veneer of a framing device. This is the case in Mary Shelley's *Frankenstein* (first published in 1818), for example, in which Walton's letters to his sister convey Victor Frankenstein's tragic tale; it is likewise the case in Henry James's *The Turn of the Screw* (1898), in which the story is told by way of letters sent to the ostensible storyteller, Douglass—notably, James doesn't reestablish the frame at the end, choosing instead to end the story with the ambiguous death of the child Miles; and it is also more or less the case in Stoker's *Dracula* (1897) in which journals, including Jonathan Harker's account of being a sort of damsel in distress held captive by the vampiric count, play a central role in conveying information. The letters and journals in these works are presented to the reader as the means through which the tale is conveyed.

In other instances, the conceit of the found manuscript plays a less central, but still important, role in revealing an occulted history and fleshing out the details of the narrative that shape the protagonist's and reader's understanding of the former's situation. This is the situation in Ann Radcliffe's *The Romance of the Forest* (1791) in which the protagonist, Adeline, discovers a manuscript written by someone being held captive inside a now-ruined abbey (who, remarkably, turns out to be her father!).[1] The most convoluted variant on this formula is almost certainly Charles Maturin's *Melmoth the Wanderer* (1820), which is told through a series of nested stories-within-stories that reveal the supernatural existence of the titular Melmoth, who sold his soul to the devil in exchange for an extended existence and who now (unsuccessfully) seeks someone to assume the pact for him so he can avoid eternal perdition.

These found manuscripts themselves divide into two categories: those that, like the one in Radcliffe's *The Romance of the Forest*, rehearse a tragic but ultimately mundane history of violence that resonates in some respect with the protagonist's imperiled situation and reveals the perfidy of appearances, and those, as in *Frankenstein*, *Melmoth*, and *Dracula*, that tell an incredible tale of events and creatures that exceed what science and physics tell us is possible. The former conforms to our understanding of reality; the latter necessitates a reformulated understanding of how the universe works—one that includes reanimated corpses, vampires, unnatural longevity as a result of Faustian bargains, and so on. In both cases though—whether the revelation is terrestrial tragedy or diabolical forces—the interpolation of the manuscript is a kind of uncanny disordering of the present for the protagonist and/or the reader. In a self-referential way, books that foreground the uncanny power of books make clear the thing-power inherent in narrative itself: The book is revealed both as a *reality manipulator* that shifts understandings of the past and present and, in some cases, the rules that govern the universe, and as an *affect generator* that causes characters and readers to react in particular ways. All narratives in this sense can be construed as performative, constructing understandings and evoking affect. Texts within texts often highlight this agency of the written word by showing us the responses of characters to the discoveries shared with the reader, and Gothic narrative in particular emphasizes the evocation of affect through recovered narratives of violence and the supernatural. The recovered manuscript acts on both characters and readers, reformulating knowledge and manipulating feeling.

Corrupting Books

More active than the found manuscript and much more specifically connected to the Gothic are accursed books, the first variant of which I will consider as the *corrupting* book. The idea is relatively straightforward: Reading the corrupting book effects the moral degradation of the reader. In some cases, this deterioration seems the consequence of the introduction of tabooed ideas; in others, the book itself as object exerts a kind of mesmeric or magical hold over its possessor. Unlike the found manuscript, the narrative of which is shared directly with the reader, the content of the corrupting book is absorbed by a character but only described to the reader in vague terms or passed along in small snippets. (Attempting to describe corrupting content in anything other than vague terms or tiny samples would likely end up as disappointing, censurable, or both!) The two most important corrupting books in the Gothic literary tradition—leading up to H. P. Lovecraft's grimoire the *Necronomicon*, to be discussed later together with spell books—are arguably the yellow book in Oscar Wilde's *The Picture of Dorian Gray* (1890) and the play *The King in Yellow* introduced in Robert Chambers's 1895 collection of short stories of the same name.

In *Dorian Gray*, young Dorian becomes obsessed with a "poisonous book" provided to him by aesthete Lord Henry. As Dorian first starts to read it, he considers it "the strangest book that he had ever read." "It seemed to him," the text explains, "that in exquisite raiment, and to the delicate sound of flutes, the sins of the world were passing in dumb show before him. Things that he had dimly dreamed of were suddenly made real to him. Things of which he had never dreamed were gradually revealed" (Wilde [1890] 2008, 141). Wilde's prose in attempting to describe Dorian's experience of the book then becomes especially rhapsodic:

> There were in it metaphors as monstrous as orchids, and as subtle in colour. The life of the senses was described in the terms of mystical philosophy. One hardly knew at times whether one was reading the spiritual ecstasies of some mediaeval saint or the morbid confessions of a modern sinner. *It was a poisonous book.* The heavy odour of incense seemed to cling about its pages and to trouble the brain. The mere cadence of the sentences, the subtle monotony of their music, so full as it was of complex refrains and movements elaborately repeated, produced in the mind of the lad, as he passed from chapter to chapter, a form of reverie, a malady of dreaming, that made him unconscious of the falling day and creeping shadows. (141, emphasis mine)

Dorian loses himself in the novel, and the narration tells us that, "for years, Dorian Gray could not free himself from the influence of this book" (142). Seduced by the book's decadent hedonism, Dorian abandons conventional morality to pursue pleasure and sensation. "Dorian Gray had been poisoned by a book," explains the narration succinctly (156).

Dorian, of course, has not literally been poisoned by the yellow book (a plot device pursued instead by Umberto Eco in *The Name of the Rose* [1980]). Rather, his desires have been directed and his character influenced in ways construed as contrary to social acceptability. The corrupting book is one that exerts a negative influence on its reader in light of the social expectations of a given time and place. The poisonous yellow book in *Dorian Gray* in fact has its real-world counterpart in J. K. Huysmans's *À Rebours* (*Against Nature*) (1884). In Huysmans's novel, a wealthy aesthete, Jean des Esseintes, rejects conventional bourgeois morality and devotes his life to sensual experience. Introduced as an exhibit during the trial of Oscar Wilde for sodomy in 1895, the book was castigated by the prosecution as "sodomitical" (see Fellion and Inglis 2017, 150).[2] What this highlights is our commonplace understanding of the thing-power of books, which can seduce, corrupt, entrance, horrify, surprise, amuse, and so on. (Were this not the case, there would be no lists of banned and censored books, nor would there need to be any consideration of the "age appropriateness" of books for children.) Of course, what is being addressed here is the content of the book—the ideas conveyed through written language—not the physical properties of the book itself. The words, as interpreted by a reader, are what do the corrupting, not the medium that transmits them (conventionally, bound paper; now screens of various sorts). And yet it becomes difficult to separate out the message from the medium—books are physical objects invested with a kind of aura created by their content. Reflecting this idea, the poisonous book becomes a kind of body in Gothic narrative, a shell housing a debased spirit that seduces and corrupts.

This is certainly the case with the corrupting yellow book in Robert Chambers's *The King in Yellow* (1895), and the language used to describe it is the very same as that used to characterize the yellow book in *Dorian Gray*: poisonous. In Chambers's collection of short stories, *The King in Yellow* is a forbidden play castigated for its pernicious, seductive immorality. As does Wilde, Chambers becomes particularly rhapsodic in describing the play, its history, and effect. In "The Repairer of Reputations," the collection's first story, narrator Hildred Castaigne summarizes the book, which he has unsuccessfully tried to burn, and his experience of it as follows:

> If I had not caught a glimpse of the opening words in the second act I should never have finished it, but as I stooped to pick it up, my eyes became riveted to the open page, and with a cry of terror, or perhaps it was of joy so poignant that I suffered in every nerve, I snatched the thing out of the coals and crept shaking to my bedroom, where I read it and reread it, and wept and laughed and trembled with a horror which at times assails me yet. . . . I pray God will curse the writer, as the writer has cursed the world with this beautiful, stupendous creation, terrible in its simplicity, irresistible in its truth—a world which now trembles before the King in Yellow. . . . It is well known how the book spread like an infectious disease, from city to city, from continent to continent, barred out here, confiscated there, denounced by Press and pulpit, censured even by the most advanced of literary anarchists. No definite principles had been violated in those wicked pages, no doctrine promulgated, no convictions outraged. It could not be judged by any known standard, yet, although it was acknowledged that the

supreme note of art had been struck in *The King in Yellow*, all felt that human nature could not bear the strain, nor thrive on words in which the essence of purest *poison* lurked. (Chambers 1895, emphasis mine).

In *Dorian Gray*, the yellow book is characterized as a kind of soporific drug—and Wilde interestingly emphasizes the sensual qualities of its language. It is the "cadence of the sentences, the subtle monotony of their music, so full as it was of complex refrains and movements elaborately repeated" that it induces a form of reverie in Dorian, a "malady of dreaming," as Wilde puts it, that renders Dorian unaware of the passing of time. The sensual effect of the yellow book connects it to the opium narrative that runs throughout *Dorian Gray* and the Orientalism that is associated with it—the book is an exotic drug that seduces, corrupts, and poisons.

The King in Yellow finds its grounding as well in a kind of fin-de-siècle Orientalism, although its effects are less sensual and, indeed, more threatening. The play is characterized as an "infectious disease," connecting it, on the one hand, to yellow fever and, on the other, to the "yellow peril" of the late 1800s—racist anxieties concerning Asian immigrants (see Tchen and Yeats 2014). Rather than a soporific malady of dreaming, *The King in Yellow* evokes a powerful affective response: terror, joy, tears, trembling. In "The Yellow Sign," the fourth story in the collection, Chambers again attempts to describe *The King in Yellow*, this time likening the text to "poisoned diamonds":

> Oh the sin of writing such words,—words which are clear as crystal, limpid and musical as bubbling springs, words which sparkle and glow like the poisoned diamonds of the Medicis! Oh the wickedness, the hopeless damnation of a soul who could fascinate and paralyze human creatures with such words,—words understood by the ignorant and wise alike, words which are more precious than jewels, more soothing than music, more awful than death! (Chambers 1895)

Chambers makes clear here why the content of the corrupting book is withheld from the reader—how, after all, could one actually render words "more precious than jewels, more soothing than music, more awful than death"? But he also emphasizes the curious inversion of animacy associated with Gothic objects in general: The book that poisons, and whose words sparkle and glow, paralyzes human creatures. Although Chambers associates *The King in Yellow* not with hazy incense but hard, cold jewels, there is a kind of malady of dreaming here as well, an infection of the soul that renders the body inert as the book mesmerizes. This is the flip side to my discussion in Chapter 3 of the body reduced to quasi-object when under the sway of some controlling force—and there is indeed some suggestion in Chambers's story cycle that possession of the yellow sign (a kind of symbol or glyph) opens one up to a form of mind control. While the reader of the corrupting book is seduced, drugged, mesmerized, and so on, the book itself achieves a kind of uncanny animacy, exerting control over the entranced subject. The book becomes the master, possessing its possessor. As Dorian starts to read the yellow book, the text tells us "he became absorbed" (Wilde [1890] 2008, 141). In "The Repairer of Reputations," Castaigne's eyes are "riveted to the page" (Chambers 1895) as he reads and rereads the forbidden book. This then is the nature of the corrupting book in Gothic narrative: an object that takes control of the subject, a text that transfixes and dominates its reader—an uncannily vibrant thing that reduces its reader to the status of quasi-thing shaped and manipulated by the thing-power of the book.

The Grimoire

Corrupting books in Gothic narrative exert an influence over the characters who read them, metaphorically poisoning their minds by influencing them to reject conventional standards of morality and propriety. The book assumes control, mesmerizing, pacifying, and manipulating those who delve into their pages, turning readers into quasi-objects. While in some cases the book seems to choose the reader in the sense of attracting those already open to its influence, its effect is to undermine psychological bulwarks against "immoral" thoughts, seducing and tempting the reader to abandon conformity to social expectation. Grimoires—spell books—in Gothic narrative take this challenge to conventional morality and social expectation to the next step by aligning their bearers with dark magic that violates rationalist understandings of the physical universe and turning their users into literal conduits for their power.

Grimoires are both accursed and corrupting: They require one to traffic with diabolical forces, and the power they promise invites hubris as their wielders seek control over physical matter, including other people. The bargain is generally Faustian—access to dark magic and forbidden power comes at the cost of one's soul. Grimoires also offer the clearest illustration of the performativity of Gothic books as reading the spell aloud—sometimes in conjunction with other rituals—holds the potential to alter reality as a diabolical being is summoned, the dead are revived, or matter is in some way physically manipulated from a distance. In casting the spell, one does something with words in a direct way independent of any social evaluation of the magician's status—whether one acknowledges the authority of the wizard to cast a spell has no effect on the outcome of the spell (although one gets the spell wrong at one's peril!).

The idea of spells able to influence reality or summon spiritual forces is, of course, an ancient one going all the way back to Mesopotamian cuneiform tablets and ancient Egyptian amulets. In Owen Davies's *Grimoires: A History of Magic Books* (2009), he offers an overview of notorious and influential grimoires, including the Renaissance *Key of Solomon*, the sixteenth-century *Fourth Book of Occult Philosophy* associated with Cornelius Agrippa (but not actually written by him—see Davies 2009, 50–54), and the eighteenth-century *Sixth and Seventh Books of Moses*. While commonplace in fantasy works such as the *Harry Potter* series, in which magic is accepted as the norm, books of magical spells also play an important role in Gothic narrative, where magic and diabolical forces are received as violations of the understood principles of the physical world. The most significant example here is undoubtedly American horror author H. P. Lovecraft's fictional creation *The Necronomicon*.

First introduced in Lovecraft's story "The Hound" (1924) and then referenced repeatedly in other works, including "The Call of Cthulhu" (1926), "The Dunwich Horror" (1928), *The Case of Charles Dexter Ward* (1943), *At the Mountains of Madness* (1936a), and "The Dreams in the Witch House" (1932), the book, attributed to the "mad Arab" Abdul Alhazred (Lovecraft, "The Hound," 84), purportedly contains a history of Lovecraft's "Old Ones" (his pantheon of extraterrestrial monstrosities, including Cthulhu, Yog-Sothoth, and Azathoth) and the means for summoning them. A complete account of the book was provided by Lovecraft in his "History of the *Necronomicon*" (1927), which rather dryly explains that reading the book "leads to terrible consequences" (268) and humorously proposes that it is from the *Necronomicon* that Robert W. Chambers derived the idea of his forbidden play *The King in Yellow*, published when Lovecraft was five years old. (While some have suggested Lovecraft in fact got the idea from Chambers, it appears Lovecraft didn't actually read *The King in Yellow* until 1927, and Lovecraft himself noted that Gothic literature is filled with "mouldy hidden manuscripts" that could have provided inspiration for his fictional grimoire (see Joshi, "Afterword" [2014], 420).

The *Necronomicon* is preeminent among a number of "terrible and forbidden" grimoires invented by Lovecraft and his coterie of admirers known as the Lovecraft circle. These forbidden spell books include Ludvig Prinn's *De Vermis Mysteriis*, *The Book of Eibon*, and of course Friedrich von Junzt's unforgettable *Unaussprechlichen Kulten*. As with corrupting books in general, the content of the spell book must be withheld from the reader—Lovecraft himself noted that, "if anyone were to try to write the *Necronomicon*, it would disappoint all those who have shuddered at cryptic references to it" (quoted in Joshi,

"Afterword" [2014], 419). The longest passage included from the *Necronomicon* appears in Lovecraft's "The Dunwich Horror" and challenges human exceptionalism by describing Lovecraft's "Great Old Ones," dormant extraterrestrials with godlike powers whose awakening will result in humanity's end:

> Nor is it to be thought . . . that man is either the oldest or the last of earth's masters, or that the common bulk of life and substance walks alone. The Old Ones were, the Old Ones are, and the Old Ones shall be. Not in the spaces we know, but *between* them, They walk serene and primal, undimensioned and to us unseen. . . . They walk unseen and foul in lonely places where the Words have been spoken and the Rites howled through at their Seasons. The wind gibbers with Their voices, and the earth mutters with Their consciousness. They bend the forest and crush the city, yet may not forest or city behold the hand that smites. . . . Man rules now where They ruled once; They shall soon rule where man rules now. After summer is winter, after winter summer. They wait patient and potent, for here shall They reign again. (Lovecraft [1928] 2001, 259–60)

Although not a spell, this passage encapsulates Lovecraft's "cosmicism"—his philosophy that humans are insignificant within the larger scheme of the universe where we are buffeted about by powers and forces indifferent to our existence (if not actively malevolent). Within Lovecraft's fiction, those who seek to tap into or summon these forces using the *Necronomicon* typically are morally suspect to begin with, go mad, and meet with an unfortunate end.

What references to the *Necronomicon* in Lovecraft repeatedly emphasize is its remarkable thing-power. In "The Festival" (1925) and "The Dunwich Horror" (1928) it is used to summon horrible monsters. In *The Case of Charles Dexter Ward* (1943), it is among the books that the wizard Curwen uses for unnatural longevity and the transmigration of his consciousness. The book is "forbidden" ("The Hound" [1924] 1999, 84), "unmentionable" ("The Festival" [1925] 1999, 112), "dreaded" ("The Dreams in the Witch House" [1933] 2013, 286) and "frightful" (*At the Mountains of Madness* [1936a] 2013, 240). It is "monstrous" ("The Festival," 112), both in the forbidden knowledge it imparts of the horrors of the universe and the tenuous nature of human existence and the response this knowledge evokes from its readers. Those who dabble in the *Necronomicon* are unsettled by its revelations; those who seek to use it are invariably destroyed because the powers they summon through its invocations are inhuman. To cast spells using the *Necronomicon* is to turn oneself into a kind of human lightning rod for uncontrollable cosmic forces as one summons the storm.

What has been especially interesting about Lovecraft's *Necronomicon* has been its ironic fertility. As Conny Lippert observes, with Lovecraft's blessing, Lovecraft's admirers incorporated elements of his writing, including the *Necronomicon*, into their fiction, which initiated a process of expansion, extending the sphere of the fictional grimoire's influence and helping to give it a life of its own (see Lippert 2012–13). For example, Lovecraft's friend Frank Belknap Long suggested a connection between Elizabethan magician John Dee and the *Necronomicon* in his story "The Space-Eaters" (1928), which begins with an epigraph attributed to Dee's alleged translation. Clark Ashton Smith's 1932 "The Nameless Offspring" begins with an epigraph attributed to the Arabic version of Abdul Alhazred. Manly Wade Wilson's 1937 tongue-in-cheek story "The Terrible Parchment," first published in *Weird Tales* in 1937, not only is dedicated to Lovecraft and offers a kind of history of the *Necronomicon* but explains that "lots of other W. T. [*Weird Tales*] authors—Clark Ashton Smith and Robert Bloch and so on—have taken it up" (Wellman 1937, 238). For additional confirmation of this, one need only look to Robert Bloch (e.g., his "The Shambler from the Stars," 1935), August Derleth (e.g., his novel, *The Lurker at the Threshold* [1945], which develops the background and contents of the *Necronomicon* extensively), Ramsey Campbell, who repeatedly references the *Necronomicon* in his work (e.g., "The Plain of Sound" [1964] and "The Horror From the Bridge" [1964]), Brian Lumley (*The Horror at Oakdeene* [1977]), and so on.

Not only have other authors appropriated and further developed the contents and history of Lovecraft's fictional grimoire, but various claims have been made of its actual existence, and several versions of the book have been published.[3] Lovecraft biographer L. Sprague de Camp, for example, claimed to have a copy written in the fictional language of Druriac, which he published in a very limited run in 1973. As John L. Steadman documents, a few years after de Camp's version, *Necronomicon: The Book of Dead Names* was published in 1978 claiming that the *Necronomicon* was not a single work, but rather a "compilation of magical material" and "part of a larger work from the Middle East" (Steadman 2015, 76). The work then expands on Lovecraft's minimal framework, outlining Lovecraftian entities and rituals (76–80). Also in 1978, another version of the *Necronomicon* was published—one with only loose connections to Lovecraft. Since the author of the introduction only identified himself as "Simon," this version has since been referred to as the Simon *Necronomicon* and, as Davies explains, this "well-constructed hoax" consists of "contents stitched together from printed sources on Mesopotamian myth and magic" (Davies 2009, 268). Another version, titled *Necronomicon: The Wanderings of Alhazred*, was published in 2004 by Canadian occultist Donald Tyson.

Contemporary authors and filmmakers have followed suit, using the *Necronomicon* as shorthand for a powerful, reality-altering spell book. It is the *Necronomicon*—referred to as the *Necronomicon Ex-Mortis*—that summons an evil force (known as the Kandarian Demon) in Sam Raimi's 1987 *Evil Dead II* when an audiotape recording of passages from book is played. (The book is present in the first film as well, *Evil Dead* [1981], but is referred to there as the *Naturom Demonto*). As I will address later under "living books," the *Necronomicon Ex-Mortis* literally comes alive in the third Evil Dead film, *Army of Darkness* (Sam Raimi, 1992). The Friday the Thirteenth franchise then plucks the *Necronomicon Ex-Mortis*—human face and all—directly from the Evil Dead films in *Jason Goes to Hell: The Final Friday* (Adam Marcus, 1993).

While Drew Goddard's *The Cabin in the Woods* (2012) doesn't apparently include the *Necronomicon* itself in its basement full of accursed objects, it does appear to have collected the tape recorder from *The Evil Dead* that includes

Figure 13. The *Necronomicon Ex-Mortis* in *Army of Darkness*

Figure 14. The Necronomicon in *Jason Goes to Hell: The Final Friday*

passages from it that summon a demon. Stephen King, who acknowledges his debt to and affection for Lovecraft in many places, alludes to the *Necronomicon* in his 1987 *The Eyes of the Dragon*, in which the evil wizard Randall Flagg owns a massive grimoire written on the Plains of Leng by a man named Alhazred—in Lovecraft, the author of the *Necronomicon* is Abdul Alhazared, and the Plains of Leng is a mythical place of converging realities. Reading from Flagg's spell book can drive one insane. In King's later Lovecraft-meets-Mary Shelley mash-up, *Revival* (2014), he turns not to Lovecraft's *Necronomicon*, but instead borrows his *De Vermis Mysteriis* as a source of power and insight for primary antagonist Charles Jacobs as he seeks to penetrate the veil between life and death. In a neat little metafictional twist, one of King's characters explains that Lovecraft's "fictional" *Necronomicon* was in fact based in part on the real *De Vermis Mysteriis*, which is characterized as "the most dangerous book ever written" (King 2014, 337). In a more humorous vein, Lovecraft's *Necronomicon* is repurposed as a kind of telephone directory for supernatural entities called the *Necrotelicomnicon* in Terry Pratchett's Discworld franchise, and an episode of *The Simpsons* has former U.S. Presidential candidate Bob Dole read from the *Necronomicon* to the Springfield Republican Party just before they resolve to destroy the environment ("Brawl in the Family," S13, E7, 2002). In perhaps the most surprising appearance of the *Necronomicon*, it features in an episode of the medical drama *House* (Hugh Laurie) as House and his team investigate a strange illness afflicting a medieval reenactment group ("Knight Fall," S6, E18, 2010).

Lovecraft's *Necronomicon* is exemplary of the thing-power of the grimoire in that reading from it can summon fantastic monsters. In addition, the knowledge it conveys undoes both rationalist conceptions of the universe and any sense of human exceptionalism. In Lovecraft's Gothic fiction and other works of Gothic horror, spells work and can summon monsters and manipulate matter. All of this seems the stuff of horror and fantasy, except that it reflects back at us in a darkly parodic way commonplace understandings of how books and language function. That books can corrupt, can "cast a spell" over the reader, and can "change the world" are all familiar ideas and clichés. Performative grimoires simply highlight the uncanny agency we already afford books, making clear the thing-power with which they have always been invested.

That the *Necronomicon* should have proliferated to such an extent in post-Lovecraft fiction, film, and media indeed makes clear the power of books—even fictional ones—to alter reality. Like *The King in Yellow*, Lovecraft's *Necronomicon* has "infected" other authors, spreading out and influencing still more readers. And perhaps the most interesting transformation it has enacted is upon itself. Despite Lovecraft's caution that attempts to actually write the *Necronomicon* can only result in disappointment, as is mentioned earlier it nevertheless has been attempted several times. The *Necronomicon* is now a "real" book. It has in a sense dreamed itself into existence—which, one might suggest, is the nature of narrative itself.

Worth mentioning here is one other grimoire of sorts that finds its parallel with the *Necronomicon* as a spell book that summons malevolent entities—and that is the pop-up book *Mister Babadook* from Jennifer Kent's 2014 film *The Babadook*. Within the film, Amelia Vanek (Essie Davis) is a widow raising her troubled son Sam (Noah Wiseman) on her own after the death of her husband. The situation in the film deteriorates after Amelia starts to read the unsettling *Mister Babadook* book to Sam. Strange things subsequently begin to happen within the home—weird sounds are heard, doors open and close by themselves, and so on—which Amelia attributes to Sam, while Sam attributes them to the Babadook. Amelia tries to dispose of the book—she rips it up, she burns it—but each time it magically reassembles itself and returns. Amelia's mental health deteriorates until she finally confronts the monstrous Babadook, locking it into the basement.

The Babadook is a good example of a horror film that can easily be interpreted as an allegory—in this case, depression as a result of unresolved mourning. Amelia is raising Sam on her own because her husband, Oskar (Ben Winspear), was killed in a car crash while driving her to the hospital when she went into labor. A straightforward interpretation of the film is that she has harbored resentment toward her son ever since and has never come to grips with the loss of her husband. This is the opinion of Wael Khairy (among others), who writes that "the malevolent Babadook is basically a physicalized form of the mother's trauma. . . . I believe, the Babadook embodies the destructive power of grief. Throughout the film, we see the mother insist nobody bring up her husband's name. She basically lives in denial. Amelia has repressed grief for years, refusing to surrender to it" (Khairy 2014). From this perspective, the Babadook is a metaphor for depression that increasingly takes control of Amelia as she is forced to grapple with her son's seemingly aberrant behavior and her own unresolved mourning.

There is much to recommend this interpretation of the film, and it makes perfect sense on a thematic level. However, for allegories to be effective as narratives, they must also engage their audiences on the literal level, and a horror movie that fails to evoke an affective response from viewers, instead presenting itself as a thinly veiled metaphor for intellectual appreciation, is likely to be a disappointment as a horror movie. I would suggest that the locus of horror within at least the first two-thirds of *The Babadook* is not the Babadook as a metaphor for depression, but the uncanny materiality of the horrifying pop-up book that names the antagonist. The film may indeed be about depression, but it is also, simultaneously and just as much, *about a book*—one that is held, read, torn, burned, and increasingly despised. It is a poisonous book that infects the household and elicits bad dreams. *The Babadook* is a horror film that has at its center a *dreadful book*—a book that evokes dread from its readers and auditors as both Amelia and the viewer realize that this is not a good book, not a book for children, not a happy book. In discussing his design for the pop-up book with the film, production designer Alexander Juhasz explains that "I had to keep the simple, graphic aesthetic of a children's book while subverting the images with the unsettling evil presence of the monster lurking beneath [its] pages" (Seigh 2016). But the book does not just contain a monster—the book *is* the monster, or at least an avatar of it, and the images within the book are arguably the most arresting parts of the film.

However, as with other Gothic narratives emphasizing the thing-power of books, the pop-up book within *The Babadook* is simply an exaggeration of the power that we already attribute to books. It tells parents to carefully vet the books they read to children or allow children themselves to read because, while physical books can be destroyed, the impressions they create can be indelibly imprinted into memory. Amelia tries to tear up and burn the book, but it keeps coming back. It sticks to her and her son and won't go away. Like a spell, it conjures up nightmares because, in the end, fictional narratives are always conjurations, bringing something into being that has the potential to haunt the reader or viewer for a long time.

Figure 15. Amelia reads *Mister Babadook* to Sam

The Portal

Perhaps the oddest riff on Lovecraft and the *Necronomicon* is John Carpenter's 1994 film *In the Mouth of Madness*, the title of which alludes to Lovecraft's *At the Mountains of Madness* (1936a) and that is filled with Lovecraftian references. Within the film, protagonist John Trent (Sam Neill) tells an incredible tale of a book—the titular *In the Mouth of Madness*—the reading of which not only drives readers insane but releases an ancient race of monstrous beings. Most interesting (and confusing) about the film is the ontological status of the protagonist, John, who discovers himself in the end to be a character within a book whose scripted actions have seemingly helped bring about the end of the world.

Reading *In the Mouth of Madness* apparently opens a portal between worlds or dimensions, allowing monstrous creatures access to our reality. Book as portal in Gothic narrative is the third of the four variants of the accursed book, and it literalizes the familiar metaphor of books as doorways to other worlds. This conceit is more common in fantasy—particularly works for children—than in Gothic horror. In Michael Ende's *The Neverending Story* (*Die unendliche Geschichte* [1979]), for example, protagonist Bastian Balthazar Bux discovers that the magical land of Fantastica described in the book is real and is transported there; books transport the two protagonists of Mary Pope Osborne's *Magic Tree House* series either into the past or into the books (it's never really clear which); in J. K. Rowling's *Harry Potter and the Chamber of Secrets* (1998), the diary of Tom Riddle somehow allows an avatar of Lord Voldemort to magically manifest in Harry's present. In a different medium, the video for '80s New Wave hit "Take on Me" (1985) by Norwegian band A-ha features a young woman reading a comic book in a coffee shop who is invited into the world of the comic when a pencil-drawn hand reaches out for her.

In Gothic narrative, the book as portal is typically presented as a violation of the rationalist worldview that prevails at the start and usually facilitates the entrance of some kind of horrific being and/or access to some other dimension of horror. A straightforward use of the book-as-portal conceit in Gothic narrative is Roman Polanski's film *The Ninth Gate*, his 1999 adaptation of Arturo Pérez-Reverte's 1993 novel *The Club Dumas*. Within the film, protagonist Dean Corso (Johnny Depp) is an unorthodox scholar-*cum*-detective hired by a wealthy occultist to acquire and compare the three extant copies of a book adapted from another purportedly written by the devil himself: *The Nine Gates of the Kingdom of Shadows*. "Correctly interpreted with the aid of the original text and sufficient inside information," explains Corso's employer, Boris Balkan (Frank Langella), "they're reputed to conjure up the Prince of Darkness in person." The problem for Balkan, however, is that his copy of *The Nine Gates* hasn't worked—the devil hasn't appeared—so he suspects the book may not be authentic. Over the course of the narrative, Corso works out that the key to the puzzle of the *Nine Gates* is not the text, but rather the engravings. The book has nine of them, and three in each of the extant volumes differ from the others, notably in being signed "LCF" (suggestive of Lucifer). Once Corso assembles all nine LCF illustrations, a portal opens for him, presumably to hell.

The book as portal conceit is closely tied to use of a grimoire to summon a supernatural entity or open some kind of gate between worlds. The difference is that, rather than a means to an end, the book as portal is itself the doorway between worlds. Rather than being used to cast a spell, the book *is* the spell that causes changes in or to the material world, as well as to its readers, when read—and this agency of the book then circumscribes that of its reader. At the end of *In the Mouth of Madness*, John Trent discovers that he has always been playing the part scripted for him from the start. He has no real agency; instead, he is simply a character in a book. At the end of *The Ninth Gate*, Corso has solved the puzzle introduced by Balkan, and the answer has forced upon him a reconceptualization of the universe. From a man whose only faith was in money, he has transformed into one who now believes in a larger universe of powers and forces, including Satan, and presumably God, for whom human beings are pawns in the contest for control of the universe. The Gothic book-as-portal reveals that there are other worlds and dimensions, but that they are inhospitable to humanity. Even when the revelation is of the existence of a transcendental plain, this is nevertheless Lovecraftian cosmic dread: the antihumanist undoing of anthropocentrism in the face of powers and forces that dwarf human comprehension and agency.

The Living Book

The final variant of the accursed book is the form demonstrating the most agency: the living book. As per its designation, the living book is a book that acts in ways suggesting consciousness. It is in some sense alive—it may choose its reader, move, bite, change, or speak. This may be because the book is inspirited and serves as the container or prison for some other entity or because the book itself is the entity (and in some cases, it is difficult to tell). Often, living books are part of the animistic world of fantasy, in which objects of various sorts exhibit agency: the *Monster Book of Monsters* in the *Harry Potter* series, for example, will bite the hand that holds it unless its spine is stroked to soothe it, while in the library of Unseen University in Terry Pratchett's *Discworld* series, books have to be chained to their shelves to protect visitors. In the comedy/horror film *Hocus Pocus* (Kenny Ortega, 1993), the Sanderson sisters' spell book has a human eye on the cover that sleeps and wakes, while in P. C. Hodgell's *Kencyranth* series, the Book Bound in Pale Leather occasionally gets goosebumps and shows veins.

Straddling the line between horror and comedy is Clive Barker's playful *Mister B Gone* (2007). Narrated by a demon named Jakabok Botch, the conceit of the novel is that the demon is trapped in the book the reader is holding and is speaking directly to the reader. He was imprisoned in the book in the fourteenth century, he explains, after being discovered eavesdropping on a discussion between heaven and hell over how to divide up the rights to various forms of print publication in the wake of Johannes Gutenberg's invention of the printing press. Botch repeatedly tries to convince the reader to burn the book, pleading, threatening, and offering bribes. In the end, though, he admits to the reader unmoved by his plight that burning the book would have set him free to kill the reader, and he instead counsels the reader to pass the book along to someone they hate.

An example of an exceptionally feisty living book is the *Necronomicon Ex-Mortis* in Sam Raimi's *Army of Darkness* (1992), a work that also walks the line between horror and comedy. Within the film, protagonist Ash (Bruce Campbell), having been transported to a fantasy version of the Middle Ages at the end of *Evil Dead II* (Sam Raimi, 1987), can only return to his own world with the assistance of the *Necronomicon Ex-Mortis*. After various misadventures, Ash discovers a sort of altar with three versions of the book. While the first tries

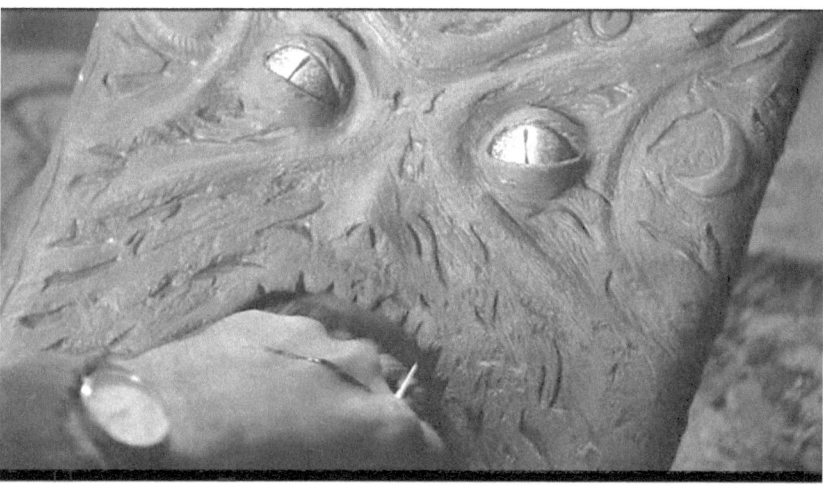

Figure 16. Ash being attacked by one of the books in *Army of Darkness*

to suck him into a kind of wormhole, the second comes to life, biting his fingers and then flying into the air and literally attacking him.

Margaret Irwin's short story "The Book" (1930) presents a particularly dark version of the living book narrative. Within the narrative, protagonist Mr. Corbett falls under the sway of a mysterious manuscript written in Latin—a remnant on his bookshelf of his uncle's theological library that "appeared to be an account of some secret society whose activities and rituals were of a nature so obscure, and, when not, so vile and terrible, that Mr. Corbett would not at first believe that this could be a record of any human mind" ([1930] 2011, 187). As his familiarity with the book grows, he discovers that new text mysteriously begins appearing at the end of the book. At first, he receives financial advice, and his speculations are extremely profitable. However, the book then begins to make other demands. "But presently, interspersed with these [financial] commands, were others of a meaningless, childish, yet revolting character such as might be invented by a decadent imbecile, or, it must be admitted, by the idle fancies of any ordinary man who permits his imagination to wander unbridled" ([1930] 2011, 189). If the directions are ignored, Mr. Corbett's financial dealings turn sour. The commands get progressively darker. First, Mr. Corbett is commanded to kill the family dog, which he attempts but is unsuccessful in doing. Then he is commanded to kill his eight-year-old daughter. When Mr. Corbett resists and throws the book onto the fire, something strangles him, and he is found dead in the morning with finger marks on his throat.

The final details of "The Book" suggest that the book is in some way inspirited by a debased entity—either the "soul" of a human magician or a demon of some sort. Irwin's story was published in 1930, so prior to digital communication, and thus assumes the stability of the material text—what is fantastic in the tale is that the book, a material object, changes on its own. New messages appear at the end of a late seventeenth-century manuscript in the same "crabbed" handwriting that constitutes the rest of the text, and nothing in the story suggests anything other than a supernatural explanation. The uncanniness of the tale thus inheres in the animacy of the book that changes, addresses, and directs its reader. The conceit here is, however, a hyperbolic variant of the idea of the corrupting book that renders in stark relief real-world anxieties concerning the uncanny animacy of *all* books. All books are in a sense "alive," conveying information to readers and prompting them to act, feel, reflect, and imagine.

One final living book narrative to consider here is Thomas Ligotti's short story "Vastarien," from *Songs of a Dead Dreamer* ([1986] 2010), which explores the ways in which books choose their readers, rather than the other way around. The tale centers on protagonist Victor Keirion, whose name not only resonates with the title of the book he finds, *Vastarien*, but can be interpreted as signaling Victor's desire to transcend the flesh—victory over the carrion—and leave the world of material reality behind. For Victor, "the only value of this world lies in its power—at certain times—to suggest another" (Ligotti). Entirely in keeping with Victoria Nelson's proposition in *The Secret Life of Puppets* that modern human beings retain a residual desire for the transcendental—one that used to find satisfaction through religion, but now is assuaged by speculative media—Victor looks to books to fulfill this need, searching for just the right one, which he discovers in a store called the Librairie de Grimoires. The book, *Vastarien*, depicts another world, one filled with the wonder that Victor finds lacking in the "real" world. In fact, according to Victor, the book does not just describe Vastarien, but *is* Vastarien: "The book, indeed, did not merely describe that strange world but, in some obscure fashion, was a true composition of the thing itself, its very form incarnate" (Ligotti). The store's proprietor, with some cajoling by a mysterious other man, allows Victor to purchase *Vastarien* at a reasonable price because "the book has found its reader" (Ligotti). As the similarity between the names "Victor Keirion" and "Vastarien" suggests, Victor is meant for the book and the book for him—the proprietor of Librairie de Grimoires claims not to have known he had it on his shelves until Victor discovered it. In the end, convinced that a mysterious force, having accessed his beloved Vastarien through him, is consuming it, Victor is confined to an asylum—where the orderlies describe the book as empty: "nothing, nothing written anywhere" (Ligotti).

Ligotti's "Vastarien" is in some ways the inverse of Irwin's "The Book." Rather than a demonic force dictating actions in the "real world," Victor is instead transported to his other world—one that appears more real to him than the material world of his mundane existence. And instead of text being added to the magical book, at the end of "Vastarien" it is subtracted—Victor feels Vastarien is being consumed, and, to his orderlies, his book contains nothing but empty pages. Despite these opposite polarities, however, in both cases the books seem to choose their readers because of the promise they hold for fulfillment. Mr. Corbett, who seems in some ways morally compromised from the start, discovers "with a slight shock that Mrs. Corbett had always bored him. [His son] Dickey he began actively to dislike as an impudent blockhead, and the two girls were as insipidly alike as white mice" (Irwin [1930] 2011, 185). Even prior to his discovery of the accursed text, he reads "with feverish haste as though he were seeking for some clue to knowledge, some secret key to existence which would quicken and inflame it, transform it from its present dull torpor to a life worthy of him and his powers" (185). It is in this state that he is attracted to the forbidden manuscript that tempts him with the possibility of "a discovery that should alter his whole life" (186). Victor Keirion, too, as noted, finds his world disenchanted and bland. Vastarien, in contrast, is a place of wonder in which "every formation suggested a thousand others, every sound disseminated everlasting echoes, every word founded a world" (Ligotti). Both Mr. Corbett and Victor find what they seek in books, but with disastrous consequences. Mr. Corbett ultimately resists the corruption of his soul compelled by the book, but at the cost of his life. Victor, in contrast, is driven mad by the apparent dissolution of his treasured fantasy world. In both stories, to achieve one's desire results in one's destruction—both Mr. Corbett and Victor are undone by living books, books that select their owners rather than being chosen by their readers.

Tales of living books that choose their readers literalize commonplace expressions such as that a book "spoke to me" or "appeared at just the right moment" and are another way that books within Gothic narrative, whether considered narrowly in the sense of actual books or broadly as written messages in any form, are always endowed with agency. While the body, as discussed in the preceding two chapters, may be the preeminent Gothic thing, books within Gothic narrative inevitably assert thing-power as they seduce, corrupt, transport, direct, attack, and effect changes to the material world. And even more clearly than the body in Gothic narrative, Gothic books enact a kind of Thing

Theory that resonates with critical paradigms asserting the depths, agency, and "vibrancy" (cf. Bennett 2010) of material objects. Books are in some senses easy to animate because we already attribute thing-power to books in the ways we discuss them. Books can be dangerous, mesmerizing, corrupting, inspiring, and so on. Gothic narratives of corrupting and accursed books therefore make plain that the human relationship to the nonhuman is not a one-way street or simple hierarchy of subject/object. Books in this sense are exemplary of Gothic objects, highlighting the instability of the subject/object dichotomy and the uncanny animacy of things.

6
Building
Bigger on the Inside

In this final chapter of this study on Gothic things, our attention shifts from bodies and books to buildings—that is, to the human experiences of place and architecture. Haunted houses have received their fair share of critical scrutiny.[1] In this chapter, however, I'm less interested with the ghost that materializes in the Gothic castle (or house or other structure) than in the castle itself as a space that creates the conditions for the haunting. In some cases—the more familiar narrative of the haunted house—the building houses the ghost and serves as the precondition for its materialization; in other cases—more interesting from the point of view of this study—it is the house itself that does the haunting, exerting a kind of unsettling agency that undoes the animate/inanimate subject/object dichotomies. In both cases, however, haunted house narratives highlight the *uncanny agency of place*. As with the other types of Gothic things addressed in this study, haunted houses are the exceptions that prove the rule as they emphasize the active role that place plays in the constitution of human experience. What narratives of haunted and haunting houses (and other types of buildings) make clear is not only that all places are haunted, but that all places also *haunt*—that is, to adapt the language used throughout this study, places exert what we may refer to as "place-power" that actively shapes human affect and understanding.

From Space to Place

What I am calling place-power—the agency of place—has been curiously downplayed in the tradition of humanistic geography associated with Yi-Fu Tuan, which explores how space becomes place primarily in terms of what we might consider human cognitive colonization of a given location. For Tuan in *Space and Place* (1977), space is abstract and undifferentiated (6). It is "that which allows movement" (6), and its openness has a threatening quality. Space becomes place through a process of objectification. "Place," in contrast, is "whatever stable object catches our attention" (161). Where space is associated with movement, "place is pause" (6). In the time that our attention is arrested, a kind of cognitive colonization of location occurs as affect is elicited and meaning is superimposed. As Robert T. Tally Jr. explains in his summary of Tuan in *Topophrenia* (2018), "Place . . . by definition is associated with a certain way of seeing that might well be called 'critical,' even 'literary critical,' inasmuch as interpretation, evaluation, and analysis of its meaning, functioning, and effects are presupposed the moment a given portion of space becomes recognizable as place" (18). Put concisely, space becomes place when it is transformed into a meaningful object for a human subject.

Tally, in his overview of Tuan, notes the egocentrism of this interpretive process that relies on the perceiver's "subjective experience" to create meaning (19), and his own approach to "geocriticism" retains this subjective emphasis in which places "are invested with profoundly affective or emotional content for the subject that perceives, moves about, and in the broadest sense inhabits" them (20); however, Tally also acknowledges that the transformation of space into place is more complicated. Spaces may be apprehended subjectively, but they are only comprehensible as places "when located within or in reference to a non- or suprasubjective ensemble of spatial relations, sites, networks, circuits, and so on" (24). Put differently, places are not isolated and discrete, but nodes within existing networks. Tally explains further that "if, as Tuan insists, place is defined in part as a site imbued with meaning, therefore subject to interpretation and thus an appropriate subject for literary criticism, it also needs to be understood that the language used to describe and to interpret place itself engenders or conditions the place. The place is a text, but one that is necessarily informed, and indeed formed, by other texts as well" (24). Summing up his approach, Tally asserts that "after all, a place is only a place because of the ways in which we, individually and collectively, organize space in such a way as to mark the *topos* as special, to set it apart from the spaces surrounding and infusing it. Our understanding of a particular place is determined by our own experiences, by our point of view, including our biases and our wishful thinking" (40).

Perhaps Tuan, Tally, humanistic geography, and geocriticism assume it goes without saying, but it is nevertheless remarkable that what is omitted from a consideration of what makes a place a place are the qualities of the place itself. As explained by Tuan and Tally, the epistemological colonization of space that transforms it into place has everything to do with the perceiving subject's orientation and seemingly nothing to do with the qualities of that which is perceived. The perceiving subject is active, the space perceived not only wholly passive, but almost absent in these descriptions. But there must be something of the space to arrest the perceiver's attention in the first place in order to initiate the transformation into place. We might therefore revise Tally's conclusion as follows: After all, a place is only a place because something of that place—what Roland Barthes might characterize as the punctum—"catches" the perceiver (see Barthes, *Camera Lucida* [1982], 27 and *passim*). Once attention is arrested, sensory details such as shape, size, color, texture, sound, and smell conspire with memories, associations, biases, and so on to evoke affect as interpretation is overlaid upon location. Humans invest places with meanings, but the qualities of the places themselves play an active role in influencing interpretation and affect. Places are never just "there," passive substrates for human cognitive colonization; they actively assert themselves, in a sense seeking out their perceivers. *Something of the space causes the perceiver to pause, and the qualities of that space then help shape interpretation.*

While curiously underplayed in humanistic geography and geocriticism, an awareness of place-power is central to that school of geography called psychogeography and to architecture and has also entered the popular consciousness through the Chinese notions of *shi* and *feng shui*. Psychogeography, as explained by Merlin Coverly in *Psychogeography* (2018), was a 1950s outgrowth of avant-garde French Lettrism of the 1940s and 1950s. As defined by French philosopher Guy Debord in 1955 in his "Introduction to a Critique of Urban Geography," psychogeography attempts to study "the precise laws and specific effects of the geographical environment, consciously organized or not, on the emotion and behavior of individuals" (quoted in Coverly 2018, 14). Coverly explains that psychogeography "describes the point at which psychology and geography collide, a means of calibrating the behavioural impact of place" (14). Associated particularly with urban environments, the practitioners of psychogeography sought to "uncover the true nature of that which lies beneath the flux of the everyday"—to overcome the "banalization" of the everyday and recover a sense of surprise and mystery (17). As Coverly explains, psychogeography was associated with "the act of urban wandering; the spirit of political radicalism; allied to a playful sense of subversion and governed by an inquiry into the ways in which we can transform our relationship to the urban environment." "The entire project," continues Coverly, "is then further coloured by an engagement with the occult, and is one that is as preoccupied with excavating the past as it is with recording the present" (18).

Perhaps because architecture concerns man-made structures in particular, rather than space and place writ large, architectural theory has been more attentive to place-power and the active role buildings play in eliciting intellectual and affective responses than traditional geography. Going all the way back to ancient Rome, Vitruvius, for example, in his *The Ten Books of Architecture* (likely the first century B.C.E., the only treatise on Classical architecture surviving in its entirety), identified the three essential elements necessary for a well-designed building as "firmness," "commodity," and "delight" (*firmitas, utilitas,* and *venustas*; see "Firmness, Commodity, and Delight" [2011]). Firmness has to do with stability—whether or not the building will come down around your ears. Commodity has to do with how successfully the building fulfills its intended objectives. And delight, of course, has to do with aesthetics—a well-constructed building should not only be functional, but pleasing to the eye. Consideration of delight then quickly segues into contemplation of various sensory qualities, including color, line, texture, balance, proportion, and so on. The experience of architecture, therefore, has to do with both intellectual appraisal of how solid the building is and the extent to which it does what it is supposed to do, as well as the affect it elicits.

Geoffrey Broadbent's meditation on architecture, *Design in Architecture: Architecture and the Human Sciences* (1973), suggests, however, that firmness and commodity should in fact be subsumed under the umbrella of delight, which Broadbent introduces as "the fundamental condition of architecture" (viii). While not quite affect theory, Broadbent's point is that our overall feeling about a building—whether we delight in it or not—is a combination of intellectual appraisal and affective response to the building's qualities. As part of this evaluation, Broadbent notes that buildings excite the senses beyond the visual. In addition to looking at buildings, people "touch them, hear sounds, feel warm or cold within them. Each building even has a characteristic smell" (viii). And the meaningfulness of architecture is then complicated still further by personal experience and associations. Broadbent explains that differences in personal taste will make it difficult for the architect to please everyone. In addition, individuals will also apply their personal values: "not merely monetary values, but values also in terms of symbolism, of what buildings ought to look like, what other buildings they seemed to resemble, whether they appeared bright and cheerful, dignified, efficient and so on" (xii). "People," Broadbent continues, "will read such meanings into our buildings whether we want them to or not, however 'functional' or aesthetically neutral the architect tries to make them" (xii). The conclusion Broadbent derives from this is that "the building itself, the object of our perception, is constant, a physical *thing* which is quite unchanged by our perceiving it. But the lifetime of experience which, respectively, we bring to the perceiving of it, is different for each of us and this accounts for the differences in our perceptions of it" (ix).

Broadbent's commentary is useful here because, contra Tuan's and Tally's more general considerations of place, his meditation on the ways we experience buildings highlights the interactive nature of the relationship. A building is not some *tabula rasa* awaiting our imaginative colonization; instead, it is an object with qualities that participate in eliciting intellectual and affective responses from perceivers—responses that will also be shaped and inflected by personal experiences and associations. And, of course, this analysis can be extended to natural environments, as well. The meaningfulness of a swamp, for example, for someone moving through it, will be shaped by many factors including temperature, humidity, sun and shade, smell, sound, and the texture of the ground or boat. These qualities will then combine with the perceiver's tastes, experiences, associations, and, indeed, physical disposition to create an overall experience of place—someone young, healthy, dressed properly, and raised in proximity to the swamp will experience its qualities very differently from someone infirm and unfamiliar with the environment. None of this is surprising—and that's the point: The qualities of places—whether man-made or natural—play an active role in structuring our experiences of them. *Spaces are never passive objects simply there and then endowed with meaning*; they assert themselves in ways both obvious and subtle and, in an act of reciprocal creation, create their perceivers as perceivers in the process.

Of note here as well is Gaston Bachelard's *Poetics of Space*, first published in 1958, because it presents another approach to thinking about place-power. *The Poetics of Space* outlines what Bachelard refers to as "topoanalysis," which he defines as "the systematic psychological study of the sites of our intimate lives" (Bachelard [1958] 1994, 8). What Bachelard then offers is a phenomenological exploration of the meaning of domestic spaces and their furnishings, as well as larger outdoor spaces, that find frequent expression in poetry and literature. For our purposes in this chapter on houses that haunt, it is notable that Bachelard regards the house as "a privileged entity for a study of phenomenological study of the intimate values of inside space" (3) because the house is bound up with notions of shelter, comfort, memory, dreams, and so on. Bachelard addresses the house along a vertical axis, with the cellar characterized as the "*dark entity* of the house" (18), a space of darkness and memory, and the attic as that which, in reaching toward the sky, strives to break free of earthly bonds. Importantly, Bachelard is not addressing actual homes; rather, his inquiry is into the symbolic and archetypal meanings of architecture. However, Bachelard's contention that "a house that has been experienced is not an inert box. Inhabited space transcends geometrical space" ([1958] 1994, 47), is one we can extend not only to all houses in poetry and literature, but to all houses in the "real world," as well. Houses and other architectural structures, as will be developed later, are always "bigger on the inside"—spaces of memory and experience that exert place-power as they structure our experiences of them and elicit affective responses.

This emphasis on the qualities of place as evocative of affect is also at the heart of the Chinese concepts of *shi* and *feng shui*. As explained by Bennett, *shi* refers to "the style, energy, propensity, trajectory, or élan inherent in a specific arrangement of things" (2010, 35). Similar in some ways to atmosphere, *shi* is the "dynamic force" (35) created by a specific configuration of things and, for Bennett, reflects the agency of the assemblage—the way that a particular configuration of things exerts itself. *Feng shui* then is the art of managing *shi*—of creating spatial arrangements and layouts that influence the flow of *shi* in favorable ways (see Cho 2019). While the underlying theory of invisible forces or vital energy that must be balanced for human health and well-being is speculative, one need not subscribe to the belief in them to accept that the qualities of particular places—their layouts, orientations, accoutrements, and so on—combine to evoke affective responses ranging from delight to dread. Places, finally, through the complex amalgamation of sensory perception, intellectual apprehension, memory, and association, have a character, feeling, "aura," or "vibe." They may be comfortable or ominous, melancholy or cheerful, cold or caring. What is interesting about the ideas of *shi* and *feng shui* is that, rather than the perceiver transforming space into place through the act of apprehension, it is the space that acts on the experiencer of it, influencing the well-being of both in ways that escape conscious detection. Poorly organized places can make one sick, whereas well-organized ones promote health. This is where the Gothic comes into play for us because at the heart of the genre is a kind of literary *feng shui* in which buildings exert place-power, inverting the subject/object dichotomy in the way that Gothic things invariably do by assuming uncanny life as they freeze, mortify, and frustrate characters deprived of agency. A consistent theme of the Gothic since its origins has been the power of place to create the experience of haunting.

Haunted Houses

Despite the obvious awareness that Gothic tales of ghosts and hauntings often depend on architecture to such an extent that the haunted house story is a well-established subgenre of supernatural fiction and a building is part of the title of many Gothic works ("The Fall of the House of Usher," *The Haunting of Hill House, Hell House, The House on Haunted Hill,* Disney's *The Haunted*

Mansion, The House of Leaves, and so on), something curious happens when scholars and critics turn their attention to Gothic tales of hauntings and haunted houses: that which is often most immediately striking—the physical geography of the space—quickly retreats into the background as haunting is established not as a function or extension of architecture, but rather of memory.[2] The house is there at the start and throughout as the horizon of possibility, but is never quite in focus, and it quickly becomes a metaphor for psychic space. Leslie Fiedler's overview of the Gothic in his famous *Love and Death in the American Novel* ([1960] 1992) illustrates this slippage into metaphor:

> Beneath the haunted castle lies the dungeon keep: the womb from whose darkness the ego first emerged, the tomb to which it knows it must return at last. Beneath the crumbling shell of paternal authority, lies the maternal blackness, imagined by the gothic writer as a prison, a torture chamber—from which the cries of the kidnapped anima cannot even be heard. The upper and lower levels of the ruined castle or abbey represent the contradictory fears at the heart of gothic terror: the dread of the super-ego, whose splendid battlements have been battered but not quite cast down—and of the id, whose buried darkness abounds in dark visions no stormer of the castle had even touched. (132)

Fiedler's analysis here is the Gothic version of Bachelardian topoanalysis, inflected more obviously by way of Freud. The castle, mansion, or house represents the psyche as plotted along a vertical axis. The dungeon/cellar/basement below represents the unconscious, the repository of darkest fears and desires, while the upper levels stand for authority, order, obedience, and conformity. The castle or house, then, merely becomes the physical backdrop against which the drama of contending historical and psychological forces plays out.

This is similarly the case in other studies of the Gothic (excellent though they may be in many respects), such as Kate Ferguson Ellis's *The Contested Castle: Gothic Novels and the Subversion of Domestic Ideology* (1989), in which the titular "castle" is used almost entirely as a metonym for "family." Marie Mulvey-Roberts's *The Handbook of the Gothic* ([1998] 2009) lacks entries for house, castle, or setting altogether, and its discussion of Gothic architecture instead addresses the "Gothic Revival" in British architecture in the late eighteenth and nineteenth centuries. This is similarly the case with David Punter's *A New Companion to The Gothic* (2012). Glennis Byron and Dale Townshend's *The Gothic World* (2013) has a cluster of excellent essays called "Gothic Spaces," none of which, however, actually focuses on the roles architecture plays within Gothic narrative—for example, Nicole Reynolds's "Gothic and the Architectural Imagination, 1740–1840" looks at the ways Gothic literature drew inspiration from Gothic architecture, and Tamara Wagner's "Gothic and the Victorian Home" considers how the Gothic invades the domestic realm in Victorian fiction. Eve Kosofsky Sedgwick—later so important to affect theory—initially seems as though she is going to challenge this psychogeographic model in *The Coherence of Gothic Conventions* (1986) by shifting the emphasis from depth to surface. She explains in her first chapter that critics have often attempted to explain the recurrence of Gothic conventions by "privileging the spatial metaphor of depth . . . taking the metaphor to represent a model of the human self" (11). Sedgwick proposes instead a different spatial model: one that emphasizes that, within the Gothic, "the strongest energies inhere in the surface" (12). And yet, while emphasizing her approach to the Gothic as a "spatial model" (12), Sedgwick remains focused on figurative rather than literal spaces.

Even studies that attend specifically to haunted houses ironically tend to have little to say about the houses themselves. Dale Bailey's *American Nightmares: The Haunted House Formula in American Popular Fiction* (1999) is a case in point. In Bailey's introductory chapter, "Welcome to the Funhouse: Gothic and the Architecture of Subversion," he foregrounds the centrality of setting to the Gothic genre: "In few other genres does setting play such a significant and defining role. . . . In gothic fiction, setting is destiny—and it's been so from the first" (4). Bailey notes that contemporary haunted house narratives follow a particular formula involving a "sentient and malign" house into which a family enters and is forced to confront supernatural encroachments and familial fault lines (6). Bailey then shifts away in his introduction from thinking about architecture and focuses instead on haunted house narratives as metaphors for "the clash between American ideals and realities" (6); his case study to develop this thesis, curiously, is American realist author William Dean Howells's *The Rise of Silas Lapham*—which includes no "actual" ghosts and is seldom categorized as Gothic. Rebecca Janicker's *The Literary Haunted House: Lovecraft, Matheson, King and the Horror in Between* (2015) addresses space more directly, but mainly in generic terms: "troubled spaces" (18), the space of the home or domestic space, "haunted suburbia," and so on. And her focus is on how her chosen authors and texts, as in Bailey's study, "use haunting to engage with history and ideology" (20).

Most attentive to the roles of houses in haunted house narratives—and most congruent with the present study—is Barry Curtis, who, in *Dark Places: The Haunted House in Film* (2008), explores how narratives of haunting establish the agency of the house. While attentive to the ways in which ghosts and narratives of hauntings "have served as powerful metaphors for persistent themes of loss, memory, retribution and confrontation with unacknowledged and unresolved histories" (10), Curtis also bears in mind throughout the ways that setting is primary and structures these engagements with ideological issues. Curtis observes that "all houses are haunted—by memories, by the history of their sites, by their owners' fantasies and projections or by the significance they acquire for agents or strangers. Houses inscribe themselves within their dwellers, they socialize and structure the relations within families, and provide spaces for expression and self-realization in a complex interactive relationship." Put more succinctly, "haunted houses are both possessed and possessing" (66)—they are owned and yet, in a way, own their owners. "The archetype of the haunted house," then, for Curtis "is a place where the past is still alive and capable of making temporal connections that appear as spatial coordinates" (40). The particular configuration of the haunting is a product of the specific architecture of the space haunted.

Gothic Houses

My argument is that not only is there no haunted house without the house, but that the room or building is as important to the haunting as the ghost. It is true that the meaning of "house" in Gothic narratives often quickly inclines toward "family," including ancestors, lineage, patrimony, inheritance, and the like—which, in part, may explain why architecture in such discussions is given short shrift. But questions concerning these issues are often catalyzed precisely by an uncanny physical structure that makes clear that haunting is every bit as much a function of architecture as memory. Even in Gothic tales that have an "actual" ghost, the ghost is inevitably articulated through the uncanny agency of the physical structure. Put succinctly, what marks a haunting is the unsettling liveliness of the house. In more conventional Gothic tales, the living presence of the past finds expression directly through architecture in the present. In more modern narratives, the house is haunted by the uncanny agency of matter itself.

Indeed, the Gothic as a genre itself finds its origins in a story about a haunted castle—although the relationship between ghost and physical structure is unique. Horace Walpole's *The Castle of Otranto* ([1764] 2014) opens with a prophecy: "The castle and lordship of Otranto should pass from the present family, whenever the real owner should be grown too large to inhabit it" (17). The playful absurdity of *Otranto* is to literalize this prophecy in the form of a gigantic phantom that cannot be accommodated by the castle. First, usurper Manfred's son Conrad is crushed by a giant helmet; then an immense foot and part of a leg are witnessed in a chamber; a huge sword is delivered, and the narrative culminates with the appearance of the apparition of Alfonso, poisoned by Manfred's grandfather, whose titanic size collapses much of the castle: "The walls of the castle behind Manfred were thrown down with a mighty force, and the form of Alfonso, dilated to an immense magnitude, appeared in the centre of the ruins" (103).

Haunting in *Otranto* is thus represented—at least in part—as a discontinuity in *scale* between physical space and an inhabitant of that space. The castle is literally too small for the ghost of Alfonso, who is only represented synecdochally—a helmet, a foot, a sword—until the very end when the materialization of his full form explodes the castle walls. While this incompatibility in size quickly shades into metaphor—the "house" of Manfred in the sense of family and lineage is overtaken by past sins, and the bulwarks protecting his illegitimate reign crumble—the ghost of Alfonso primarily finds expression in relation to the constricting space of the castle, and, in order for the ghosts of the past to be put to rest, the castle walls literally have to come down. The repressed past can no longer be contained, and the house—in both senses of the word—crumbles.[3]

Otranto is unique in having the ghost be bigger than the castle. Typically, ghost and house (or castle or hotel or asylum, etc.) overlap, with the space of the haunting mapped onto the building and its grounds and both ghost and building expanding in uncanny ways that circumscribe human agency. What characters in Gothic narratives involving ghosts and hauntings (whether or not the ghost turns out to be "real") experience—and what readers and viewers experience vicariously—is what we could call *architectural dread* as the spaces through which the characters move are perceived as ominous, unstable, irrational, and often malevolent. Particularly in tales of ghosts in which an entire structure is presented as haunted rather than a specific room, the haunting fills the space like a mist, suffusing the entire house or castle. Although the ghost may coalesce in particular locations at specific moments, the entire building is haunted.

Roger Luckhurst has discussed what I am referring to as architectural dread in connection specifically with corridors. He observes in "Corridor Gothic" that "the corridor is everywhere in Gothic fiction and has become particularly pervasive in contemporary horror film" (2018, 296), and then he proceeds to offer a history of the development of the corridor as an architectural space, a quick overview of its ubiquity in Gothic literature and horror film, and a consideration of the affect elicited by the corridor as "interstitial space" (307). As concerns affect, Luckhurst detaches the corridor from the Freudian model of the uncanny: "Where Freud offers a psychology of depth, of vertical archaeological strata . . . , the horizontal plane of the corridor resists the straited metaphors that turn basements or attics into spaces of depth" (304). The corridor instead, asserts Luckhurst, referencing the famous scenes from Kubrick's *The Shining* (1980) of Danny (Danny Lloyd) pedaling his Big Wheel through the hallways of the haunted Overlook Hotel, is framed by Kubrick's camera as a "space of anticipatory *Angst*" (305). Luckhurst further asserts that this affective shift from the uncanny to *Angst* reflects a twentieth-century shift toward exploring "the dread engendered by public or institutional corridors" (306).

Luckhurst's approach is useful here because, rather than slipping rapidly from a consideration of physical space to its metaphoric connotations (although that slippage occurs toward the end of his essay as he shifts to "corridors of power"), he focuses on the space itself: its history and the affect associated with it. The corridor can't be uncanny because it was never homely to begin with. Something similar is often the case in Gothic narratives of haunted castles, mansions, asylums, and so on—although I would call it dread rather than *Angst* because it is more object-oriented. What oppresses in narratives of haunted buildings is often first and foremost the ponderous size and weight of the building itself: place-power. The scale of the structure renders it intimidating and inhospitable. It is alien from the start; even before any specific phenomena of haunting manifest, the house already haunts, and the haunting then becomes an expression of the alien quality of the house itself.

While ghosts can haunt small spaces, consider where they are most commonly encountered in fiction and film: castles, mansions, asylums, hospitals, hotels, and other large buildings. The mansion in 1999's *The Haunting* (Jan de Bont), the asylum in the film *Session 9* (Brad Anderson, 2001), and the Overlook

Figure 17. Harlaxton Manor, used as the exterior for 1999's *The Haunting*

Figure 18. Danvers State Mental Hospital used for the film *Session 9*

Hotel in Kubrick's version of King's *The Shining* are cases in point. Why such large spaces? This is because, as in *Otranto*, haunting is often a function of scale—in most cases, however, the discontinuity is between the immense size of the space and much smaller size of the protagonist. The haunting begins with a sense of physical disorientation in space as the character(s) attempt to negotiate a labyrinth-like interior that keeps getting bigger as more turns are taken, new rooms negotiated, trap doors and hidden passages uncovered, and new levels investigated. Such buildings are "unhomely" right from the start, anathema to human comfort because of their vastness, their emptiness, their coldness, their twists and turns and shadows that limit perception, and the

Figure 19. The Overlook Hotel in *The Shining*

mysteries they conceal. The first manifestation of the haunting is in relation to physical space perceived as confusing, inhospitable, daunting, and/or malevolent. Architectural dread precedes and catalyzes the materialization of the ghost.[4]

Stories of hauntings set in less imposing locations are nevertheless similarly about the uneasy human inhabitation of physical space, although they are generally more easily assimilable to Freudian interpretation through the lens of the *unheimlich* as a comfortable or familiar space becomes strange—bringing out the latent alien element always already present in the homely. Often before any ghost is even glimpsed in Gothic narrative, the haunting reveals itself through the manipulation of physical space. Possessions disappear and reappear in different places, doors and windows open and close on their own, furniture moves, appliances go on and off, and the physical space itself is reconfigured. Of course, these things happen in real life, too, as we forget where we've put something or as things slide, shift, short out, break, or move as a result of entirely natural forces. Gothic narrative, however, ascribes a kind of malevolent intentionality to these changes, amplifying the types of uncertainty we confront on a daily basis in relation to space and the objects occupying it. In the film *The Sixth Sense* (M. Night Shyamalan, 1999), for example, the mother (Lynn Sear, played by Toni Collette) of a boy who can see and speak with ghosts is finally convinced of the existence of ghosts when she turns around in her kitchen to discover all the cupboards have suddenly opened.

In Sam Raimi's *Evil Dead II* (1987), the malevolent force terrorizing protagonist Ash (Bruce Campbell) causes the entire cabin to come to life as a mounted stag's head, a table lamp, curtains, books, sofa cushions, a wall clock, and so on

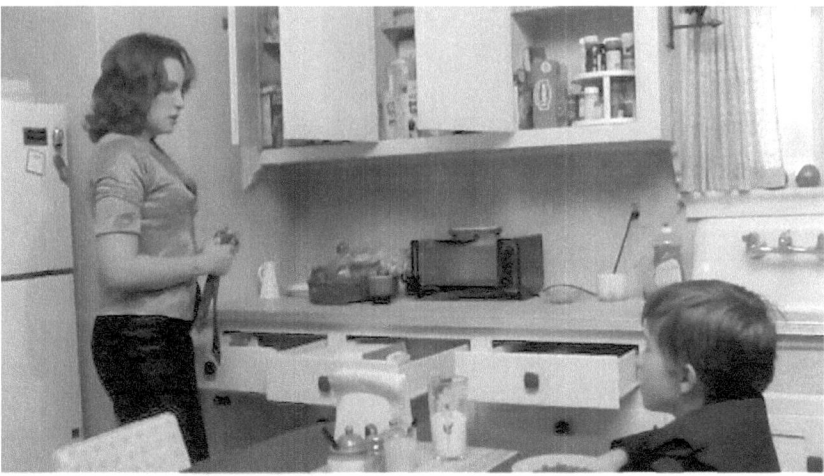

Figure 20. Drawers and cabinets open by themselves in M. Night Shyamalan's *The Sixth Sense*

Figure 21. Ash confronts a world of animate things in *Evil Dead II*

all move and mock the now-isolated and unstable Ash while the camera careens wildly, giving the impression that the entire space is shifting. In both films, the supernatural manifests through alterations of the physical space as drawers and cabinets open, objects move, and the world tilts.

Part of the uncanniness of Gothic narratives of ghosts, hauntings, and other supernatural manifestations is also the sense that architecture has become permeable as boundaries between outside and inside dissolve. In some cases, as in *The Amityville Horror* (Stuart Rosenberg, 1979), *Candyman* (Bernard Rose, 1992), and Stephen King's novel version of *The Shining* (1977), this may involve the invasion of insect life as flies or bees swarm within a house or building, seeming to come out of nowhere. In other cases, it may involve the encroachment of plant life, as in the infamous "violated by the woods" scene in *Evil Dead* (Sam Raimi, 1981) or the tree that crashes through the children's bedroom window in *Poltergeist* (Tobe Hooper, 1982). More often than not, though, the dissolution of physical boundaries is conveyed through the sense of a lack of not just privacy but safety as walls and doors serve as no impediment to incorporeal phantoms. This is exemplified within film by the ubiquity of bathroom scenes in which something appears in a mirror or manifests while someone is in the shower or bathtub. Not only is the bathroom a space of vulnerability, but bathrooms also tend to be hard, slippery spaces of porcelain, tile, and glass.[5] When the ghost or other supernatural terror invades the bathroom, it highlights the absence of safety and privacy afforded by walls. Architecture is undone as both firmness and commodity, to refer back to Vitruvius, are compromised.

Gothic space is also elastic—it expands and contracts in response to human encroachment. In Gothic literature, there is always the sense that buildings keep growing, stretching out into the darkness—that, looking ahead to the discussion of *House of Leaves*, the building is impossibly bigger on the inside than on the outside. There is always more to explore in the haunted castle or house, more passageways to be traversed, chambers to be discovered, and secrets revealed beneath trapdoors and bricked-up walls. In film, this sense of expanding space is conveyed particularly well through dolly zoom shots that cause space to seem to stretch when the camera zooms in or out while physically moving in the other direction. Alfred Hitchcock famously used this effect in *Vertigo* (1958) to convey the crippling vertigo Jimmy Stewart's character experiences when looking down from high places. In the horror film, the effect is often literalized as some supernatural agency seeks to torment a protagonist by causing a hallway literally to stretch. This is the case in *Poltergeist*, for example, as the mother, Diane Freeling (JoBeth Williams) seeks to rescue her children from their room, and similar scenes of stretching hallways are pervasive in contemporary horror (see, for example, *The People under the Stairs* [Wes Craven, 1991], *The Descent* [Neil Marshall, 2005], and *Insidious* [James Wan, 2010]).[6]

As Luckhurst addresses, shots of long corridors—as in *The Shining*—are staples of contemporary horror. As the camera advances, explains Luckhurst, "it multiplies anticipatory fear from the off-screen space of the doorways and voids it passes," and the length "allows things to advance or recede ominously from the viewer" (2018, 302). Roman Polanski uses expressionistic corridor shots to reveal his characters' psychic states (Luckhurst 2018, 303), David Lynch uses them to "evoke anticipatory fear" (303), and Stanley Kubrick uses them to convey the eerie sense of "anticipatory *Angst*" (305). But corridor dread in Gothic

Figure 22. The stretching hallway in *Poltergeist*

narrative doesn't pertain just to what is to come, but also to anxiety about what is: the human inhabitation of space. Scenes of stretching hallways are not just phenomenological reflections of their characters' terror; they are presented as literal alterations of a space rendered unstable through supernatural agency. The stretching hallway is, of course, the stuff of nightmares—the inability to move or reach one's destination despite one's efforts. But it also reflects in exaggerated form the very real experiences of negotiating long corridors of airports, government buildings, universities, hotels, shopping malls, hospitals, and so on in heightened affective states such as anxiety or dread. The stretching hallway thus reflects our own experiences not just of diminished scale as the space dwarfs us, but also of the suspicion of a kind of malign agency of space that extends purposefully, complicating our passage from point A to point B—which is very much the stuff of Freud's uncanny.

Haunted house narratives, however, one might reasonably object, do not always involve castles, grand mansions, hotels, and endless corridors. They may instead be humble homes, shacks, even individual rooms within a home. Space and architecture, nevertheless, continue to exert place-power and remain central to the experience of the haunting for characters and audience. Setting is never just setting—it is intimately interconnected with plot, influencing the action in terms of character possibilities. Isolated cabins in the woods or decrepit shacks by the roadside, for example, elicit architectural dread from the moment they are first depicted for both characters and readers/viewers because they are—quite reasonably—spaces of danger that could contain a variety of

Figure 23. The perfect vacation spot? The cabin from *The Evil Dead*

real-world threats ranging from violent or deranged people to rotting floorboards, animals, and rusty nails—and the conventions of genre then lead us to expect that the initial dread usually experienced by characters and shared by readers and viewers will be amplified by mysterious phenomena working in concert with spooky surroundings. In such instances, architecture not only foreshadows haunting from the start but influences how it manifests.

Haunted houses need not be old and decrepit, however; in the end, the main prerequisite is some kind of traumatic history associated with the building or the space on which it is built. Indeed, this is the haunted house formula at its most basic: building + tragic past. Through exploration of the haunted building, the tragic history is unearthed. But house and haunting are not separable; *the haunting is a characteristic or affordance of the house,* like worn floorboards, rusty pipes, or cracked tile, that reflects the house's history. From this perspective, all houses are—or will become—haunted, metaphorically bigger on the inside, marked by and gesturing toward the histories of land on which they are built and of those who have inhabited the house. Gothic narratives of haunted houses finally are exaggerated tales of place-power, making clear how places assert agency, acting—sometimes powerfully—upon those who interact with them.

Houses That Haunt

Whether or not they contain an "actual" ghost, all places thus "haunt"—assert themselves, "stick" to us, elicit affective responses, and shape interpretations. Haunted houses in Gothic narrative are in this way the exception that proves the rule: They are hyperbolic representations of the kind of place-power all buildings assert. For the remainder of this chapter, I would like to focus on haunted house narratives that foreground the Gothic's intimate interconnections with contemporary Thing Theory through a focus on place-power. These are unconventional ghost stories for the most part because the house is what haunts—but in haunting they make clear that all houses are haunted and, by virtue of being haunted, in turn haunt those who interact with them.

No Affinity with the Air of Heaven: "The Fall of the House of Usher"

A useful starting point for any consideration of houses that haunt is Edgar Allan Poe's 1839 Gothic tale "The Fall of the House of Usher"—a story that complicates interpretation by everywhere overlapping the dual meanings of the term "house" referring both to physical structure and family lineage. Although many different approaches have been taken to interpreting the story, for our purposes it is convenient to consider it as an example of place-power and architectural dread. As Bailey observes, despite the ambiguity of meaning embedded in the title (house or family?), "we are introduced to the cracked facade of the mansion long before the neurasthenic figures of Roderick and Madeline Usher make their appearance" (Poe [1839] 1996, 21)—and the house is very much part and parcel of the oppressive atmosphere of the landscape in which it is situated.

While in keeping with the geography of Poe's tales in general, where the setting for "The Fall of the House of Usher" falls on the map is ambiguous; nevertheless, the setting is described in detail, with an emphasis on the affect evoked by it from the observer. The house is located within a "singularly dreary tract of country" and sits on the edge of a "black and lurid tarn" amid "sedges" and "white trunks of decayed trees" (317). The unnamed narrator fancies that "about the whole mansion and domain there hung an atmosphere peculiar to themselves and their immediate vicinity—an atmosphere which had no affinity with the air of heaven, but which had reeked up from the decayed trees, and the gray wall, and the silent tarn—a pestilent and mystic vapour, dull, sluggish, faintly discernible, and leaden-hued" (319).

The house, too, is described in detail—and, as has often been noted, in a way that anthropomorphizes it. It has "bleak walls" and "vacant eye-like windows" (317). Focusing on the house in more detail, the narrator explains that

> its principal feature seemed to be that of an excessive antiquity. The discoloration of ages had been great. Minute fungi overspread the whole exterior, hanging in a fine tangled web-work from the eaves. Yet all this was apart from any extraordinary dilapidation. No portion of the masonry had fallen; and there appeared to be a wild inconsistency between its still perfect adaptation of parts, and the crumbling condition of the individual stones. In this there was much that reminded me of the specious totality of old wood-work which has rotted for long years in some neglected vault, with no disturbance from the breath of the external air. Beyond this indication of extensive decay, however, the fabric gave little token of instability. Perhaps the eye of a scrutinizing observer might have discovered a barely perceptible fissure, which, extending from the roof of the building in front, made its way down the wall in a zigzag direction, until it became lost in the sullen waters of the tarn. (319–20)

The house is comparable to a head with eye-like windows, the crack suggestive of mental instability. Further, there is an inconsistency between the decayed parts and still-standing totality.

The appearance of the house, together with the general milieu in which it stands, depresses the narrator's spirits. "With the first glimpse of the building," he recalls, "a sense of insufferable gloom pervaded my spirit" (317). He is afflicted with "an utter depression of soul which I can compare to no earthly sensation more properly than to the after-dream of the reveller upon opium—the bitter lapse into everyday life—the hideous dropping off of the veil." "There was an iciness," he continues, "a sinking, a sickening of the heart—an unredeemed dreariness of thought which no goading of the imagination could torture into aught of the sublime" (317). The house and environment exert place-power over the narrator from the moment of his arrival and lead him to reflect on the ways that "there are combinations of very simple natural objects which have the power of thus affecting us" (317). The narrator is a vibrant materialist *avant la lettre*.

Again and again, as a number of critics have noted, the story emphasizes atmosphere.[7] This is sometimes in relation to mood, as when the narrator explains, "I felt I breathed an atmosphere of sorrow. An air of stern, deep, and irredeemable gloom hung over and pervaded all" (321) or when he refers to the "oppressive atmosphere" of the vault in which Lady Madeline's body is placed (329). Just as frequently, however, these references are to literal atmospheric effects: physical environment and climactic conditions. As noted previously, the narrator claims to perceive "reek[ing] up from the decayed trees, and the gray wall, and the silent tarn—a pestilent and mystic vapor" (319). As the story proceeds toward its conclusion, the wind picks up and a strange glow rises from the tarn:

> A whirlwind had apparently collected its force in our vicinity; for there were frequent and violent alterations in the direction of the wind; and the exceeding density of the clouds (which hung so low as to press upon the turrets of the house) did not prevent our perceiving the lifelike velocity with which they flew careering from all points against each other, without passing away into the distance. . . . But the under surfaces of the huge masses of agitated vapour, as well as all terrestrial objects immediately around us, were glowing in the unnatural light of a faintly luminous and distinctly visible gaseous exhalation which hung about and enshrouded the mansion. (331)

The narrator, attempting to calm the agitated Roderick Usher, suggests that the glow may have its "ghastly origin in the rank miasma of the tarn" (331).

Atmosphere conspires with architecture in the story most significantly in Roderick's theory concerning the "the sentience of all vegetable things" (327) that focuses on the house. Reflecting the narrator's own initial thoughts about the ability of particular organizations of things to evoke affect, the narrator explains that, for Roderick, "The conditions of the sentience had been here, he imagined, fulfilled in the method of collocation of these stones—in the order of their arrangement, as well as in that of the *fungi* that overspread them, and of the decayed trees which stood around—above all, in the long undisturbed endurance of this arrangement." The persistence of this arrangement over time then creates an atmosphere that itself affects those who enter it: "Its evidence—the evidence of the sentience—was to be seen, [Roderick] said . . . in the graduate yet certain condensation of an atmosphere of their own about the waters and the walls. The result was discoverable, he added, in that silent, yet importunate and terrible influence which for centuries had moulded the destinies of his family, and which made *him* what I now saw him—what he was" (327–28). Proto-Thing Theorist Roderick Usher here not only outlines a theory of the animacy of objects, but also asserts the role that place-power plays in shaping human character and deportment. The House of Usher—the family lineage—has been shaped by the house itself—a house that has achieved a kind of sentience and creates its own atmosphere.

Haunting, finally, might otherwise be expressed in "Usher" as atmosphere. There is no ghost in "The Fall of the House of Usher" in the traditional sense of some discrete, identifiable entity with a particular tragic history that could in some way be exorcised. Instead, *architecture and environment together exercise agency though evocation of affect*. Tarn, fungus, decay, miasma, wind, weather, and so on create conditions so powerfully affecting that sentience is ascribed to the house. Walker goes so far as to trace Roderick's "state of terror" in the story "back to the stagnant tarn and its miasmic 'atmosphere'" (1996, 589). The House of Usher might today be described as a "sick house"—one that, through atmospheric conditions, makes those within it ill.[8] Bailey suggests that the house in Poe's tale is the antagonist: "An obscure conjunction of architecture and geometry has endowed the house with a malign will and intelligence utterly distinct from any merely human revenant" (1999, 22). This, however, feels exaggerated. Unlike Hill House, to be addressed later, the Usher House never seems to act with intentionality. It is not "hungry" and does not "target" its inhabitants in any particular way; instead, it—together with the surrounding environment—exerts place-power, demonstrating the ways, as Taylor notes, "'we' are subjects of/to our surroundings" (Taylor 2007, 213) and how "affects or atmospheres might actually reside in things and then possess persons, rather than the other way around" (214). What haunts in "Usher" is, as Brink puts it, a "multifarious atmosphere *generated* by objects" (Brink 2016) as the story "baldly present[s] the degree of 'influence' that places have over persons" (Taylor 216).

Vile and Diseased: Hill House

One hundred and twenty years after Poe's story, but very much a lineal literary descendant, Shirley Jackson's 1959 *The Haunting of Hill House* arguably set the template for the contemporary narrative of the house that haunts. Within the story, an anthropologist investigating paranormal phenomena, Dr. John Montague, invites several people to join him in the titular Hill House in hopes of gathering evidence to confirm the existence of the supernatural. Primarily told from the perspective of Eleanor Vance, a woman who has led a sheltered and unexciting life, those present experience a range of peculiar phenomena—a cold spot outside the nursery, pounding on doors and walls, strange messages conveyed by paint and Ouija Board, and so on. At the end of the narrative, Eleanor, forced to leave by the other members of the party because she appears to be succumbing to the influence of the house, crashes her car into the same tree where an accident had killed a previous owner—whether her death is suicide or a result of supernatural manipulation by the house is left unresolved.

While Eleanor is clearly the story's protagonist and her experience negotiating social interactions under the pressure of the house the story's focus, the star of the story—and its most active player—is the house itself. In the famous opening and closing passages, the house is personified and conflated with the ghost that haunts it. The story begins:

> No live organism can continue for long to exist sanely under conditions of absolute reality; even larks and katydids are supposed, by some, to dream. Hill House, not sane, stood by itself against its hills, holding darkness within; it had stood so for eighty years and might stand for eighty more. Within, walls continued upright, bricks met nearly, floors were firm, and doors were sensibly shut; silence lay steadily against the wood and stone of Hill House, and whatever walked there, walked alone. (Jackson 1959, 3)

While this precise passage is challenging to parse, the gist of it seems to be that sanity depends on occasional breaks from reality in the form of fantasy—to stay sane, one must dream. Hill House doesn't afford that break from reality—there is no escaping the pressures it exerts, which results in insanity. What is particularly curious about the passage is that, on the one hand, the house is personified: "Hill House, not sane, stood by itself against the hills, holding darkness within." On the other hand, though, the living house is inhabited by an unknowable presence: "Whatever walked there, walked alone." The house somehow is both alive *and* haunted.[9]

Jackson never finally resolves this tension between a house that is haunted and one that itself does the haunting. However, it is clear that the house exerts place-power over Eleanor. Having fantasized on her drive to Hill House about the exciting experience she is about to have, her first glimpse of the house—reminiscent of the narrator's first glimpse of the Usher House in Poe's story—undoes those expectations: "The house was vile. She shivered and thought, the words coming freely to her mind. Hill House is vile, it is diseased; get away from here at once" (33). This sense of the house being alive—and evil—is then amplified further in the first paragraph of the second chapter, which interestingly highlights the idea that Hill House is far from unique; all buildings exert place-power:

> The face of Hill House seemed awake, with a watchfulness from the blank windows and a touch of glee in the eyebrow of a cornice. Almost any house, caught unexpectedly or at an odd angle, can turn a deeply humorous look on a watching person; even a mischievous little chimney, or a dormer like a dimple, can catch up a beholder with a sense of fellowship; but a house arrogant and hating, never off guard, can only be evil. This house . . . reared its great head back against the sky without concession or humanity. It was a house without kindness, never meant to be lived in, not a fit place for people or for love or for hope. Exorcism cannot alter the countenance of a house. Hill House would stay as it was until it was destroyed. (34–35).

Particularly useful for our purposes here, Jackson emphasizes the animacy of objects. Almost any house, she says, can strike us as lively and as manifesting human qualities. Hill House is a case in point, although a profoundly negative example: it is "arrogant and hating," "a house without kindness"—and these are not qualities that can be expunged through exorcism. Hill House will continue to haunt as long as the house stands, and then persist in haunting until memory fades away.

In attempting to explain why the house affects those within in the way that it does, Dr. Montague introduces directly an analogue of the idea I am calling "place-power."

> I need not remind you, I think, that the concept of certain houses as unclean or forbidden—perhaps sacred—is as old as the mind of man. Certainly there are spots which inevitably attach to themselves an atmosphere of holiness and goodness; it might not then be too fanciful to say that some houses are born bad. Hill House, whatever the cause, has been unfit for human habitation for upwards of twenty years. What

it was like before then, whether its personality was molded by the people who lived here, or the things they did, or whether it was evil from its start are all questions I cannot answer. No one knows, even, why some houses are called haunted. (70)

When asked by Luke, a member of the investigatory party, what else one might call Hill House other than haunted, Dr. Montague replies, "Well—disturbed, perhaps. Leprous. Sick. Any of the popular euphemisms for insanity. A deranged house is a pretty conceit" (70–71).

The discussion here echoes the opening passage—"Hill House, not sane"—and reflects not only Eleanor's initial reaction to the house as "vile" and "diseased," but the narrator's characterization of the house as "not a fit place for people." Whatever presence may or may not stalk the halls of Hill House, the narrative always returns to the house itself—its "clashing disharmony" of parts (38), the "poorly executed engravings arranged with unlovely exactness" (38), its "pressing silence" (41), its "deliberate" cold spot (120), its "unbelievably faulty design which left it chillingly wrong in all its dimensions, so that the walls seemed always in one direction a fraction longer than the eye could endure, and in another direction a fraction less than the barest possible tolerable length" (40). What haunts in Hill House is finally the house itself—a house that, like any other house, exerts place-power, affecting those within its walls, "attacking" their weaknesses and not permitting imagination or illusion as an explanation.

Hill House not only serves as the template for the subcategory of haunted house stories in which what haunts is the house, it actually theorizes place-power for us, suggesting in this case that negative aesthetics—an absence of balance, harmony, and proportion of parts—abetted by tragic or traumatic history can contribute to the sense that a house is vile, diseased, sick, or deranged and then, through a process of affective contagion, infect those who interact with the space. Sick Building Syndrome is, of course, a real thing—it is a medical condition in which people feel sick in a building for no apparent reason (see Stolwijk 1991). This generally can be traced to things like poor air quality, molds, or allergies to chemicals used in construction. In Gothic narratives of houses that haunt, while atmospheric conditions can certainly play a role in influencing mood and limiting the abilities of characters to draw accurate interpretations, a conclusion that seeming supernatural phenomena can all be chalked up to straightforward real-world factors such as carbon monoxide or fungus is often disappointing—although common both to children's literature and detective stories. And, although Hill House has a curious cold spot, I am not attempting to explain the strange goings-on there as resulting from a faulty HVAC system, which I think would betray entirely the narrative's emphasis at the start, end, and throughout on the unknowable nature of Hill House's haunting presence. However, what I do think is important about Jackson's theorization of place-power is that it bears out the fundamental premise of this study: Gothic narratives offer anxious, hyperbolic representations of what we already understand concerning the agency of things and places. Jackson's vile, diseased, evil, leprous house is not categorically different from "normal" houses and buildings; rather, it is the exception that proves the rule that all houses act on their inhabitants and, when marked by history, are not just haunted but actively haunt.

Hungry Houses: Burnt Offerings

If some houses are vile and diseased, others are hungry—at least, that's the premise of Dan Curtis's 1976 horror film *Burnt Offerings*, based on a 1973 novel of the same name by Robert Marasco. Within the film, the Rolf family—writer Ben Rolf (Oliver Reed), his wife Marian (Karen Black), and their son Davey (Lee H. Montgomery)—rent a shabby neo-classical Victorian mansion for the summer. The rental comes with the odd condition from the owners—brother and sister Arnold and Rosalyn Allardyce (Burgess Meredith and Eileen Heckart, respectively)—that their elderly mother will continue to live in her upstairs room and the Rolfs will bring meals up to her (which will be left outside her door because she is obsessed with privacy). That the rental price for the summer is too good to be true is, of course, borne out by the film (one always gets more than one bargains for in horror novels and films!).

As the family occupies the house for the summer, a variety of odd occurrences takes place: Davey hurts his knee and a dead plant starts to grow; Ben cuts his hand and a burned-out lightbulb works again; after Ben's elderly aunt dies (Elizabeth Rolf, played by Bette Davis), plants revive and bloom in the conservatory—the pattern quickly becomes clear to the viewer: After each injury or accident, the house restores itself. In the end, the threatened family determines to leave; Marian enters the house to inform Mrs. Allardyce, who has never been shown. When Marian fails to return, Ben goes in after her, only to discover that his wife through some kind of supernatural agency has assumed Mrs. Allardyce's place. Ben dies from a fall from an attic window, and Davey is crushed by a falling chimney as the house renews itself, and the film ends with the Allardyce siblings returning to their restored home.

If *Hill House* offers an exaggerated representation of a sick building, *Burnt Offerings* gives us a hyperbolic picture of home ownership, as well as of the kind of psychic projection of animacy onto objects outlined in Jörg Kreienbrock's

Malicious Objects, Anger Management, and the Question of Modern Literature (2012). In *Burnt Offerings*, the house is shown to be literally hungry and requiring the life force of its inhabitants to sustain itself. As the Rolfs get injured and die, the house renews itself. While houses do not repair themselves (yet!), the film otherwise offers a remarkably accurate representation of caring for an older home or building requiring constant upkeep and repair. The conveyance of energy in such cases is, indeed, literal as substantial energy is invested in maintenance. Injuries can happen, and, while old houses and buildings don't derive sustenance directly from blood, they certainly can suck up money.

In such circumstances, it is quite natural to project feelings of animosity onto the house itself. The apartment, house, or building becomes what Kreienbrock refers to as a "malicious object": "Malicious objects refuse to disappear into their automatic, unconscious functionality and instead remain stubbornly conspicuous. Endowed with agency, these cunning and perfidious intruders into the lifeworld of the subject seem to actively interrupt his or her intentions, unleashing anger and rage against the object. The malicious object in any case is something the subject experiences as recalcitrant, obtrusive, and vexing" (2012, 1). The house in *Burnt Offerings* is literally a malicious object—it thrives on the harm inflicted on its inhabitants.[10] In this, it functions as a literalization of the commonplace experience of an object that seems to seek to thwart or vex the subject. As with my consideration of *Hill House*, I do not wish here to undercut the affective power of a horror film such as *Burnt Offerings* by suggesting a mundane parallel, but part of the power of Gothic narratives of

Figure 24. The Dunsmuir House in Oakland, California—the mansion in *Burnt Offerings*

animate things and place-power is that they confirm the suspicions we have harbored all along. The house really is trying to drive us crazy!

The Fall of the House of Ayres: **The Little Stranger**

The impossibilities of maintaining an old home that will not repair itself with a severely constrained budget, limited help, and minimal technical know-how are also dramatized by Sarah Waters's 2009 novel *The Little Stranger*. While in some ways a more traditional ghost story than either Jackson's *Hill House* or Curtis's *Burnt Offerings*, as in both, it is really about a house that may be haunted but that most definitely haunts.

The story, in fact, focuses from the very start on a house that haunts the novel's narrator, Dr. Faraday. Set in rural Warwickshire, England, in 1947 and told from the perspective of Faraday, a middle-aged bachelor with working-class origins, the narrative opens with Faraday recalling his first impressions of Hundreds Hall, an eighteenth-century estate hosting a celebration for the local community. "I first saw Hundreds Hall when I was ten years old," begins Faraday (1). "I recall most vividly the house itself, which struck me as an absolute mansion," he continues, and then goes on to lovingly recount details of the house and the "thrill" it gave him: "I mean the thrill of the house itself, which came to me from every surface—from the polish on the floor, the patina on wooden chairs and cabinets, the bevel of a looking-glass, the scroll of a frame" (2).

Faraday's recollections of Hundreds Hall, we learn, were prompted by his being summoned there years later to attend to a housemaid whose ailments, he concluded, were a performance because she wished to leave service in a house haunted by a "bad thing." What astonished Faraday, however, was not the idea of a haunting, but rather the contrast between his memories of the grandeur of the house and its current dilapidated state, which he dwells on in great detail. "The garden," he recalls, "was a chaos of nettle and bindweed." Walking with Roderick Ayres, the young lord of the manor who has been physically injured and psychologically scarred during a crash as a pilot during World War II, Faraday remembers that "there was a faint but definite whiff of blocked drains. The windows we passed were streaked and dusty; all were closed and most were shuttered" (6). The interior, too, was a pale, shabby comparison to its former magnificence: "I saw with dismay that a horde of schoolboy vandals might have been at work on the plaster . . . for chunks had fallen away, and what was left was cracked and discoloured. The rest of the wall was not much better. There were several fine pictures and mirrors, but also darker squares and oblongs where pictures had obviously once hung. One panel of watered silk was ripped, and someone had patched and darned it like a sock" (16).

As a consequence of his house call, Faraday strikes up an acquaintance—and then a romance of sorts—with Caroline Ayres, sister to Roderick—frequently discussing with her the house's decline. In language suggesting *Burnt Offerings*, Caroline describes the estate as follows: "Hundreds is lovely! But it's sort of a lovely monster! It needs to be fed all the time, with money and hard work" (62). Returning to this theme later, Caroline cautions Faraday about becoming too invested in the house: "Do you remember when I told you about this house, when I showed you around it? It's greedy. It gobbles up all our time and energy. It'll gobble up yours, if you let it" (138). Caroline here is not speaking about the "bad thing" within the house, but simply the way an old house requires constant upkeep and frequent infusions of cash. "Hundreds Hall is such a drain on us," Caroline tells Faraday. "It's hardly worth staying for [Roderick]" (137).

For his part, Faraday—who we learn on the first page of the novel has in a sense been gobbled up by the house ever since he visited as a boy—considers that the declining state of the house parallels the diminished fortunes of the family: "It was as if the house were developing scars of its own, in response to [Roderick's] unhappiness and frustration—or to Caroline's, or her mother's—perhaps, to the griefs and disappointments of the whole family. The thought was horrible" (137). Roderick Ayres as presented in *The Little Stranger* is in many respects a direct literary descendent of Roderick Usher. He—and his sister and their mother—live in a house that appears at times to exhibit a form of sentience and with which the fortunes of the family are intertwined to such an extent that it is difficult to tell whether the house is an avatar of the family or vice versa. As in Hill House—another reference point in thinking about Hundreds Hall—the house is perceived as acting upon its inhabitants: "The house is playing parlour games with us, I think," Caroline tells Faraday. "She lifted her voice, and spoke into the stairwell. 'Do you hear me, house? It's no good your teasing us! We simply shan't play.'" (283). Georges Letissier notes the animacy of the house when he writes that "the house is anthropomorphized by being on several occasions identified as the active subject holding the characters as puppets or mannequins in its grip" (2017, 45).

Of note as well is the fact that, to the extent that the house teases, it does so through the uncanny animacy of objects—which Roderick perceives as supernatural malevolence, most notably in his account of an animate shaving mirror that he confesses to Faraday, who then passes the story along to the reader. The passage is worth quoting at some length because of how clearly it presents a picture of Gothic thing-power and the upending of the world that occurs when objects exert agency:

> Rod stood perfectly still, in that still room, and watched as the shaving-glass shuddered again, then rocked, then began to *inch its way across the washing-stand towards him*. It was just, he said, as if the glass were walking—or, rather, as if it were in that moment discovering its own *ability* to walk. . . . "It was the most sickening thing I ever saw," said Rod. . . . "It was all the more sickening, somehow, for the glass being such an ordinary sort of object. If—I don't know, but if some *beast* had suddenly appeared in the room, some spook or apparition, I think I would have borne the shock of it better. But *this*—it was hateful, it was *wrong*. It made one feel as though everything around one, the ordinary stuff of one's ordinary life, might all at any moment start up like this, and—overwhelm one. . . ." All the time that Rod had been watching the glass make its shuddering way toward him, sick with horror at what, to me, he kept calling the *wrongness* of the thing. Part of this wrongness was his sense that the glass was acting somehow impersonally. It had, God knew how, become animate; but he had the feeling that what was animating it was blind, thoughtless motion. (150)

Roderick here not only recalls a terrifying upending of the world but offers a pithy explanation of why Gothic objects provoke such anxiety: "It made one feel as though everything around one, the ordinary stuff of one's ordinary life, might all at any moment start up like this, and—overwhelm one." This is precisely why New Materialism and the Gothic are mirror reflections of one another. The unsettling of the distinction between the animate/inanimate, subject/object dichotomies induces epistemological vertigo as it undercuts anthropocentrism.

In the end, *The Little Stranger* does suggest the possibility that there is a kind of ghostly presence in the house—a "bad thing" that animates objects, starts fires, makes noises, and so on—and one explanation that is dangled before the reader is that the house is haunted by the ghost of Mrs. Ayres's first daughter, who died of diphtheria at age eight. But, at the same time, what haunts in the novel is the house—the mansion that symbolizes for Faraday the class status from which he is perpetually barred even should he marry into the family.[11] The haunting is expressed through the house and is inextricably intertwined with it. My argument here, though, has been that this is the case with every house: The house is haunted by a past that has marked and shaped it; and, in turn, the house haunts, expressing place-power by evoking affect from and shaping interpretation by those who interact with it.

A House That Leaves

To end this study of Gothic things, I turn my attention to one of the most dazzling—and daunting—examples of Gothic thing-power: Mark Z. Danielewski's *House of Leaves* (2000). As anyone familiar with *House of Leaves* knows well, the novel is unconventional in its presentation of a convoluted narrative. Framed by first-person narrator Johnny Truant's account of assembling and evaluating a manuscript authored by a now-dead blind man named Zampanò that studies a documentary film (that may or may not exist) called *The Navidson Record*, the novel interweaves Zampanò's summary of and commentary on the film, Truant's commentary on Zampanò's report and autobiographical details concerning how it affects him, copious footnotes—some of which have their own notes—intertwining references to real and fictional sources, and additional notes from anonymous editors. At the heart of the novel, though, is the story of a house that is paradigmatic of all Gothic objects in that it is disturbingly bigger on the inside than on the outside—and, in this case, this paradoxical discrepancy is literal.

The *Navidson Record*—the possibly fictional documentary film summarized and analyzed by Zampanò (and then conveyed by Truant)—chronicles the experiences of photojournalist Will Navidson, his partner, Karen Green, and their two children, along with assorted others, including Will's brother Tom, as they explore the unstable space of the Navidson's Virginia home. The situation begins when the Navidson family discovers a door and a small closet space where before there had only been a wall. A second door then appears leading to the children's room. "The puzzling part," according to Zampanò's narrative, as relayed by Truant (as if the mysterious hallway and doors were not puzzling enough on their own!) "comes when Navidson measures the internal space. He carefully notes the length of the new area, the length of both bedrooms and the factors in the width of all the walls. The result is anything but comforting. In fact it is impossible. . . . The width of the *house* inside would appear to exceed the width of the *house* as measured from the outside by 1/4" (30).[12]

The interior space, however, doesn't stay just slightly larger than the exterior dimensions; rather, it grows—dramatically. The *Navidson Record* documents Will's investigations into the unstable and expanding interior of his home. Part of it (as summarized by Zampanò and relayed by Truant), for example, depicts the following:

> Navidson pushes ahead, moving deeper and deeper into the house, eventually passing a number of doorways leading off into alternate

passageways or chambers. . . . No matter how far Navidson proceeds down this particular passageway, his light never comes close to touching the punctuation point promised by the converging perspective lines. . . . Finally, Navidson stops in front of an entrance much larger than the rest. It arcs high above his head and yawns into an undisturbed blackness. His flashlight finds the floor but no walls and, for the first time, no ceiling. Only now do we begin to see how big Navidson's house really is. (64)

"Big," however, becomes a significant understatement as the interior swells to impossible—inhuman—proportions. At one point, the time it takes a coin to fall to the bottom of an enormous spiral staircase suggests Navidson has descended 54,545 miles—almost seven times the diameter of the Earth: house as hyperobject (305). Later, during what is referred to as "Exploration #5," Navidson brings a bike and covers "anywhere from 240 to 300 miles at a time" for day after day (425), traveling thousands of miles of featureless hallways lit only by the lamp on the front of his bike. Eventually, he is left, alone, in the endless black interior of the house, standing on an ash black slab, apparently supported by nothing: "darkness below, above, and of course darkness beyond" (464). Whereas Caroline in *The Little Stranger* refers to being "gobbled up" by the house as a metaphor for being preoccupied by it, Will Navidson has seemingly been gobbled up literally—swallowed by a house that defies logic and physics. In the end, he does reemerge, although how he manages to return is left unexplained.

Space within the Navidson house not only apparently extends into infinity but is also profoundly unstable. A door and hallway appear out of nowhere and are located by the different characters on different walls—it is first described as being on the north wall (4) and later on the west wall (an inconsistency pointed out by Truant in a footnote on page 57). The spiral staircase past what the characters call the Great Hall, first estimated at 13 miles in length, later appears to be no more than 100 feet (159). Near the end of *The Navidson Report*, parts of the house collapse inward (341) and the floor drops away, revealing only blackness (343). "Everything here is constantly shifting," states Navidson while exploring the house's interior (164)—an instability that affects one of the characters as a kind of sea sickness (164).

The Navidson Report—the documentary footage of Will Navidson's explorations into the impossibly large and unstable interior space of his home—then becomes the focal point of all manner of speculation within the novel, as well as the catalyst for considerations of related topics, such as the perception of space, echoes, and labyrinths and the relationship between sign and referent.

In an almost Brechtian way, the novel in its Zampanò sections, in particular, and through its playful metatextuality as a whole, seeks to estrange the reader from the powerful affective force of Navidson's experience navigating the impossible inner dimensions of his house. Summary of *The Navidson Report* is repeatedly interrupted by Zampanò, who offers long-winded analysis of particular scenes and shots, academic discursions on related topics, background, context, and so on, copiously footnoted in what often is obvious parody of academic writing. In one section, for example, Zampanò offers a technical discussion of the phenomenon of echoes, including the formula for calculating resonance frequencies (49–50). The narrative itself then playfully and insistently foregrounds its status as a constructed artifact not only through different fonts, unusual textual arrangements that complicate reading, and the interplay of real and fictional sources, but also through the overall Chinese box structure that has Truant summarizing Zampanò summarizing and reflecting on *The Navidson Report*. We, as readers, can appreciate the correspondence between book and house established by the title; the book is a house constructed of leaves—that is, pages. And both the novel, *The House of Leaves*, and the physical structure the novel takes as its focus are comparable in being "bigger on the inside." A book is a "house" that contains worlds, and the house in *House of Leaves* contains a universe within its walls.

This playful correspondence between book and house is then triangulated by way of one of the book's privileged conceits, the labyrinth, emphasized in particular in Chapter IX. In relating both the house and *The Navidson Record*, Zampanò foregrounds their mazelike structures: "From the outset of *The Navidson Record*, we are involved in a labyrinth, meandering from one celluloid cell to the next, trying to peek around the next edit in hopes of finding a solution, a centre, a sense of whole, only to discover another sequence, leading in a completely different direction, a continually devolving discourse, promising the possibility of discovery while all along dissolving into chaotic ambiguities too blurry to ever completely comprehend" (114). Zampanò's prose, then, having already included a Derridean-length footnote on Jacques Derrida's deconstruction of center and periphery (including quoting the French), devolves entirely into a parody of academic writing when he continues, "In order to fully appreciate the way the ambages unwind, twist only to rewind, and then open up again, whether in Navidson's house or the film—*quae itinerum ambages occursusque ac recursus inexplicabiles*—we should look to the etymological inheritance of a word like 'labyrinth'" (114). At this point, *The Navidson Record* has been left far behind.

In asking us to consider film footage as labyrinth, the novel—as has been often remarked in the criticism—then implicitly asks us to take the obvious next step and consider the novel itself as a labyrinth, which certainly seems an apt description of a narrative that winds in directions impossible to foresee in advance. Kröger, for example, notes the book's "complicated labyrinth of narrative structure" (Kröger 2009, 149). Hamilton, foregrounding Danielewski's creative use of typography, notes that Danielewski "creates a labyrinth with his form as well as his themes" (Hamilton 2008, 5) and that "The entire *House of Leaves* is a maze of footnotes, fact, and fiction" (8). There is no straightforward path through *House of Leaves*, and the affective force of the Navidson sections is conveyed in bursts like a pulsar as the novel continually refocuses its lens, rather than a consistent gravitational attraction that pins the reader to the ground of the narrative.

And yet, what the novel withholds or obscures with one hand, it restores with the other, offering the reader a model of the affective power of narrative in the form of Johnny Truant. As suggested by his name, Truant is in a sense deliberately absent—refusing to tell the story he presumably is trying to tell in anything like a straightforward way. Instead, he constantly interweaves his own story together with that of *The Navidson Record* through lengthy footnotes that go on for pages and convey Truant's deteriorating mental state as he worked to assemble Zampanò's materials into the book we presumably have in our hands. Just like Navidson, Truant descends increasingly into a kind of unplumbable dark interior space, his transformation precipitated—like Navidson's—by the impossible inconsistencies of the house.

"Horror has caused this," writes Truant. "But where horror? Why horror? Horror of what?" (Danielewski 2000, 494). The horror Truant experiences is arguably the horrific underside to New Materialism and Thing Theory that has been mined by the Gothic for over two centuries. "Objects," writes Timothy Morton in *Hyperobjects*, using a metaphor of which he is particularly fond, "are like Doctor Who's Tardis, a time-traveling spaceship that is bigger on the inside than it is on the outside" (Morton 2013a, 79). And across what Morton calls the "rift" between objects as perceived and understood by us and their real qualities that exist independently of being perceived is the "strange stranger," the unknown. For Quentin Meillassoux, in *After Finitude*, across the rift is the "the great outdoors": "that outside which [is] not relative to us . . . existing in itself regardless of whether we are thinking of it or not; that outside which thought could explore with the legitimate feeling of being on foreign territory—of being entirely elsewhere" (Meillassoux 2008, 7). The world is not just there for us and does not disappear when we close our eyes. Glossing this idea in *Alien Phenomenology*, Ian Bogost writes that "once we put down the trappings of culture and take the invitation into that great outdoors, a tremendous wave of surprise and unexpectedness would overwhelm us—a 'global ether' of incredible novelty and unfamiliarity. As Latour sums up, 'If you are mixed up with the trees, how do you know they are not using you to achieve their dark design?'" (Latour 2001, 38).

This moment of surprise and unexpectedness could be, on the one hand, the Vibrant Materialism of Jane Bennett's assemblage of debris in *Vibrant Matter*—her glimpse of "a culture of things irreducible to the culture of objects" (Bennett 2010, 5). On the other, though, getting lost in the woods of the great outdoors and encountering the strange stranger can be the stuff of nightmare—and this is the horror that Johnny Truant experiences and that is arguably at the heart of *House of Leaves*. *House of Leaves* is a ghost story in which what haunts is the house—and more so than any of the other texts discussed here, it certainly exerts place-power, expressing a kind of agency through its various transformations and the effects it has on those who investigate them. But what arguably haunts Truant most is the malign suspicion that the Navidson house is not unique, not some violation of time and space, but rather the general condition of things. What if all houses are houses of leaves, houses *that* leave, that are bigger on the inside, that cannot be pinned down or fully known? What if all objects are labyrinths that go on and on? Truant's horror is what I think, then, with Luckhurst's consideration of corridors in mind, can properly be called *Angst*, but with a very specific twist. If we think of *Angst* as objectless dread, Truant is *Angst*-ridden over the prospect of losing objects or, more specifically, of having always already lost them. In *Alien Phenomenology*, Bogost summarizes the Object-Oriented Ontologist perspective that "all objects recede interminably into themselves" (2012, 9). In *The Navidson Report*, Will Navidson attempts to follow them all the way down, but fails. Truant's response to the Navidson Report is to lose himself in what Morton calls the ontological "abyss" separating objects from one another and from their own qualities (see Morton 2013a, 79). In this sense, *The Navidson Report* is a cursed object that acts as a kind of portal, precipitating Truant into the Great Outdoors of Gothic Objects.

In the end, the Navidson house, like Hundreds Hall, Hill House, and the house in *Burnt Offerings*, is a ghost story in which, as Kröger appreciates, what haunts is the house itself (2009, 154). What haunts the reader or viewer, however, is the prospect that these haunting homes are not exceptions, but rather simply exaggerations of the norm: all homes, as Curtis writes of haunted houses in film, in particular, are both possessed and possessing (Curtis 2008, 66). They are haunted by memories, histories, associations, fantasies, and projections of their owners and "inscribe themselves within their dwellers" (34). As "complex ecology[ies] of past and present, interior and exterior," they exert place-power over those who interact with them, eliciting affect and provoking interpretation.

None of this is new—architects consider how the organization and aesthetics of their structures will influence those who utilize and occupy them, and the premise of both psychogeography and *feng shui* is that environment affects mood and behavior. This awareness of "place-power" is similarly an extension of twenty-first-century Thing Theory. But the Gothic insistence that not only are all homes haunted, but that all homes haunt, compels the uncanny realization of diminished human importance. The Gothic, yet again, is shown to express the anxiety underlying New Materialist optimism. Architectural dread is the flipside to vibrant materialism demonstrating the typical Gothic inversion in which when things come to life, human beings are treated like things.

Epilogue
The Ominous Matter of One's Ordinary Life

In Sarah Waters's *The Little Stranger* (2009), as summarized in Chapter 6, Rod Ayres recounts to Dr. Faraday his terrified response to the uncanny animacy of his shaving glass: "But *this*—it was hateful, it was *wrong*. It made one feel as though everything around one, the ordinary stuff of one's ordinary life, might all at any moment start up like this, and—overwhelm one" (150). Rod's sense of a world turned upside down is a pithy encapsulation of the argument of this book: What the Gothic does is to take the ordinary stuff of our ordinary lives—our clothes, books, houses, toys, bodies, and so on—and overwhelm us with them by giving them uncanny life, making them seem hateful and wrong: the ordinary made ominous. This is the menace of the Gothic, as well as its profundity: It asserts that the world is not some passive substrate to be acted upon by human beings who are in control of everything; instead, the Gothic shows us the thing-power and place-power of the world. We are possessed by the objects and spaces we interact with every bit as much as we possess them. The Gothic's representation of this entanglement of human beings and the material world is generally hyperbolic and invested with dread; however, the anxiety it evokes is connected to very real anxieties about things expressing agency and, inversely, people being reduced to the status we typically afford things.

The Gothic thus shows us that twenty-first-century New Materialism is not particularly new. Since its origins in the eighteenth century, Gothic materialism has emphasized the hidden depths of objects, the "vibrancy" of things, and the entanglement of human and nonhuman actants in Latourean networks. This is no doubt why practitioners of the nonhuman turn seem drawn toward the dark side, even when their orientation ostensibly is toward hope. Gothic tales of what I've referred to as "ominous matter," however, have the potential to elicit such a powerful affective response because they tap into deep-seated anxieties about circumscribed human autonomy. What the Gothic highlights for us is just how hard the nonhuman pivot is to make because what the Gothic explores is human fragility, blindness, and impotence—and the centrality of the Gothic to twenty-first-century culture is, as I note in the Introduction, arguably the boomerang effect of the nonhuman turn making clear the challenges theoretical paradigms seeking to undercut anthropocentrism must confront. For every vibratory tableau of objects on a storm drain grate there is a cellar full of cursed objects in a cabin in the woods.

In Gothic narrative, human beings are always, finally, trying to save themselves: to stave off madness and destruction, to resist being reduced to the status of a thing. This may involve putting ghosts to rest, escaping the villain, defeating the monster, restoring the "natural order," putting right what has gone wrong, and so on. In many cases, they are successful—although the protagonists often do not emerge unscathed. In other cases, darkness triumphs. However the end comes, the period leading up to it in Gothic narrative is always chaotic as transgression tends toward tragedy: the protagonist is trapped, tormented, uncertain, tortured. This is the chaos in which we perceive ourselves to be enmeshed in the twenty-first century, haunted by the past, contending with monsters, tending toward apocalypse. Everything is unstable, and we—the human—feel ourselves to be threatened and encroached upon from all sides.

A prominent strain of New Materialist/Speculative Realist/OOO discourse would have us embrace our "humiliation"—Timothy Morton's word for our status in comparison to the expansiveness of hyperobjects (see *Hyperobjects* [2013a], 17)—that is, to undo human exceptionalism, embrace our entanglement with the material world, and wonder at the unexpected depths and dignity of objects. Often, this orientation is associated with an ethical stance—the necessity of careful stewardship of the environment, respecting the lives of animals, celebrating human physiological and cultural diversity. The Gothic is the antagonistic counternarrative to this position, responding with horror to the perceived humiliation of the human and asking how humiliation could evoke anything other than Lovecraftian cosmic dread. The Gothic is the story of our moment, arguably the privileged lens through which we view our twenty-first-century experience, and perhaps the most Gothic realization the centrality of the Gothic to contemporary life compels is how intimately intertwined anthropocentrism is to apocalypse. We are so overwhelmed with dread at the thought of our diminished importance that we resist acting to save ourselves. The transgressive Gothic narrative of thing-power and place-power currently being written is a central—maybe *the* central—story of our moment, and it insistently asks us to consider how the story will end.

Acknowledgments

This project has been developing for several years, and I have tried out material incorporated here in various places. Much of chapter 1 was developed for Justin Edwards, Rune Graulund, and Johan Höglund's *Dark Scenes from Damaged Earth: The Gothic Anthropocene* collection. Material on *Twin Peaks* in chapter 2 came from my chapter "Wondrous and Strange: The Matter of *Twin Peaks*," in *Return to Twin Peaks: New Approaches to Materiality, Theory, and Genre on Television*, edited by me and Catherine Spooner. Material on Edgar Allan Poe's "Berenice" in chapter 3 started as a presentation at the sixth annual conference of the Gesellschaft für Fantastikforschung e.V. at the Eberhard Karls Universität Tübingen and was subsequently included in the conference proceedings *Wissen in der Fantastik: Vom Suchen, Verstehen und Teilen*, edited by Meike Uhrig, Vera Cuntz-Leng, and Luzie Kollinger, as "Blasphemous Knowledge."

As I was finishing up work on this manuscript, the Covid-19 epidemic was in full swing and my university library was shut down, making it difficult to obtain many book chapters and secondary articles. During this chaotic time, I was continually impressed by and thankful for the generosity of other scholars who provided me directly with materials otherwise unobtainable. Thanks in particular should go to Scott Peeples, Justin Wigard, and David Willingham, who helped me get ahold of valuable secondary sources. The virus has been terrible; however, the community I have witnessed among scholars around the world has been heartening.

This project benefited from attentive reading and extremely useful feedback from Natania Meeker and Kevin J. Wetmore Jr., and Aldene Fredenburg's close eye prevented me from making some embarrassing mistakes. Thanks as well go to Richard Morrison for his continued support of me and my work and to the rest of the excellent team at Fordham University Press, including Eric Newman and Kem Crimmins, for making the book possible.

Notes

3. Body-as-Thing

1. As I outline in my *Scare Tactics: Supernatural Fiction by American Women*, the category of the female Gothic at its most broad simply serves to designate Gothic fiction written by women; however, it is more commonly addressed as a "form of critique of the oppressiveness of patriarchal constraints" (Weinstock 2010, 11). See also Weinstock 2010, 10–14.

2. Kelly Hurley addresses these anxieties concerning the integrity and stability of the human body in relation to late nineteenth-century Gothic literature, in particular, noting that the "ruination" of the human body "in the most violent, absolute, and often repulsive terms, is practiced insistently, almost obsessively, in the pages of British Gothic fiction at the end of the nineteenth century and the beginning of the twentieth" (Hurley 1996, 3). Undergirded by anxieties related to scientific discourse redefining the idea of the "human," Gothic fiction of the period dwelt on the "abhuman" (3), a "not-quite-human subject, characterized by its morphic variability, continually in danger of becoming not-itself, becoming other" (3–4).

3. Hurley's discussion of the "abhuman" connects in some ways with what Stephen Bruhm calls "the Gothic body" in his consideration of nineteenth-century Romantic fiction. The Gothic body for Bruhm is one whose pain is "on excessive display" (Bruhm 1994, xvii) for readers of literature and viewers of art, and his project contemplates the complications of aestheticizing pain. On the horror film and affect, see Reyes's *Horror Film and Affect* (2016) and Hanich's *Cinematic Emotion in Horror Films and Thriller* (2010).

4. On *Texas Chainsaw Massacre*, see, for example, Merritt (2010). On *Night of the Living Dead*, see Lightning (2010). On *Hostel*, see the chapter devoted to the film and its sequel in Bernard (2014).

5. As Andrea Goulet remarks in an interesting essay related to "tooth decay" in late nineteenth-century French literature, Freud considered tooth loss within dreams as symbolic of "castration in punishment for onanism" (Goulet 2017, 199). This leads into a relatively straightforward psychoanalytic interpretation of "Berenice" in which Egaeus's punishment of his cousin is a projection of his own guilt/shame.

6. Not surprisingly, criticism of Poe's "Berenice" has often focused on gender, situating Berenice in relation to other women in Poe's fiction and the violence to which they are subject. See, for example, Doyle (1993), Renzi (2012), and Keetley (2005). This is very much to the point of my analysis to follow, which foregrounds the dangerous ramifications of reducing human beings to objects.

7. My interpretation of the story runs contrary to that of Scott Peeples who, in *Edgar Allan Poe Revisited* (Peeples 1998), argues that Berenice's teeth are different in kind than the other objects on which Egaeus has fixated his attention (50). For Peeples, Egaeus is "entering a world of feeling," and his extraction of Berenice's teeth is because he believes them to be ideas: "He is desperate to have some essential part of her survive bodily disintegration" (51). My argument is that the teeth are not different from the other objects, but exemplary and, in their materiality, highlight the dangers of thinking bodies as objects no different in their materiality than other objects. See Peeples 1998, 50–51.

8. And in keeping with Poe's fiction, as well as the deeply entrenched misogyny of the Gothic horror tradition, "Berenice" exemplifies the ways in which women's bodies in particular are fetishized, dismembered, and violated by men within patriarchal culture. As Joan Dayan remarks in her important essay connecting Poe's representations of women to slavery, "Poe, Persons, and Property," "Poe's women, then, though adored or treasured, are never quite human" (2001, 113). See also Dayan's "Amorous Bondage: Poe, Ladies, and Slaves" (1994) for a consideration of how the language of possession in Poe's tales of unearthly women corresponds with antebellum slavery.

9. Barker, as Jay McRoy develops in his essay "There Are No Limits: Splatterpunk, Clive Barker, and the Body in-extremis," is among the "best known practitioners" of splatterpunk, "a sub-genre of horror fiction marked by 'the explicit depiction of horrific acts, including murder and every sort of mutilation of the body' (Tucker, 33)" (McRoy 2002, 131). In his essay, McRoy considers the politics of Barker's novel *The Hellbound Heart*, its adaptation as the film *Hellraiser*, and another of Barker's films, *Nightbreed*, finding *Nightbreed* to be the most progressive in its embracing of monstrous hybridity. See McRoy. "The Midnight Meat Train" (1988), despite its barbed critique of American capitalism, has received very little critical attention. Bernard Perron compares Barker's story to its comic and cinematic adaptations in "Drawing (to) Fear and Horror: Into the Frame of Clive Barker's *The Midnight Meat Train* and *Dread* Comic and Film Adaptations" (2017). Gary Hoppenstand offers some limited attention to the story

in his *Clive Barker's Short Stories: Imagination as Metaphor in the Books of Blood and Other Works* (2013).

10. That "The Midnight Meat Train" regards the butchering of human beings for meat as repulsive is clear; however, whether we are also supposed to regard the story as a rejection of the butchering of animals for meat is uncertain. Barker has self-identified on Twitter as a vegetarian, writing in 2012 that "being a vegetarian has lost me more friends than being a gay man" (Barker, "Being a Vegetarian"). Whether he was a vegetarian in 1984 when *Books of Blood, vol. 1*, was published is uncertain. Interestingly, the 2008 cinematic adaptation of the story, directed by Rhuhei Kitamura and produced by Barker, presents main protagonist Leon as a vegan, allowing the narrative more clearly to reject using both humans and animals as meat. In general, the Gothic maintains an attitude of human exceptionalism and regards both the emergence of the animal within the human (as with werewolf narratives) and the treatment of the human as an animal (as in tales of abuse and confinement) with dread.

11. Although, as critics have pointed out, restoration of Regan's subjectivity reinserts her into the matrix of patriarchal heteronormativity that circumscribes female agency. See, for example, Olney (2014).

12. As the language here no doubt suggests and a consideration of *White Zombie* makes clear, possession narratives have affinities with slave narratives, although the racial subtexts are seldom as clear as they are in Halperin's film, in which voodoo master Legendre mesmerizes predominantly black bodies to serve as labor in his Haitian sugar mill. Indeed, although it is outside of the scope of this study, nineteenth-century Romantic tales of mesmerism (or "animal magnetism") such as those by Hawthorne and Poe could usefully be explored in relation to American slavery. With a plot involving a white woman who is presumed dead but is really "zombified," *White Zombie* also has interesting connections with Poe's "Berenice" and other tales of women who seem to return from the dead.

13. On masks in horror films, see Doug Bradley's *Sacred Monsters: Behind the Mask of the Horror Actor* (1996) and Alexandra Heller-Nicholas's *Masks in Horror Cinema: Eyes Without Faces* (2019).

14. Despite the association of the hockey mask with Jason, he doesn't in fact put it on until the third installment of the franchise, *Friday the 13th Part III* (Steve Miner [1982]); amusingly, Michael Myer's mask in the *Halloween* franchise is actually a *Star Trek* Captain Kirk mask spray painted white.

15. Heller-Nicholas's discussion of masks focuses on their role in ritual, the power they afford the wearer, and the kinds of transformations they catalyze (2019).

4. Thing-as-Body

1. On the zombie's violation of discrete categories, see Sarah Juliet Lauro's introduction to her *Zombie Theory: A Reader* (2017), as well as her essay with Karen

Embry, "A Zombie Manifesto: The Nonhuman Condition in the Era of Advanced Capitalism," contained in the same volume.

2. See, for example, Giorgio Agamben's *Homo Sacer: Sovereign Power and Bare Life* (1998), Achille Mbembe's *Necropolitics* (2019), and Judith Butler's *Precarious Life: The Powers of Mourning and Violence* (2004).

3. In Theodore Ziolkowski's survey of haunted portraits, he proposes three categories: portraits tied to a particular place (*genius loci*), those that foreshadow future events (*figura*), and those that have a magical connection to to their model (*anima*). While Ziolkowski's study consists primarily of plot summaries, his chapter on haunted portraits highlights their ubiquity in Gothic narrative (1977). Jakub Lipski notes that animated portraits in Gothic narrative negotiate "the binaries of past and present, self and other, real and unreal, beyond the obvious entanglement with the issues of what belongs to animate and what inanimate matter" (2017, 66). For a more general consideration of the "counterfeit" relationships between portraits and referents in *Hamlet* and *Otranto*, see Hogle (1994).

4. Naomi Miyazawa (2017) connects Poe's "The Oval Portrait" to daguerreotypes and photographs used to preserve images of the dead.

5. "The Mezzotint" (James 1904a) takes as its focus, as per the title, a mezzotint, a print made from an engraved steel or copper plate rather than a photograph; however, the principle is the same.

5. Book: How to Do Things with Words

1. In Jonathan Dent's analysis of the found manuscript in *The Romance of the Forest*, he interprets the fragmented manuscript as indexing the profound disruption to narratives of progress caused by the French Revolution. In this case, the specific story conveyed by the manuscript ironically calls into question the extent to which the past can be known: "The fractured manuscript that features in *The Romance of the Forest* reveals a past that is not entirely governable by reason and rational frameworks and shows how, with the outbreak of the French Revolution at the end of the eighteenth century, the past seemed more unknowable than ever" (Dent 2012, 20).

2. Noting that the "power of the book" had particular resonance at the end of the nineteenth century when "the sacred properties of the Bible and prayer-book were being called into question" (2013, 160), Peter Raby explores the influence of Huysmans on Wilde and fin-de-siècle anxieties concerning corrupting books.

3. Lippert notes that Lovecraft's *Necronomicon* has "been borrowed, used and altered to such an extent that . . . certainty of its fictitiousness has been compromised" (Lippert 2012–13, 41).

6. Building: Bigger on the Inside

1. See, for example, Barry Curtis's *Dark Places: The Haunted House in Film* (2008), Rebecca Janicker's *The Literary Haunted House: Lovecraft, Matheson, King*

and the Horror in Between (2015), and Dale Bailey's *American Nightmares: The Haunted House Formula in American Popular Fiction* (1999).

2. Susan Poznar makes this point when she writes of houses and castles of the Gothic that "scholars of the Gothic traditionally link these ill-fated habitations to the ruined fortunes of an etiolated, decadent, or irresponsible aristocracy and its historically diminishing power, to anti-Catholic sentiment, or to more generalized mistrust of antiquated religious institutions that presumably wield a moribund but still menacing power" (Poznar 2015, 144). "Almost always," she continues, "architectural instability or aberration represents dynastic weakness, vice, tragedy, or crime and is therefore intelligible" (144). The physical space itself is quickly superseded in such interpretations by its symbolism. Hill House in Jackson's *The Haunting of Hill House* (1959), according to Poznar, is an exception to this rule. Poznar's assertion concerning the conventional scholarly approach to buildings in Gothic fiction is borne out by S. L. Varnado and Maria M. Tatar. Varnado interprets castles in Gothic fiction as "ideograms," which he defines as a "symbolic phrase that, by analogy, suggests the numinous experience" (1987, 10). The "haunted castle," he argues, is "the unifying ideogram of Gothic literature," suggesting that which "lies hidden behind the world of material reality" (32). The castle is merely a kind of scrim or screen on which flickering images of the numinous can be projected. Tatar's "The Houses of Fiction: Toward a Definition of the Uncanny" (1981) addresses a number of works, starting with Walpole's *Otranto* and including Hawthorne's *The House of the Seven Gables* and Dickens's *Oliver Twist*, but focuses almost entirely on "house" as family rather than physical structure.

3. In keeping with the critical tendency to look past the literal role of physical structures within Gothic narrative in order to attend to them as symbols, Gretchen Cohenour (2008), referencing Elaine Showalter and Claire Kahane, argues that the castle in *Otranto* "represents a domestic space that mirrors the maternal (M)other, making it a pivotal image that reflects eighteenth-century paranoia about contamination of bloodlines and property ownership" (73). In contrast, in a short article in *The Explicator*, Maureen Gokey (2019) argues that *Otranto* pits the masculine space of the castle against the subversive feminine space of the caverns beneath it. For an interesting consideration of engraved illustrations of *Otranto* that attempt to visualize Walpole's descriptions, see Lindfield (2017).

4. For David Punter, this irrationality of space is a reflection of the Gothic's power to disorder our understanding of reality in general. In his introduction to *Spectral Readings* (1999), he writes, "Just as Gothic castles from Udolpho to Gormenghast exist in a world where there are no maps, where halls, corridors and stairways go on for ever, where rooms that were there in the night have vanished by morning, so Gothic itself challenges that very process of map-making by means of which we might hope to reduce the world to manageable proportions" (4).

5. Emma Fraser notes the ubiquity of bathroom violence in horror films, as well as its gendered nature. See her "Horror, Femininity, and the Vulnerability of Bathrooms" (2019).

6. For an overview and examples of the dolly zoom shot, see John Francis McCullagh's "The Cinematic Power of Hitchcock's Dolly Zoom Technique" (2018).

7. On this point, see, for example, Brink, 2016.

8. See "Sick Building Syndrome" (n.d.) for a definition for and symptoms of the condition. See also Stolwijk (1991).

9. In keeping with general trends in Gothic criticism, critics have generally looked past the literal presence of the house in *Hill House* and explored its symbolism. Michael T. Wilson, for example, referencing S. L. Varnado's consideration of Gothic castles as ideograms (see note 2), sees the house as a stage where anxieties concerning the nature of reality and the afterlife play out: the house as "liminal figuration between mercifully clouded mortal perception and that of unendurable reality" (Wilson 2015, 115). For Richard Pascal, what Hill House offers is not an encounter with the ineffable, but a picture of the dysfunctional American family and terrible parenting—the *"unfamily"* (2014, 465) in which children and mothers contend with domineering fathers amid shifting cultural understandings of family and individualism.

10. In her analysis of *Burnt Offerings*, Dara Downey (2015) interprets the film as participating in a particular horror film tradition representing the entrapments of domestic space for women. The hungry house thus becomes in her reading an avatar for patriarchal ideology that tricks women into domestic subjugation by leading them to think that traditional marriage and motherhood will offer fulfillment.

11. Issues of social class are obviously central to the novel and have accordingly been focal points of critical attention in analyses of *The Little Stranger*. Georges Letissier argues that, in the novel, "the ghost romance tropes the topic of the extinction of the Ayres's dynasty, and by extension the disappearance of a social class tightly bound up with the British establishment, more specifically the Army and the fading glory of the Empire" (2017, 42). Ann Heilmann notes in a wide-ranging essay that "Hundreds Hall is a focal point for fractured identities and frustrated desires, but here members of the new professional class born from domestic service covet not subjection to but, rather, the possession of the old-time privilege bestowed by a hereditary house" (2012, 40). Barbara Braid speculates that Dr. Faraday himself, who covets Hundreds Hall and the class status associated with it, is, in a sense, behind the hauntings. "Is it possible that his other self, his Hyde, went to Hundreds Hall to punish his fiancée for rejecting him?" she questions (2013, 144)—a question she answers in the affirmative.

12. The two instances of "house" set here in italic appear in a blue font in the original text.

Works Cited

Agamben, Giorgio. 1998. *Homo Sacer: Sovereign Power and Bare Life.* Stanford, Calif.: Stanford University Press.
Alaimo, Stacy. 2010. *Bodily Natures: Science, Environment, and the Material Self.* Bloomington: Indiana University Press.
———. 2018. "Trans-Corporeality." In *Posthuman Glossary*, edited by Rosi Braidotti and Maria Hlavajova, 435–37. London: Bloomsbury.
Allewaert, Monique. 2013. *Ariel's Ecology: Plantations, Personhood, and Colonialism in the American Tropics.* Minneapolis: University of Minnesota Press.
Austin, J. L. [1962] 1975. *How to Do Things with Words.* 2nd ed. Cambridge, Mass.: Harvard University Press.
Ayers, Sheli. 2004. "*Twin Peaks*, Weak Language and the Resurrection of Affect." In *The Cinema of David Lynch: American Dreams, Nightmare Visions*, edited by Erica Sheen and Annette Davison, 93–106. London: Wallflower Press.
Bachelard, Gaston. [1958] 1994. *The Poetics of Space.* Translated by Maria Jolas. Boston: Beacon Press.
Bailey, Dale. 1999. *American Nightmares: The Haunted House Formula in American Popular Fiction.* Bowling Green, Ohio: Bowling Green State University/Popular Press.
Barker, Clive. [1984] 1988. "The Midnight Meat Train." In *Clive Barker's Books of Blood. Omibus ed.* 1:28–51. London: Sphere.
———. [1988] 2014. *Cabal.* North Carolina: Crossroad Press. Digital ed.
———. 2007. *Mister B Gone.* New York: HarperPerennial.
———. 2012. "Being a Vegetarian Has Lost Me More Friends Than Being a Gay Man." Tweet, February 23. https://twitter.com/RealCliveBarker/status/172852961234534400.
Barthes, Roland. 1982. *Camera Lucida: Reflections on Photography.* Translated by Richard Howard. New York: Hill and Wang.

Behar, Katherine, ed. 2016. *Object-Oriented Feminism*. Minneapolis: University of Minnesota Press.
Bennett, Jane. 2001. *The Enchantment of Modern Life: Attachments, Crossings, and Ethics*. Princeton: Princeton University Press.
———. 2010. *Vibrant Matter: A Political Ecology of Things*. Durham, N.C.: Duke University Press.
Bernard, Mark. 2014. *Selling the Splat Pack: The DVD Revolution and the American Horror Film*. Edinburgh: Edinburgh University Press.
Blatty, William Blatty. 1971. *The Exorcist*. New York: Bantam.
Bloch, Robert. 1935. "The Shambler from the Stars." *Weird Tales* 26(3) (September), 368–75.
Bloom, Clive. 2012. "Horror Fiction: In Search of a Definition." In *A New Companion to the Gothic*, edited by David Punter, 211–23. Malden, Mass.: Wiley-Blackwell.
Bogost, Ian. 2009. "What Is Object-Oriented Ontology? A Definition for Ordinary Folk." December 8. http://bogost.com/writing/blog/what_is_objectoriented_ontolog/.
———. 2012. *Alien Phenomenology, or What It's Like to Be a Thing*. Minneapolis: University of Minnesota Press.
Botting, Fred. 1996. *Gothic*. London and New York: Routledge.
Bovsun, Mara. 2008. "Lost Boys of Texas." *Daily News*, June 28. https://www.nydailynews.com/news/crime/lost-boys-texas-article-1.292434.
Bradley, Doug. 1996. *Sacred Monsters: Behind the Mask of the Horror Actor*. London: Titan.
Braid, Barbara. 2013. "What Haunts Hundreds Hall? Transgression in Sarah Waters' *The Little Stranger*." In *Crossroads in Literature and Culture*, edited by Jacek Fabiszak, Ewa Urbaniak-Rybicka, and Bartosz Wolski, 135–45. Berlin and New York: Springer.
Braidotti, Rosi. 2013. *The Posthuman*. Medford, Mass.: Polity Press.
Brassier, Ray. 2007. *Nihil Unbound: Enlightenment and Extinction*. New York: Palgrave Macmillan.
Brink, Dennis Meyhoff. 2016. "Affective Atmospheres in the House of Usher." *Journal of the Short Story in English* 66 (Spring). https://journals.openedition.org/jsse/1695.
Broadbent, Geoffrey. 1973. *Design in Architecture: Architecture and the Human Sciences*. London and New York: John Wiley & Sons.
Brown, Bill. 2001. "Thing Theory." *Critical Inquiry* 28(1) (Autumn): 1–22.
Bruhm, Steven. 1994. *Gothic Bodies: The Politics of Pain in Romantic Fiction*. Philadelphia: University of Pennsylvania Press.
Bryant, Levi R. 2011. *The Democracy of Objects*. Ann Arbor, Mich.: Open Humanities Press.
Butler, Judith. 2004. *Precarious Life: The Powers of Mourning and Violence*. New York: Verso.
Byron, Glennis, and Dale Townshend, eds. 2013. *The Gothic World*. London and New York: Routledge.

Campbell, Ramsey. [1964] 1996. "The Plain of Sound." In *The New Lovecraft Circle*, edited by Robert M. Price, 3–15. New York: Ballantine.

———. [1964] [2011. "The Horror from the Bridge." In *The Inhabitant of the Lake & Other Unwelcome Tenants*, by Ramsey Campbell. Hornsea, East Yorkshire: PS Publishing. http://weirdfictionreview.com/2011/12/the-horror-from-the-bridge/.

Carroll, Nöel. 1990. *The Philosophy of Horror: or, Paradoxes of the Heart*. New York: Routledge.

Chambers, Robert. 1895. *The King in Yellow*. https://www.gutenberg.org/files/8492/8492-h/8492-h.htm.

Cho, Anjie. 2019. "What Are the Basic Principles of Feng Shui?" December 9. https://www.thespruce.com/what-is-feng-shui-1275060.

Clasen, Mathias. 2017. *Why Horror Seduces*. New York: Oxford University Press.

Cohen, Jeffrey Jerome. 1996. "Monster Culture (Seven Theses)." In *Monster Theory: Reading Culture*, edited by Jeffrey Jerome Cohen, 3–25. Minneapolis: University of Minnesota Press.

Cohenour, Gretchen. 2008. "A Man's Home Is His Castle: Bloodlines and *The Castle of Otranto*." *EAPSU Online: A Journal of Critical and Creative Work* 5: 73–87.

Cole, Andrew. 2013. "The Call of Things: A Critique of Object-Oriented Ontologies." *Minnesota Review* 80: 106–18.

Colebrook, Claire. 2014. *Death of the Posthuman: Essays on Extinction*. Vol. 1. London: Open Humanities Press.

Coverly, Merlin. 2018. *Psychogeography*. Harpenden, UK: OldCastle.

Curtis, Barry. 2008. *Dark Places: The Haunted House in Film*. London: Reaktion.

Danielewski, Mark Z. 2000. *House of Leaves: A Novel*. New York: Pantheons.

Davies, Owen. 2009. *Grimoires: A History of Magic Books*. Oxford and New York: Oxford University Press.

Dayan, Joan. 1994. "Amorous Bondage: Poe, Ladies, and Slaves." *American Literature* 66(2) (June): 239–73.

———. 2001. "Poe, Persons, and Property." In *Romancing the Shadow: Poe and Race*, edited by J. Gerald Kennedy and Liliane Weissberg, 106–26. Oxford and New York: Oxford University Press.

Del Pilar Blanco, María, and Esther Peeren, eds. 2013. *The Spectralities Reader: Ghosts and Haunting in Contemporary Cultural Theory*. London: Bloomsbury.

DeFazio, Kimberly. 2014. "The Spectral Ontology and Miraculous Materialism." *Red Critique* (Winter/Spring). http://redcritique.org/WinterSpring2014/spectralontologyandmiraculousmaterialism.htm.

Dent, Jonathan. 2012. "'The Anguish and Horror of Her Mind Defied All Control': The Fragmented Manuscript and Representations of the Past in Ann Radcliffe's *The Romance of the Forest* (1791)." *Victoriographies* 2(1): 15–30.

Derleth, August. [1945] 2003. *The Lurker at the Threshold*. New York: Carroll & Graf.

Derrida, Jacques. 1988. "Signature, Event, Context." In *Limited Inc.*, by Jacques Derrida. Translated by Jeffrey Mehlman, 1–23. Evanston, Ill.: Northwestern University Press.

———. 2006. *Specters of Marx: The State of Debt, the Work of Mourning & the New International*. New York: Routledge.

———. 2016. *Of Grammatology*. Translated by Gayatri Chakravorty Spivak. Baltimore: The Johns Hopkins University Press.

Downey, Dara. 2015. "Locating the Specter in Dan Curtis's *Burnt Offerings*." In *Cinematic Ghosts: Haunting and Spectrality from Silent Cinema to the Digital Era*, edited by Murray Leeder, 143–58. London: Bloomsbury.

Doyle, Jacqueline. 1993. "(Dis)Figuring Woman: Edgar Allan Poe's 'Berenice.'" *Poe Studies: History, Theory, Interpretation* 26 (1–2) (June): 13–21.

du Maurier, Daphne. [1938] 2006. *Rebecca*. New York: William Morrow.

Eco, Umberto. [1980] 2014. *The Name of the Rose*. Boston: Mariner.

Edwards, Rob. 2009. "Pharaohs Left Behind a Radioactive Curse." *New Scientist*. October 23. https://www.newscientist.com/article/mg16422092-700-pharaohs-left-behind-a-radioactive-curse/.

Elliott, Kamilla. 2012. *Portraiture and British Gothic Fiction: The Rise of Picture Identification, 1764–1835*. Baltimore: The Johns Hopkins University Press.

Ellis, Kate Ferguson. 1989. *The Contested Castle: Gothic Novels and the Subversion of Domestic Ideology*. Champaign: University of Illinois Press.

Ende, Michael. [1979] 1993. *The Neverending Story*. Translated by Ralph Manheim, New York: Puffin.

Fellion, Matthew, and Katherine Inglis. 2017. *Censored: A Literary History of Subversion & Control*. Montreal, Quebec: McGill-Queen's University Press.

Fiedler, Leslie. [1960] 1992. *Love & Death in the American Novel*. New York: Anchor.

"Firmness, Commodity, and Delight: Architecture in Special Collections." 2011. *University of Chicago Library*. https://www.lib.uchicago.edu/collex/exhibits/firmness-commodity-and-delight/.

Fisher, Mark. 2016. *The Weird and the Eerie*. London: Repeater.

Ford, Sarah Gilbreath. 2020. *Haunted Property: Slavery and the Gothic*. Jackson: University Press of Mississippi.

Fraser, Emma. 2019. "Horror, Femininity, and the Vulnerability of Bathrooms." *SyFyWire*. October 17. https://www.syfy.com/syfywire/horror-femininity-and-the-vulnerability-of-bathrooms.

Freud, Sigmund. 2003. *The Uncanny*. 1919. Translated by David McLintock. New York: Penguin.

Goddu, Teresa A. 2014. "The African American Slave Narrative and the Gothic." In *A Companion to American Gothic*, edited by Charles L. Crow, 71–83. John Wiley & Sons.

Gokey, Maureen. 2019. "Subterranean Spaces and Female Subversion in Walpole's *Castle of Otranto*." *Explicator* 77(2): 43–46.

Goulet, Andrea. 2017. "Tooth Decay: Edgar Allan Poe and the Neuro-déca'dent'isme of Villiers and Huysmans. *Nineteenth-Century French Studies* 45(3–4): 198–218.

Groom, Nick. 2012. *The Gothic: A Very Short Introduction.* Oxford: Oxford University Press.
Grusin, Richard, ed. 2015. *The Nonhuman Turn.* Minneapolis: University of Minnesota Press.
Halberstam, Judith (Jack). 1995. *Skin Shows: Gothic Horror and the Technology of Monsters.* Durham, N.C.: Duke University Press.
Hamilton, Natalie. 2008. "The A-Mazing House: The Labyrinth as Theme and Form in Mark Z. Danielewski's *House of Leaves.*" *Critique: Studies in Contemporary Fiction* 50(1): 3–16.
Hanich, Julian. 2010. *Cinematic Emotion in Horror Films and Thrillers: The Aesthetic Paradox of Pleasurable Fear.* New York: Routledge.
Haraway, Donna. 1991. "A Cyborg Manifesto: Science, Technology, and Socialist-Feminism in the Late Twentieth Century." In *Simians, Cyborgs and Women: The Reinvention of Nature*, by Donna Haraway, 149–81. New York: Routledge.
———. 1992. "The Promises of Monsters: A Regenerative Politics for Inappropriate/d Others." In *Cultural Studies*, edited by Lawrence Grossberg, Cary Nelson, and Paula A. Treichler, 295–336. New York: Routledge.
———. 2016. *Staying with the Trouble: Making Kin in the Chthulucene.* Durham, N.C.: Duke University Press.
Harman, Graham. 2005. *Guerrilla Metaphysics: Phenomenology and the Carpentry of Things.* Chicago: Open Court.
———. 2011. *The Quadruple Object.* Winchester, UK: Zero.
———. 2012. *Weird Realism: Lovecraft and Philosophy.* Winchester, UK: Zero.
Harris, Derrick. 2016. Rev. of *Dark Ecology: For a Logic of Future Coexistence*, by Timothy Morton. *Environmental Philosophy* 13(2) (Fall): 303–6.
Hawthorne, Nathaniel. [1851] 2005. *The House of the Seven Gables.* New York: W. W. Norton.
Heilmann, Ann. 2012. "Specters of the Victorian in the Neo-Forties Novel: Sarah Waters's *The Little Stranger* (2009) and Its Intertexts." *Contemporary Women's Writing* 6(1): 38–55.
Heller-Nicholas, Alexandra. 2019. *Masks in Horror Films: Eyes without Faces.* Cardiff: University of Wales Press.
Hilton, Leon. 2013. Review of *Animacies: Biopolitics, Racial Mattering, Queer Affect*, by Mel Y. Chen. *Bio/Zoo* 10(1) (Winter). https://hemisphericinstitute.org/en/emisferica-101/10-1-book-reviews/animacies-biopolitics-racial-mattering-and-queer-affect.html.
Hird, Myra J. 2017. "Proliferation, Extinction, and an Anthropocene Aesthetic." In *Posthumous Life: Theorizing Beyond the Posthuman*, edited by Jami Weinstein and Claire Colbrook, 251–69. New York: Columbia University Press.
Hogle, Jerrold E. 1994. "The Ghost of the Counterfeit in the Genesis of the Gothic." In *Gothick Origins and Innovations*, edited by Allan Lloyd Smith and Victor Sage, 23–33. Leiden: Rodopi.

Hoppenstand, Gary. 2013. *Clive Barker's Short Stories: Imagination as Metaphor in the Books of Blood and Other Works*. Jefferson, N.C.: McFarland.
Hurley, Kelly. 1996. *The Gothic Body: Sexuality, Materialism, and Degeneration at the* Fin de Siècle. Cambridge and New York: Cambridge University Press.
Huysmans, J. K. [1884] 2004. *Against Nature (À Rebours)*. New York: Penguin Classics.
Irwin, Margaret. 2011. "The Book." In *The Weird: A Compendium of Strange and Dark Stories*, edited by Ann and Jeff VanderMeer, 183–91. New York: Tor.
Jackson, Shirley. 1959. *The Haunting of Hill House*. New York: Penguin.
Jackson, Zakiyyah Iman. 2013. "Animal: New Directions in the Theorization of Race and Posthumanism." *Feminist Studies* 39 (3): 669–85.
———. 2020. *Becoming Human: Matter and Meaning in an Antiblack World*. New York: New York University Press.
Jacobs, W. W. 1902. "The Monkey's Paw." https://americanliterature.com/author/w-w-jacobs/short-story/the-monkeys-paw.
James, Henry. [1898] 1999. *The Turn of the Screw*. New York: W. W. Norton.
James, M. R. 1904a. "The Mezzotint." https://www.thin-ghost.org/items/show/145.
———. 1904b. "Oh, Whistle, and I'll Come to You, My Lad." https://www.fadedpage.com/books/20130332/html.php.
Janicker, Rebecca. 2015. *The Literary Haunted House: Lovecraft, Matheson, King and the Horror in Between*. Jefferson, N.C.: McFarland.
Jentsch, Ernest. [1906] 1997. "On the Psychology of the Uncanny." *Angelaki: Journal of the Theoretical Humanities* 2(1): 7–16.
Joshi, S. T. 2014. "Afterword to Lovecraft's 'History of the *Necronomicon*.'" In *Lovecraft and a World in Transition*, by S. T. Joshi, 419–21. New York: Hippocampus Press.
Keetley, Dawn. 2005. "Pregnant Women and Envious Men in 'Morella,' 'Berenice,' 'Ligeia,' and 'The Fall of the House of Usher.'" *Poe Studies: History, Theory, Interpretation* 38: 1–16.
Khairy, Wael. 2014. "Film Analysis: 'The Babadook.'" *The Cinephile Fix*. November 22. https://cinephilefix.com/2014/11/22/film-analysis-the-babadook/.
King, Stephen. [1972] 2011. "The Mangler." In *Night Shift*, by Stephen King, 115–44. New York: Anchor.
———. [1973] 2011. "Trucks." In *Night Shift*, by Stephen King, 197–222. New York: Anchor .
———. [1977] 2013. *The Shining*. New York: Anchor.
———. [1980] 2016. "The Monkey." In *Skeleton Crew: Stories*, by Stephen King, 159–202. New York: Scribner.
———. 1983a. *Christine*. New York: Signet.
———. [1983b] 2002. *Pet Sematary*. New York: Gallery.
———. 1986. *It: A Novel*. New York: Pocket.
———. 1987. *The Eyes of the Dragon: A Novel*. New York: Viking.
———. 1991. *Needful Things*. New York: Signet.
———. [2002] 2017. *From a Buick 8*. New York: Gallery.

———. 2012. *The Stand*. New York: Anchor.
———. 2014. *Revival*. New York: Gallery.
Kreienbrock, Jörg. 2012. *Malicious Objects, Anger Management, and the Question of Modern Literature*. Bronx, N.Y.: Fordham University Press.
Kristeva, Julia. 1982. *Powers of Horror: An Essay on Abjection*. Translated by Leon S. Roudiez. New York: Columbia University Press.
Kröger, Lisa. 2009. "*House of Leaves*: A Postmodern Retelling of Shirley Jackson's *The Haunting of Hill House*." *Journal of the Georgia Philological Association* (December): 149–56.
Latour, Bruno. 2001. *The Pasteurization of France*. Translated by Alan Sheridan. Cambridge, Mass: Harvard University Press.
———. 2012. "Love Your Monsters: Why We Must Care for Our Technologies as We Do Our Children." *Breakthrough Institute* (February 14). https://thebreakthrough.org/journal/issue-2/love-your-monsters.
Lauro, Sarah Juliet, ed. 2017. *Zombie Theory: A Reader*. Minneapolis: University of Minnesota Press, vii–xxiii.
Lauro, Sarah Juliet, and Karen Embry. 2017. "A Zombie Manifesto: The Nonhuman Condition in the Era of Advanced Capitalism." In *Zombie Theory: A Reader*, edited by Sarah Juliet Lauro, 395–412. Minneapolis: University of Minnesota Press.
LeFanu, Sheridan. [1872] 1989. *Carmilla: The Penguin Book of Vampire Stories*. Edited by Alan Ryan, 71–137. New York: Penguin.
Letissier, Georges. 2017. "Hauntology as Compromise between Traumatic Realism and Spooky Romance in Sarah Waters's *The Little Stranger*." In *Trauma and Romance in Contemporary British Literature*, edited by Jean-Michel Ganteau and Susana Onega, 34–50. New York: Routledge.
Lewis, Matthew. [1796] 2016. *The Monk*. Edited by Nick Groom. Oxford: Oxford University Press.
Lightning, Robert K. 2000. "Interracial Tensions in *Night of the Living Dead*." *CineAction* 53: 22–29.
Ligotti, Thomas. [1986] 2010. "Vasterien." In *Songs of a Dead Dreamer*, by Thomas Ligotti. Burton, Mich.: Subterranean Press. Kindle edition.
Lindfield, Peter N. 2017. "Imagining the Undefined Castle in *The Castle of Otranto*: Engravings and Interpretations." *Image[&]Narrative* 18 (30): 46–63.
Lippert, Conny. 2012–13. "Lovecraft's Grimoires: Intertextuality and the *Necronomicon*." In *Working with English: Medieval and Modern Language, Literature and Drama* 8: 41–50.
Lipski, Jakub. 2017. "Moving Pictures: The Animated Portrait in *The Caste of Otranto* and the Post-Walpolean Gothic." *Image[&]Narrative* 18 (3): 64–79.
Long, Frank Belknap. 1928. "The Space-Eaters." *Weird Tales* 11(1). https://en.wikisource.org/wiki/The_Space-Eaters.
Lovecraft, Howard Phillips. [1922] 1999. "The Hound." *The Call of Cthulhu and Other Weird Stories*, edited by S. T. Joshi, 81–88. New York: Penguin.

———. [1925] 1999. "The Festival." In *The Call of Cthulhu and Other Weird Stories*, edited by S. T. Joshi, 109–18. New York: Penguin.
———. [1926] 1999. "The Call of Cthulhu." In *The Call of Cthulhu and Other Weird Stories*, edited by S. T. Joshi, 139–69. London: Penguin.
———. [1927] 2010. "History of the *Necronomicon*." In *The Other Gods and More Unearthly Tales*, edited by Jeffrey Andrew Weinstock, 267–69. New York: Barnes & Noble.
———. [1928] 2001. "The Dunwich Horror." In *The Thing on the Doorstep and Other Weird Stories*, edited by S. T. Joshi, 206–45. New York: Penguin.
———. [1932] 2013. "The Dreams in the Witch House." In *H. P. Lovecraft: The Classic Horror Stories*, edited by Roger Luckhurst, 285–319. New York: Oxford.
———. [1936a] 2013. *At the Mountains of Madness*. In *H. P. Lovecraft: The Classic Horror Stories*, edited by Roger Luckhurst, 182–284. New York: Oxford University Press.
———. [1936b] 2009. "The Shadow Out of Time." In *At the Mountains of Madness and Other Weird Tales*, edited by Jeffrey Andrew Weinstock, 265–320. New York: Barnes & Noble, Inc.
———. [1936c] 1999. "The Shadow Over Innsmouth." In *The Call of Cthulhu and Other Weird Stories*, edited by S. T. Joshi, 268–335. New York: Penguin.
———. [1943] 2001. *The Case of Charles Dexter Ward*. In *The Thing on the Doorstep and Other Weird Stories*, edited by S. T. Joshi, 90–205. New York: Penguin.
———. 1973. *Supernatural Horror in Literature*. New York: Dover..
Luckhurst, Roger. 2018. "Corridor Gothic." *Gothic Studies* 20(1–2) (November): 295–310.
Lumley, Brian. 1977. *The Horror at Oakdeene*. Sauk City, Wisc.: Arkham House.
MacCormack, Patricia. 2020. *The Ahuman Manifesto: Activism for the End of the Anthropocene*. London: Bloomsbury.
Machen, Arthur. [1894] 2020. *The Great God Pan*. In *The Great God Pan and Other Horror Stories*, edited by Aaron Worth, 9–54. Oxford: Oxford University Press.
Mandel, Emily St. John. 2014. *Station Eleven*. New York: Alfred A. Knopf.
Maturin, Charles. [1820] 2008. *Melmoth the Wanderer*. Edited by Douglas Grant. Oxford and New York: Oxford University Press.
Mbembe, Achille. 2019. *Necropolitics*. Durham, N.C.: Duke University Press.
McCullagh, John Francis. 2018. "The Cinematic Power of Hitchcock's Dolly Zoom Technique." *Beat* (December 14). https://www.premiumbeat.com/blog/hitchcocks-dolly-zoom-filmmaking-technique/.
McRobbie, Linda Rodriguez. 2013. "The Strange and Mysterious History of the Ouija Board." *Smithsonian Magazine* (October 27). https://www.smithsonianmag.com/history/the-strange-and-mysterious-history-of-the-ouija-board-5860627/.
McRoy, Jay. 2002. "There Are No Limits: Splatterpunk, Clive Barker, and the Body in-extremis." *Paradoxa* 17: 130–50.
Meillassoux, Quentin. 2008. *After Finitude: An Essay on the Necessity of Contingency*. Translated by Ray Brassier. London and New York: Continuum International.

Miéville, China. 2016. "Afterword: Interview with China Miéville." In *The Age of Lovecraft*, edited by Carl H. Sederholm and Jeffrey Andrew Weinstock, 231–44. Minneapolis: University of Minnesota Press.

Melville, Herman. [1852] 1996. *Pierre: or, The Ambiguities*. Edited by William Spengemann. New York: Penguin.

Mendlesohn, Farah. 2008. *Rhetorics of Fantasy*. Middletown, Conn.: Wesleyan University Press.

Merritt, Naomi. 2010. "Cannibalistic Capitalism and other American Delicacies: A Bataillean Taste of *The Texas Chainsaw Massacre*." *Film-Philosophy* 14(1): 202–31.

Mills, Sandra. 2018. "Discussing Dolls: Horror and the Human Double." In *The Palgrave Handbook to Horror Literature*, edited by Kevin Corstorphine and Laura R. Kremmel, 249–58. New York: Palgrave.

Miyazawa, Naomi. 2017. "Poe, The Portrait, and the Daguerreotype: Poe's Living Dead and the Visual Arts." *Poe Studies* 15: 88–106.

Mori, Masahiro. [1970] 2012. "The Uncanny Valley." Translated by Karl F. MacDorman and Norri Kageki. *IEEE Robotics and Automation* 19(2): 98–100.

Morton, Timothy. 2007. *Ecology without Nature: Rethinking Environmental Aesthetics*. Cambridge, Mass.: Harvard University Press.

———. 2010. *The Ecological Thought*. Cambridge, Mass.: Harvard University Press.

———. 2013a. *Hyperobjects: Philosophy and Ecology after the End of the World*. Minneapolis: University of Minnesota Press.

———. 2013b. *Realist Magic: Objects, Ontology, Causality*. Ann Arbor, Mich.: Open Humanities Press.

———. 2016. *Dark Ecology: For a Logic of Future Coexistence*. New York: Columbia University Press.

Mulvey-Roberts, Marie, ed. [1998] 2009. *The Handbook of the Gothic*. 2nd ed. New York: New York University Press.

Nelson, Victoria. 2001. *The Secret Life of Puppets*. Cambridge, Mass.: Harvard University Press.

Newitz, Annalee. 2006. *Pretend We're Dead: Capitalist Monsters in American Pop Culture*. Durham, N.C.: Duke University Press.

Olney, Ian. 2014. "Unmanning *The Exorcist*: Sex, Gender and Excess in the 1970s Euro-Horror Possession Film." *Quarterly Review of Film and Video* 31(6): 561–71.

Pascal, Richard. 2014. "Walking Alone Together: Family Monsters in 'The Haunting of Hill House.'" *Studies in the Novel* 46(4): 464–85.

Peeples, Scott. 1998. *Edgar Allan Poe Revisited*. New York: Twayne.

Perron, Bernard. 2017. "Drawing (to) Fear and Horror: Into the Frame of Clive Barker's *The Midnight Meat Train* and *Dread* Comic and Film Adaptations." In *Clive Barker: Darker Imaginer*, edited by Sorcha Ní Fhlainn, 85–109. Manchester: Manchester University Press.

Phillips, Wesley. 2012. "The Future of Speculation?" *Cosmos and History: The Journal of Natural and Social Philosophy* 8(1): 289–303.

Poe, Edgar Allan. [1835] 1996. "Berenice." In *Poe: Poetry, Tales, & Selected Essays*, edited by Patrick F. Quinn and G. R. Thompson, 225–33. New York: Library of America.

———. [1835] 2015. "Letter to Thomas W. White." April 30. In *Edgar Allan Poe Society of Baltimore*, December 17. Online: accessed August 17, 2015. http://www.eapoe.org/works/letters/p3504300.htm.

———. [1839] 1996. "The Fall of the House of Usher." In *Poe: Poetry, Tales, & Selected Essays*, edited by Patrick F. Quinn and G. R. Thompson, 317–36. New York: Library of America.

———. [1842] 1996. "The Oval Portrait." In *Poe: Poetry, Tales, & Selected Essays*, edited by Patrick F. Quinn and G. R. Thompson, 481–84. New York: Library of America.

Poznar, Susan. 2015. "Rocking and Reeling through the Doors of Miscreation: Disequilibrium in Shirley Jackson's *The Haunting of Hill House*." In *Monsters and Monstrosity from the Fin de Siècle to the Millennium*, edited by Sharla Hutchison and Rebecca A. Brown, 144–65. Jefferson, N.C.: McFarland.

Punter, David. 1999. "Introduction: of Apparitions." In *Spectral Readings: Toward a Gothic Geography*, edited by Glennis Byron and David Punter, 1–8. New York: Macmillan.

———, ed. 2012. *A New Companion to the Gothic*. Malden, Mass.: Wiley-Blackwell.

Raby, Peter. 2013. "Poisoned by a Book: The Lethal Aura of *The Picture of Dorian Gray*." In *Oscar Wilde in Context*, edited by Kerry Powell and Peter Raby, 159–67. Cambridge and New York: Cambridge University Press.

Radcliffe, Ann. 1826. "On the Supernatural in Poetry." *New Monthly Magazine* 7: 145–52.

———. [1791] 2009. *The Romance of the Forest*. Edited by Chloe Chard. Oxford and New York: Oxford University Press.

Radford, Benjamin. 2014. "Mystery of the Hope Diamond Curse." *LiveScience*, April 30. https://www.livescience.com/45239-hope-diamond-curse.html

Renzi, Kristen. 2012. "Hysteric Vocalizations of the Female Body in Edgar Allan Poe's 'Berenice.'" *ESQ: A Journal of Nineteenth-Century American Literature and Culture* 58(4) [229]: 601–40.

Reyes, Xavier Aldana. 2016. *Horror Film and Affect: Towards a Corporeal Model of Viewership*. New York: Routledge.

Reynolds, Nicole. 2013. "Gothic and the Architectural Imagination, 1740–1840." In *The Gothic World*, edited by Glennis Byron and Dale Townshend, 85–97. London and New York: Routledge.

Rowling, J. K. 1998. *Harry Potter and the Chamber of Secrets*. London: Bloomsbury.

Sagan, Carl. 1985. *Contact: A Novel*. New York: Gallery.

Saldanha, Arun J. J. 2009. "Back to the Great Outdoors: Speculative Realism as Philosophy of Science." *Cosmos and History: The Journal of Natural and Social Philosophy* 5(2). https://www.cosmosandhistory.org/index.php/journal/article/view/118.

Saler, Michael. 2012. *As If: Modern Enchantment and the Literary Prehistory of Virtual Reality*. Oxford and New York: Oxford University Press.

Schneider, Steven J. 2009. "The Paradox of Fiction." *Internet Journal of Philosophy*. June 9. http://www.iep.utm.edu/fict-par/.

Sconce, Jeffrey. 2000. *Haunted Media: Electronic Presence from Telegraphy to Television*. Durham, N.C.: Duke University Press.

Sears, John. 2011. *Stephen King's Gothic*. Cardiff: University of Wales Press.

Sedgwick, Eve Kosofsky. 1986. *The Coherence of Gothic Conventions*. New York: Methuen.

Seigh, Steve. 2016. "Ink & Pixel: The Babadook." *JoBlo*, Nov. 10, 2016. https://www.joblo.com/ink-pixel-the-babadook-697/.

Shaviro, Steven. 2015. "Speculative Realism—A Primer." *Terremoto* 2 (June 1). https://terremoto.mx/article/speculative-realism-a-primer/.

Shelley, Mary Wollstonecraft. [1818] 1993. *Frankenstein or The Modern Prometheus: The 1818 Text*, edited by Marilyn Butler. Oxford and New York: Oxford University Press.

Shomura, Chad. 2017. "Exploring the Promise of New Materialism." *Lateral: Journal of the Cultural Studies Association* 6(1) (Spring). https://csalateral.org/issue/6-1/forum-alt-humanities-new-materialist-philosophy-promise-new-materialisms-shomura/

Shuker, Karl P. N. 1996. *The Unexplained: An Illustrated Guide to the World's Natural and Paranormal Mysteries*. London: Carlton.

"Sick Building Syndrome." n.d. *Healthline*, https://www.healthline.com/health/sick-building-syndrome#prevention.

Simon, Joshua. 2013. *Neomaterialism*. Berlin: Sternberg Press.

Smith, Andrew, and William Hughes. 2003. "Introduction: Enlightenment Gothic and Postcolonialism." In *Empire and Gothic: The Politics of Genre*, edited by Andrew Smith and William Hughes, 1–12. New York: Palgrave.

Smith, Clark Ashton. 1932. "The Nameless Offspring." *Magazine of Horror* 33. (Summer). http://www.eldritchdark.com/writings/short-stories/150/the-nameless-offspring.

Sontag, Susan. [1965] 2004. "The Imagination of Disaster." In *Liquid Metal: The Science Fiction Film Reader*, edited by Sean Redmond, 40–47. London: Wallflower Press.

Spitzer, Leo. 1952. "A Reinterpretation of 'The Fall of the House of Usher.'" *Comparative Literature* 4(4) (Autumn): 351–63.

Spooner, Catherine. 2017. *Post-Millennial Gothic: Comedy, Romance and the Rise of Happy Gothic*. London: Bloomsbury.

Stallybrass, Peter. 1998. "Marx's Coat." In *Border Fetishisms: Material Objects in Unstable Spaces*, edited by Patricia Spyer, 183–207. New York: Routledge.

Steadman, John L. 2015. *H. P. Lovecraft and the Black Magickal Tradition: The Master of Horror's Influence on Modern Occultism*. San Francisco and Newburyport, Mass.: Weiser.

Stoker, Bram. [1897] 1993. *Dracula*. New York: Penguin.
Stolwijk, J. A. 1991. "Sick-Building Syndrome." *Environmental Health Perspectives* 95 (November): 99–100.
Tally, Robert T. Jr. 2018. *Topophrenia: Place, Narrative, and the Spatial Imagination*. Bloomington: Indiana University Press.
Tatar, Maria M. 1981. "The Houses of Fiction: Toward a Definition of the Uncanny." *Comparative Literature* 33(2): 167–82.
Taylor, Matthew A. 2007. "Edgar Allan Poe's (Meta)physics: A Pre-History of the Post-Human." *Nineteenth-Century Literature* 62(2): 193–221.
Tchen, John Kuo Wei, and Dylan Yeats. 2014. *Yellow Peril! An Archive of Anti-Asian Fear*. New York: Verso.
Thacker, Eugene. 2011. *In the Dust of This Planet: Horror of Philosophy. Vol. 1*. Winchester, UK: Zero.
Thrift, Nigel. 2010. "Understanding the Material Practices of Glamour." In *The Affect Theory Reader*, edited by Melissa Gregg and Gregory J. Seigworth, 289–308. Durham, N.C.: Duke University Press.
Tompkins, Kyla Wazana. 2016. "On the Limits and Promise of New Materialist Philosophy." *Lateral: Journal of the Cultural Studies Association* 5(1) (Spring). https://csalateral.org/issue/5-1/forum-alt-humanities-new-materialist-philosophy-tompkins/.
Tracy, Ann B. *The Gothic Novel, 1790–1830: Plot Summaries and Index to Motifs*. Lexington: University of Kentucky Press, 1981.
Tsing, Anna, Heather Swanson, Elaine Gan, and Nils Bubandt, eds. 2017. *Arts of Living on a Damaged Planet*. Minneapolis: University of Minnesota Press.
Tuan, Yi-Fu. 1977. *Space and Place: The Perspective of Experience*. Minneapolis: University of Minnesota Press.
Twitchell, James. 1977. "Poe's 'The Oval Portrait' and the Vampire Motif." *Studies in Short Fiction* 14: 387–93.
VanderMeer, Jeff. 2016. "Hauntings in the Anthropocene: An Initial Exploration." *Environmental Critique* (July). https://environmentalcritique.wordpress.com/2016/07/07/hauntings-in-the-anthropocene/.
Varma, Devendra P. 1957. *The Gothic Flame: Being a History of the Gothic Novel in England; Its Origins, Efflorescence, Disintegration, and Residuary Influences*. London: A. Barker.
Varnado, S. L. 1987. *Haunted Presence: The Numinous in Gothic Fiction*. Tuscaloosa: University of Alabama Press.
Wagner, Tamara. 2013. "Gothic and the Victorian Home." In *The Gothic World*, edited by Glennis Byron and Dale Townshend, 110–20. London and New York: Routledge.
Walker, I. M. 1966. "The 'Legitimate Sources' of Terror in 'The Fall of the House of Usher.'" *Modern Language Review* 61(4) (October): 585–92.
Walpole, Horace. [1764] 2014. *The Castle of Otranto: A Gothic Story*. Edited by Nick Groom. Oxford: Oxford University Press.
Walton, Kendall. 1978. "Fearing Fictions." *Journal of Philosophy* 75(1): 5–27.

Waters, Sarah. 2009. *The Little Stranger*. New York: Riverhead.
Weheliye, Alexander G. 2014. *Habeas Viscus: Racializing Assemblages, Biopolitics, and Black Feminist Theories of the Human*. Durham, N.C.: Duke University Press.
Weinstock, Jeffrey Andrew. 2004. "Introduction: The Spectral Turn." In *Spectral America: Phantoms and the National Imagination*, edited by Jeffrey Andrew Weinstock, 3–17. Madison: University of Wisconsin Press.
———. 2008. *Scare Tactics: Supernatural Fiction by American Women*. Bronx, N.Y.: Fordham University Press.
———. 2018. "The Soul of the Matter: *Frankenstein* Meets H. P. Lovecraft's 'Herbert West—Reanimator.'" In *Adapting Frankenstein: The Monster's Eternal Lives in Popular Culture*," edited by Dennis Perry and Dennis Cutchins, 221–35. New York: Palgrave.
———. 2020. "Invisible Monsters: Vision, Horror, and Contemporary Culture." In *The Monster Theory Reader*, edited by Jeffrey Andrew Weinstock, 358–73. Minneapolis: University of Minnesota Press.
———, ed. 2020. *The Monster Theory Reader*. Minneapolis: University of Minnesota Press.
Wellman, Manly Wade. 1937. "The Terrible Parchment." *Weird Tales* 30(2): 238–42. Available at https://archive.org/details/Weird_Tales_v30n02_1937-08_sas/page/n1115/mode/2up?q=Clark+Ashton+Smith.
Wharton, Edith. [1931] 1973. "Pomegranate Seed." In *The Ghost Stories of Edith Wharton*, 219–53. New York: Scribner.
Wilde, Oscar. [1890] 2008. *The Picture of Dorian Gray*. In *Oscar Wilde: The Major Works*, edited by Isobel Murray, 47–214. Oxford and New York: Oxford University Press.
Wilson, Michael T. 2015. "'Absolute Reality' and the Role of the Ineffable in Shirley Jackson's *The Haunting of Hill House*." *Journal of Popular Culture* 48(1): 114–23.
Winter, Kari J. 1992. *Subjects of Slavery, Agents of Change: Women and Power in Gothic Novels and Slave Narratives, 1790–1865*. Athens: University of Georgia Press.
Wolfendale, Peter. 2019. *Object-Oriented Philosophy: The Noumenon's New Clothes*, Falmouth, UK: Urbanomic.
Wolf-Meyer, Matthew J. 2019. *Theory for the World to Come: Speculative Fiction and Apocalyptic Anthropology*. Minneapolis: University of Minnesota Press.
Wynter, Sylvia. 2003. "Unsettling the Coloniality of Being/Power/Truth/Freedom: Towards the Human, After Man, Its Overrepresentation—An Argument." *CR: The New Centennial Review* 3(3) (Fall): 257–337.
Ziolkowski, Theodore. 1977. *Disenchanted Images: A Literary Iconology*. Princeton: Princeton University Press.
Žižek, Slavoj. 2008. *For They Know Not What They Do: Enjoyment as a Political Factor*. New York: Verso.

Index

13 Ghosts, 49–50

abhuman, 175nn2–3
abjection, 75–76, 91, 92
actor-network theory, 3, 6, 7, 8, 20. *See also* Latour, Bruno
affect, 3, 9, 10, 11, 12, 15, 76, 87, 118, 129, 146–147, 152, 156, 161
affect theory, 7, 20, 70, 72–73, 144
Agamben, Giorgio, 178n2
Agrippa, Cornelius, 123
A-ha (band), 131
Alaimo, Stacy, 67, 73
alien. *See* extraterrestrial
Alien (1979 film), 76, 111
Aliens (1986 film), 111
Allen, Lewis, 49
Allewaert, Monique, 30–31, 94
Amenábar, Alejandro, 104
Amick, Mädchen, 63
Anderson, Brad, 86–87, 147
animal studies, 7, 20
Amityville Horror, The, 150
Annabelle (character), 108, 110, 113
Annabelle (franchise), 108–109
Annihilation (2018 film), 26
Annihilation (novel), 26
Anthropocene, 8, 12–13, 14, 15, 19; and anxiety, 8 19–52, 80, 81
anthropocentrism, 4, 6, 7–8, 10, 12–13, 19, 24, 30, 36, 39, 73, 81, 132, 164, 172
apocalypse, vii, 12, 20, 25, 32–34, 39, 172
Applegate, Royce D., 61

Aranda, Vincente, 52
architecture, 140–142, 150, 156, 179n2
Army of Darkness, 126, 126, 132–133, 133
Arnold, Newt, 54
Aronofsky, Darren, 53
Ashbrook, Dana, 58
Atmosphere, 156, 159
Austin, J. L., 115–116
automaton, 107
Ayers, Sheli, 62

Babadook, The, ix, 128–129, 130
Bachelard, Gaston, 141–142, 143
Bailey, Dale, 144, 154, 156, 178–179n1
Barker, Clive, 52, 76, 81–85, 86–87, 132, 176n9; *Cabal*, 86–87, 90; *The Hellbound Heart*, 176n9; "The Midnight Meat Train," 76, 81–85, 176–177nn9–10; *Mister B Gone*, 132; *Nightbreed*, 86, 89–90
Barthes, Roland, 139
Batman Begins, 88
Bayona, J. A., 88
Behar, Katherine, 16
Bennett, Jane, vii, viii, 1, 8, 9–12, 19, 30, 34, 35, 38–39, 40, 42, 43, 44, 53–54, 63, 67, 70, 73, 74, 79–80, 83, 136, 142, 169
Bernard, Mark, 175n4
Bertino, Bryan, 52, 88
Bettis, Angela, 112–113
Beymer, Richard, 58
ben Bezalel, Judah Loew (Rabbi), 110
Black, Karen, 160
Black Swan, 53

Blade Runner, 108, 111
Blair, Linda, 85
Blatty, William Peter, 85
Bloch, Robert, 125
Blood Spattered Bride, The, 52
Bloom, Clive 14
body, 12, 14, 27, 30–31, 40, 44, 55, 72–114, 115, 175nn2–3
Boese, Carl, 109
Bogost, Ian, 8, 9, 23, 24, 30, 31, 34–35, 38, 39, 42, 67, 73–74, 168–169
de Bont, Jan, 98, 147
book, 14, 44, 115–136; accursed, 116, 118–135; corrupting 116, 118–122; grimoire, 116, 122–129; living, 116, 126, 132–136; portal, 116, 130–132; recovered, 117–118, 178n1
Book of Eibon, The, 123
Botting, Fred, 1, 4, 44
Bovsun, Mara, 35
Boyle, Lara Flynn, 63
Bradley, Doug, 177n13
Braid, Barbara, 180n11
Braidotti, Rosi, 29
Brassier, Ray, 32, 33, 36
Brenner, Yul, 113
Brink, Dennis Meyhoff, 156, 180n7
Broadbent, Geoffrey, 140–141
Brown, Bill, 9–10
Bruhm, Stephen, 175n3
Bryant, Levi R., 30, 72, 73–74, 80
Bubandt, Nils, 8, 21–23, 29–30, 33
building, 14, 44, 137–170
Burke, Edmund, 3
Burnt Offerings (1976 film), 160–162, 161, 163, 169, 180n10
Butler, Judith, 178n2
Byron, Glennis, 143

Cabin in the Woods, The, viii–x, 52–53, 70, 126–127
Cameron, James, 111, 112
de Camp, L. Sprague, 125
Campbell, Bruce, 132–133, 149–150, 150
Campbell, Ramsey, 125
Candyman, 150
cannibalism, 72, 76, 82, 83, 84, 91, 92, 93
capitalism, 47–48, 68–69, 76, 176–177n9
Carpenter, John, 55, 76, 86, 130
Carroll, Noël, 41, 42
Castle, William, 50
Castle of Otranto, The. See Walpole, Horace
categorical confusion, 2
capitalism, 7, 76, 84–85
Chambers, Robert, 119, 120–122, 123

Chappelle, Joe, 52
Chen, Joan, 62
Chen, Mel Y., 30
Child's Play (franchise), 108
Cho, Anjie, 142
Christine (car), ix, 55–56, 67
chthulucene, 4–9, 29
Chucky (character), 108, 110, 113
Clement, Jemaine, 93
class (social), 180n11
climate change, 6, 20, 26, 32, 37
Cohen, Jeffrey Jerome, 27–28, 29, 31, 32, 38
Cohenour, Gretchen, 179n3
Cole, Andrew, 16
Colebrook, Claire, 32
Collette, Toni, 149
colonialism, 7, 31,45–48, 75, 94, 95
commodity fetishism, 16, 48, 70–71
Conjuring, The (franchise), 108–109
Contact (film), 25, 26
Corll, Dean Arnold, 34, 35
corpse, 3, 11, 34, 35, 39, 47, 48, 54, 66, 71, 72, 75, 80, 82, 83, 86, 91, 92, 93, 95, 108, 118
correlationalism, 8, 9, 11, 14, 16, 23, 36, 39, 81
Coulson, Catherine E., 62
Courtney, James Jude, 88
Coverly, Merlin, 139
Covid-19, 32
Craven, Wes, 151
Creature From the Black Lagoon, 53
Crichton, Michael, 112
Cronenberg, David, 76, 86
Cthulhu, 4–9, 13, 123
Curtis, Barry, 144–145, 169, 178–179n1
Curtis, Dan, 160, 162
cyborg, 28–29, 30
Cyborg Manifesto, A, 7, 28, 108. *See also* Haraway, Donna

Da Re, Eric, 58
Danielewski, Mark Z., 165–170
dark ecology, 37–38. *See also* Morton, Timothy
dark enchantment, 42–44, 49, 52, 57
Davies, Owen, 123, 125
Davis, Bette, 160
Davis, Don S., 63
Davis, Essie, 128
Dayan, Joan, 176n8
De Vermis Mysteriis, 123, 127
Debord, Guy, 139
deconstruction, 21, 23, 27, 28–29
Dee, John, 125
DeFazio, Kimberly, 15–16, 39

INDEX

demon, 37, 52, 62, 68, 85–87, 108, 109, 110, 117, 126, 127, 132, 134, 135
Dent, Jonathan, 178n1
Depp, Johnny, 131
Derleth, August, 125
Derrida, Jacques, 20–21, 27, 32, 50, 98, 167
Descent, The, 151
Deschanel, Mary Jo, 64
Dickens, Charles, 179n2
doll, ix, 10, 55, 72, 89, 90, 91, 95, 107–114; and voodoo, 109, 110
dolly zoom, 151, 180n6
Donner, Richard, 105
doppelgänger, 66
Dougherty, Michael, 88
Downey, Dara, 180n10
Doyle, Jacqueline, 176n6
Dracula (character), 86
Dracula (novel), 117, 118
Drag Me to Hell (film), 46
dread, 2, 6, 15, 42, 57, 59, 73, 129, 152, 153, 169, 171, 172, 177n10; architectural, 146, 149, 152, 170
Dwyer, Pip, 105

Eco, Umberto, 119
eco-criticism, vii
Edwards, Rob, 49
eerie, the, 20, 22–23, 39, 108
Elliott, Kamilla, 96–98, 116
Ellis, Kate Ferguson, 143
Embry, Karen, 177–178n1
enchantment, vii, 38, 39, 40, 42–44, 46, 48
Ende, Michael, 130
Enlightenment, The, 12, 44, 46, 47, 109
Evil Dead, 150, 152
Evil Dead II, 126, 149–150, 150
Ewing, Barbara, 55
Ex Machina (2014 film), 112
exceptionalism, 7, 17, 30, 73, 111, 124, 128, 172, 177n10. *See also* anthropocentrism
Exorcist, The, 50, 85, 177n11
Expanse, The (TV series), 25, 26
extinctionist turn, 32
extraterrestrial, 25

Family Guy, 68
fantasy (genre), 43–44, 45–46, 55–56, 87, 127, 130
Fellion, Matthew, 120
female Gothic, 74–75, 76, 175n1, 179n3
feng shui, 139, 142, 170
Fenn, Sherilyn, 58
Ferrer, Miguel, 66

Fiedler, Leslie, 143
Final Destination 3, 101, 105
Fisher, Mark, 22–23, 24, 25
Flanagan, Mike, 55
flat ontology, 13, 16, 30, 39, 73, 74, 77, 80
Fly, The (1986 film), 76
Forbes, Bryan, 112
Ford, Sarah Gilbreath, 75
Foucault, Michel, 28, 32, 44
Francis, Freddie, 55
Franju, Georges, 89
Frankenstein (novel), 75–76, 111, 112, 117, 118
Fraser, Emma, 179n5
Freud, Sigmund, 32, 42, 57, 107–108, 146–147, 149, 152, 176n5
Freund, Karl, 54
Friday the Thirteenth (franchise), 126, 177n14
Friedkin, William, 50, 85
Frost, Mark, 57
Frost, Warren, 58

Gabriadze, Leo, 50
Galvani, Luigi, 111
Gan, Elaine, 8, 21–23, 29–30, 33
Garland, Alex, 112
ghost, 21–22, 23, 24, 25, 29, 32, 37, 39, 108, 109, 110, 137, 145–146, 149, 150, 157, 162–164, 169
Ghostbusters II, 98
Gibson, Brian, 50
Girard, François, 48
Global Warming. *See* climate change
Goaz, Harry, 59
Goddard, Drew, viii–ix, 52–53, 126
Goddu, Teresa A., 74–75
Gokey, Maureen, 179n3
Goldblum, Jeff, 76
golem, 109–110, 109
Golem, How He Came into the World, 109
Gothic (genre): and aesthetics, 15; appeal of, 41–44; generic features, 143
Gothic materialism, 1–2, 3, 4, 14, 19, 40, 71, 171
Goulet, Andrea, 176n5
Great Outdoors, The, 24, 36, 168, 169
Green, David Gordon, 88
Gréville, Edmond T., 54
grimoire, ix, 116, 118, 122–129, 131, 134
Groom, Nick, 1–2, 15
Grusin, Richard, vii, 4, 7, 19–20

Halberstam, Jack, 27
Halloween (franchise), 88, 177n14

Halperin, Victor, 86, 177n12
Hamilton, Linda, 112
hands, possessed, 54
Hands of a Stranger, 54
Hands of Orlac, The, 54
Hanich, Julian, 175n3
Hannibal (TV series), 35
happy Gothic, 15
Haraway, Donna, viii, 4–9, 28–29, 108
Harman, Graham, vii, 9, 23–24, 25, 33, 35–36, 38, 59, 73, 80
Hamilton, Natalie, 168
Hannibal Lecter, 35
Harris, Derrick, 38
Harry Potter (franchise), 56, 123, 130–131, 132
Hatfield, Hurd, 99
haunted house, 137, 142–170
Haunted Mansion. See Walt Disney's Haunted Mansion
haunting, 21–23, 24–25, 26, 34, 37, 137, 142, 145, 146, 148–149, 150, 151, 153, 156, 157, 159, 162–164, 169, 170, 172, 178n3
Haunting, The (1999 film), 98, 147, 147
Haunting of Hill House, The, 142, 156, 157–160, 162, 163, 169, 179n2, 180n9
hauntology, 98
Hawthorne, Nathaniel, 97, 177n12, 179n2
Heckart, Eileen, 160
Heidegger, Martin, 10
Heilmann, Ann, 180n11
Hell House, 142
Heller-Nicholas, Alexandra, 89, 177nn13,15
Hellraiser (franchise), 52, 53, 176n9
Hellraiser: Bloodline, 52
Henriksen, Lance, 111
heterotopia, 44
Hilton, Leon, 30
Historical Materialism, 14, 16
Hird, Myra, 33
Hitchcock, Alfred, 86, 151
Hocus Pocus (1993 film), 132
Hodgell, P. C., 132
Hoffman, E. T. A., 107, 111
Hogle, Jerrold E., 178n3
Holm, Ian, 111
Hooper, Tobe, 50, 52, 76, 89–90, 150
hope, 8, 11, 16–17, 20, 27, 31, 81, 171
Hope Diamond, 45, 48
Hoppenstand, Gary, 176–177n9
horror (emotion), 3, 4, 16–17, 19, 76, 168
horror (genre), 14–15, 33, 36, 37, 41–44, 87, 127, 129
Horse, Michael, 61
Hostel, 76, 175n4

House (TV drama), 127
House of Leaves, ix, 143, 151, 165–170, 180n12
House on Haunted Hill, The, 142
Howells, William Dean, 144
Hughes, William, 12
Humanism, 27, 29, 31
humiliation, 4, 25, 73, 74, 172
Hurley, Kelly, 175nn2–3
Hurt, John, 76
Huysmans, J. K., 119–120, 178n2 (chapter 5)
hyperobject, 3–4, 6, 24–26, 37, 40, 172

I Walked With a Zombie, 94
ideogram, 179n2, 180n9
In the Mouth of Madness, 130, 131
Inglis, Katherine, 120
insanity, 86–87, 157, 159
Insidious, 151
Irwin, Margaret, 133–134, 135
IT (2017 film), 104–105

Jackson, Shirley, 49, 157, 158, 160, 162, 179n2, 180n9
Jackson, Zakiyyah Iman, 31, 75
Jacobs, W. W., 47–49
James, Henry, 117
James, M. R., 50–51, 51, 101–104, 178n5
Janicker, Rebecca, 144, 178–179n1 (chapter 6)
Jason Goes to Hell: The Final Friday, 126, 127
Jason Voorhees, 88, 177n14
Jentsch, Ernest, 107
Jones, Duane, 94
Jones, Jane, 59
Joshi, S. T., 123
Juhasz, Alexander, 129

Kahane, Claire, 179n3
Kent, Jennifer, 128
Keetley, Dawn, 176n6
Key of Solomon, 123
Khairy, Wael, 129
Kidman, Nicole, 104
King, Stephen, 11, 43, 47, 49, 55–56, 57, 67–68, 101, 104–105, 127, 146–148; *Christine*, 55–56, 67; *Eyes of the Dragon*, 127; *From a Buick 8*, 67; *IT*, 11, 101; "The Mangler," 68; *Maximum Overdrive*, 67; "The Monkey," 68; *Needful Things*, 57, 68–71; *Pet Sematary*, 47; *Revival*, 127; *The Shining*, 67–68, 147–148; *The Stand*, 49; "Trucks," 67
King in Yellow, The, ix, 119, 120–122, 123, 128
Kitamura, Rhuhei, 177n10
Kreienbrock, Jörg, 160–161
Kristeva, Julia, 75, 92

INDEX

Kröger, Lisa, 168, 169
Kubrick, Stanley, 104, 146–148, 151

Lacan, Jacques, 108
Langella, Frank, 131
LaRoche, Mary, 113
Latour, Bruno, 3, 6, 7, 8, 20, 29, 44, 115, 169, 171
Laurie, Hugh, 127
Lauro, Sarah Juliet, 93–94, 95, 177–178n1
Leatherface, 89–90
Lee, Sheryl, 58
LeFanu, Sheridn, 97
Letissier, Georges, 163, 180n11
Levine, Jonathan, 93
Lewin, Albert, 99
Lewis, Matthew, 76
Lieberher, Jaeden, 105
Lightning, Robert K., 175n4
Ligotti, Thomas, 36, 134–135
Lindfield, Peter N., 179n3
Lippert, Conny, 125, 178n3 (chapter 5)
Lipski, Jakub, 178n3
Little Stranger, The (novel), 162–164, 166, 169, 171, 180n11
Lloyd, Danny, 146–147
Long, Frank Belknap, 125
Lord, Quinn, 88
Lorre, Peter, 54
Lovecraft, H. P., ix, 4–9, 10–11, 20, 25, 33, 36, 39, 118–119, 123–128, 130, 132, 172, 178n3 (chapter 5); At the Mountains of Madness, 123, 124, 130; cosmicism of, 5–6, 20, 24, 33, 39, 132, 172; "The Call of Cthulhu," 5, 123; *The Case of Charles Dexter Ward*, 123, 124; "The Dreams in the Witch House," 123, 124; "The Dunwich Horror," 7, 124; "The Festival," 124; "History of the Necronomicon," 123; "The Hound," 123, 124; racism of, 6–7; "The Shadow Over Innsmouth," 7
Luckhurst, Roger, 146, 151–152, 169
Lugosi, Bela, 86
Lumley, Brian, 125
Lynch, Austin Jack, 59
Lynch, David, 43, 57–67, 151

MacCormack, Patricia, 32
Machen, Arthur, 76
Mad Love (film), 54
madness. *See* insanity
Mandel, Emily St. John, 32
mannequin, 55, 72, 90, 91, 95
Marcus, Adams, 126

Marion, Isaac, 93
marionette, ix, 107, 112
Marshall, James, 58
Marshall, Neil, 151
Marx, Karl, 48
Marxism, 70
mask, 72, 86, 87–90, 91, 95, 177nn13–15
Mask, The, 87
matter: displaced, 58–59; fragmented, 58, 64; inspirited, 58, 62–64; multiplied, 58, 64–65, 65; objectification, 58, 65–66; ominous 58, 59–61
Maturin, Charles, 97, 117
du Maurier, Daphne du, 97, 100–101
May (2002 film), 112–113
Mbembe, Achille, 178n2
McBryde, James, 51
McCullagh, John Francis, 180n6
McKee, Lucky, 112
McLachlan, Kyle, 58
McRobbie, Linda Rodriguez, 49
McRoy, Jay, 176n9
McTeigue, 87
Meillassoux, Quentin, 24, 36, 168
Melmoth the Wanderer, 97, 117, 118
Melville, Herman, 97
Meredith, Burgess, 55, 160
Merritt, Naomi, 175n4
mesmerism, 177n12
Michael Myer, 88
Midnight Meat Train, The (2008 film), 177n10
Miéville, China, 6
Mills, Sandra, 107
Miner, Steve, 177n14
mirror, ix, 55
miscegenation, 6–7
Miyazawa, Naomi, 178n4
Monk, The (novel), 76
"Monkey's Paw, The," 47–49
monster. *See* monstrosity
monster theory, 27–28
monstrosity, vii, 12, 20, 21 26–32, 34, 38–39, 42, 90, 129, 130, 172
Montgomery, Lee H., 160
Moorcock, Michael, 56
Moore, Alan, 87
Mori, Masahiro, 89, 108
Morton, Timothy, vii, 3–4, 6, 24–26, 33, 36, 37, 38, 73, 80, 168, 169, 172
Mulkey, Chris, 59
Mulvey-Roberts, Marie, 143
Murphy, Cillian, 88
Muschietti, Andrés, 101, 105

Nakata, Hideo, 50, 105
Nance, Jack, 58
Necronomicon, The, ix, 118–119, 123–128, 126, 127, 178n3 (chapter 5)
Neill, Sam, 130
Nelson, Victoria, 42, 43, 46, 109, 134
New Materialism, vii, viii, ix, 7, 11, 12, 13, 15–16, 19, 20, 30–31, 35–36, 39, 71, 74, 95, 164, 168, 170, 171, 172
Newitz, Annalee, 94–95
Nguyen, Trung, 5
Nicholson, Jack, 104
Night of the Living Dead, 76, 92, 94, 175n4
Nightbreed, 86, 89, 89, 90, 176n9
Ninth Gate, The, 131
Nolan, Christopher, 88
nonhuman turn, the, vii, 4, 7, 8–9, 12, 39, 73, 172
Norman Bates (character), 86
nuclear war, 32

Oakland, Norman, 86
O'Bannon, Dan, 92
Object-Oriented Feminist, 16
Object-Oriented Ontology (OOO), vii, viii, 4, 7, 11, 12, 16, 19, 23–24, 34, 35–36, 38, 39, 70, 71, 73–74, 77, 79–81, 169, 172
objects: conduits, 43, 45, 49–55, 122; cursed, 43, 45–49; imbued, 54–55; inspirited, 10, 45, 55–57, 103, 108–111; malicious, 161
Ochiai, Masayuki, 104
Oculus, 55
Olkewicz, Walter, 58
Olney, Ian, 177n11
Omen, The, 105
ominous matter, 4, 8, 9, 14, 34, 44, 51, 52, 58, 59, 66, 71, 171–172
Ontkean, Michael, 58
OOO. *See* Object-Oriented Ontology
Orientalism, 45, 47, 121
Orphanage, The, 88
Ortega, Kenny, 132
Osborne, Mary Pope, 130
Osment, Haley Joel, 104
Others, The (2001 film), 104
Ouija (film), 50
Ouija Board, ix, 14, 49–50, 157
out-side, the, 9–12, 49, 53–54

pandemic, 32
Paranormal Activity, 50
Pascal, Richard, 180n9
Peeples, Scott, 176n7
Peeren, Esther, 20–21

Peli, Oren, 50
People Under the Stairs, The, 151
Pérez-Reberte, Arturo, 131
performative utterances, 115–116, 122–123, 128
Perron, Bernard, 176–177n9
phantom. *See* spectrality
Phillips, Wesley, 16
photograph, 72, 91, 95, 100–106, 107, 178nn4–5
Picture of Dorian Gray, The, 98–100, 99, 101, 119, 121
del Pilar Blanco, María, 20–21
Pirates of the Caribbean: The Curse of the Black Pearl, 46
place, 137–139, 142
place-power, 137–138, 142, 147, 153, 154, 156, 158–160, 169, 170, 171, 172
Poe, Edgar Allan, 76, 77–82, 98–99, 100, 153–156, 158, 176nn5–8, 177n12, 178n4; "Berenice," 76, 77–82, 176nn5–8, 177n12; "The Fall of the House of Usher," 142, 153–156, 158, 163; "The Oval Portrait," 98, 100, 178n4; "William Wilson," 100
Polanski, Roman, 131, 151
Poltergeist (film), 50, 150, 151, 151
Poltergeist II: The Other Side, 50
portrait, ix, 72, 91, 95–100, 106, 178n3
possession, 85–87, 112, 177n12
posthumanism, 20, 29, 31, 71
poststructuralism, 21
Poznar, Susan, 179n2
Pratchett, Terry, 56, 127, 132
Psycho (1960 film), 86–87
psychoanalysis, 20–21, 23, 107, 108, 146–147
psychogeography, 139, 170
Punter, David, 143, 179n4
puppet, 10, 55, 72, 91, 95, 107, 109

quasi-object, 86, 87, 88, 90, 93, 121, 122
quasi-subject, 115
queer, 28

Raby, Peter, 178n2 (chapter 5)
race, 30–31, 47, 76, 84, 93–95
Radcliffe, Ann, 3, 117, 118, 178n1
Radford, Benjamin, 45
Raimi, Sam, 46, 126, 132–133, 149–150
Raiders of the Lost Ark, ix
Red Violin, The, 48
Reed, Oliver, 160
Reiser, Paul, 111
Reitman, Ivan, 98
Renzi, Kristen, 176n6

INDEX

Return of the Living Dead, 92
Reyes, Xavier Aldana, 14–15, 175n3
Reynolds, Nicole, 143–144
Ring, The, 50, 105
Ringu, 50, 105, 106
Robie, Wendy, 59
RoboCop, 111–112
robot, 10, 72, 107, 109, 111–112
Romance of the Forest, The, 117–118, 178n1
Romanticism, 16
Romero, George, 52, 76, 92, 94
Rose, Bernard, 150
Rosenberg, Stuart, 150
Roth, Eli, 76
Rowling, J. K., 130–131
Rush, Geoffrey, 46
Russell, Chuck, 87

Sagan, Carl 25
Saldanha, Arun J. J., 36
Saler, Michael, 42, 43–44, 46
Savalas, Telly, 113
Schneider, Steven J., 4142
science fiction, 5, 25, 30, 33–34, 87, 111–112
Scob, Édith, 89
Sconce, Jeffrey, 50
Scott, Jackson Robert 105
Scott, Ridley, 76, 108, 111
Sears, John, 68–69
Sedgwick, Eve Kosofsky, 1, 144
Seigh, Steve, 129
Serling, Rod, 113
Session 9, 86–87, 147, 148
Shaviro, Steven, 23–24
Shelley, Mary, 76, 111, 117, 118
shi, 139, 142
Shining, The (1980 film), 104, 146–148, 148, 151
Shomura, Chad, 31, 39
Showalter, Elaine, 179n3
Shuker, Karl, 45
Shutter (2008 film), 104
Shyamalan, M. Night, 86–87, 104, 149, 149
Sick Building Syndrome, 159, 180n8
Siegel, Kate, 55
Simon, Joshua, 16
Simpsons, The, 54, 127
Sixth Sense, The, 104, 149, 149
Skarsgård, Bill, 105
slave narrative, 74–75, 177n12
slavery, 74–75, 84, 94, 176n8, 177n12
Smith, Andrew 12
Smith, Clark Ashton, 125
Sontag, Susan, 32

space (physical), 137–139, 141, 142, 146–147, 151, 152, 165–166, 168, 179n4
Specters of Marx (Derrida), 20–21, 27, 98
spectral turn, the, 21
Spectralities Reader: Ghosts and Hauntings in Contemporary Cultural Theory, 20–21
spectrality, vii, 12, 20, 20–26, 32, 34, 37, 38
Speculative Realism, vii, viii, 4, 7, 11, 12, 19, 20, 23–24, 25, 30–31, 33, 71, 172
Spielberg, Steven, ix
splatterpunk, 176n9
Split (2016 film), 86–87
Spooner, Catherine, 15
Stallybrass, Peter, 67
Standing, John, 55
Star Trek, 177n14
Steadman, John L., 125
Stepford Wives, The (1975 film), 112
Stewart, Jimmy, 151
Stoker, Bram, 86, 117, 118
Stolwijk, J. A., 159, 180n8
strange, the, 22–23
Stranger Things, 10–11, 50
Strangers, The, 52, 88
Stratford, Tracy, 113
Strobel, Al, 62
sublime, the, 3
surprise, 9, 10, 11, 169
Swamp Thing, 30
Swanson, Heather, 8, 21–23, 29–30, 33. See also *Arts of Living on a Damaged Planet*
sympoeisis, 6, 7

Talky Tina (doll), ix, 113–114, 113
Tally, Robert T., Jr., 138–139, 141
Tamblyn, Russ, 58
Tatar, Maria M., 179n2
Taylor, Jeremy Ray, 105
Taylor, Matthew, 156
Tchen, John Kuo Wei, 121
Terminator, The (1984 film), 112
Terminator, The (franchise), 111
terror, 2, 3, 9, 10, 39, 74, 84, 97, 121, 143, 152, 156
Texas Chainsaw Massacre, The, 52, 76, 89–90, 175n4
Thacker, Eugene, 14, 15, 33, 36–37
They Live, 86
Thing, The (1982 film) 76
thing-power, vii, viii–ix, 1, 12, 19, 42, 44, 48, 54–55, 56–57, 68, 70, 77, 80, 81, 90, 100, 106, 108–109, 110–111, 114, 115, 116, 120, 122, 124, 127–128, 129, 135–136, 162–163, 165, 171, 172

Thing Theory, 9–10, 11, 13, 14, 15–17, 19, 34, 38, 39, 40, 44, 55, 57, 71, 73, 74, 75, 79–80, 81, 83, 84, 85, 100, 115, 156, 168, 170
Thrift, Nigel, 57
Tolkien, J. R. R., 56
Tompkins, Kyla Wazana, viii, x, 7, 13, 31
del Toro, Guillermo, 53
Torture Garden, 55
Tourneur, Jacques, 94
Townshend, Dale, 143
Tracy, Ann B., 96
trans-corporeality, 73
transgression, 1, 4, 12, 44, 172
Trick 'r Treat, 88
Tsing, Anna, 8, 21–23, 29–30, 33
Tuan, Yi-Fu, 137–139, 141
Turn of the Screw, The, 117
Twilight Zone, The, 50, 54, 113–114
Twin Peaks, 57–67, 71
Twin Peaks: Fire Walk With Me, 59
Twitchell, James, 98
Tyson, Donald, 125

Unaussprechlichen Kulten, 123
uncanny, the, 22–23, 26, 38, 39, 40, 42, 43, 44, 57, 68–70, 72, 81, 87, 89, 90, 103, 104, 106, 107–108, 112, 115, 116–117, 118, 122, 128, 129, 134, 145, 146–147, 148–149, 150, 152, 163, 171
uncanny valley, 89, 108
Unfriended (film), 50
Uninvited, The, 49

V for Vendetta, 87
vampire, 81, 98, 108, 118
VanderMeer, Jeff, 26
Varma, Devendra, 3
Varnado, S. L., 179n2, 180n9
Verbinski, Gore, 46, 50, 105
Verhoeven, Paul, 111–112
Vertigo, 151
Vibrant Materialism, vii, 9–12, 19, 40, 55, 70, 73, 100, 136, 155, 169, 171–172
Victor Frankenstein (character), 75–76, 111, 117
Videodrome, 86
Vitruvius, 140, 150
Von Dohlen, Lenny, 58
voodoo doll. *See* doll

Wagner, Tamara, 144
Waititi, Taika, 93
Walker, I. M., 156
Walpole, Horace, ix, 97–98, 100, 105, 117, 145–146, 148, 178n3, 179nn2–3
Walt Disney's Haunted Mansion, 95–97, 96, 142–143
Walton, Kendall, 41, 42, 43–44
Wan, James, 151
Warm Bodies, 93
Waters, Sarah, 162–164, 171, 180n11
Weber, Marx, 43
Wegener, Paul, 109
Weheliye, Alexander G., 7, 31
Weinstock, Jeffrey Andrew, 21, 26–27, 93, 111, 175n1
weird, the, 20, 22, 24, 25, 38, 39
Weird and the Eerie, The (Fisher), 22–23
weird fiction, 6, 25, 26, 36
weird realism, vii, 36
Weird Tales, 125
Welsh, Kenneth, 58
Westworld (1973 film), 112
Wharton, Edith, 50
What We Do in the Shadows (film), 93
Winspear, Ben, 128
White, Stiles, 50
White, Thomas W., 79
White Zombie, 86, 177n12
Wiene, Robert, 54
Wilde, Oscar, 98–99, 100, 101, 119–120, 121
Williams, JoBeth, 151
Wilson, Manly Wade, 125
Wilson, Michael T., 180n9
Winter, Kari J., 74, 75
Wiseman, Noah, 128
Wolf-Meyer, Matthew J., 33–34
Wolfendale, Peter, 16
wonder, 8, 9, 11, 12, 38–39, 40, 42, 43–44, 172
Wong, James, 101, 105
Wordsworth, William, 3
Wynter, Sylvia, 4, 7

Yagher, Kevin, 52
Yeats, Dylan, 121

Zabriskie, Grace, 59
Ziolkowski, Theodore, 178n3
Žižek, Slavoj, 108
zombies, 10, 20, 26, 27, 28, 37, 39, 47, 76, 80–81, 86, 91, 92–95, 94, 108, 112, 177–178n1

Jeffrey Andrew Weinstock is Professor of English at Central Michigan University and associate editor in charge of horror for the *Los Angeles Review of Books*. His most recent books include *Giving the Devil His Due: Satan and Cinema* (with Regina Hansen, Fordham, 2021), *The Monster Theory Reader* (University of Minnesota Press, 2020), and *The Cambridge Companion to the American Gothic* (Cambridge University Press, 2018). Visit him at JeffreyAndrewWeinstock.com.

www.ingramcontent.com/pod-product-compliance
Lightning Source LLC
Chambersburg PA
CBHW020409080526
44584CB00014B/1239